MW00804931

# **FREE** Study Skills Videos/DVD Offer

Dear Customer,

Thank you for your purchase from Mometrix! We consider it an honor and a privilege that you have purchased our product and we want to ensure your satisfaction.

As a way of showing our appreciation and to help us better serve you, we have developed Study Skills Videos that we would like to give you for FREE. These videos cover our *best practices* for getting ready for your exam, from how to use our study materials to how to best prepare for the day of the test.

All that we ask is that you email us with feedback that would describe your experience so far with our product. Good, bad, or indifferent, we want to know what you think!

To get your FREE Study Skills Videos, you can use the **QR code** below, or send us an **email** at studyvideos@mometrix.com with *FREE VIDEOS* in the subject line and the following information in the body of the email:

- The name of the product you purchased.
- Your product rating on a scale of 1-5, with 5 being the highest rating.
- Your feedback. It can be long, short, or anything in between. We just want to know your impressions and experience so far with our product. (Good feedback might include how our study material met your needs and ways we might be able to make it even better. You could highlight features that you found helpful or features that you think we should add.)

If you have any questions or concerns, please don't hesitate to contact me directly.

Thanks again!

Sincerely,

Jay Willis
Vice President
jay.willis@mometrix.com
1-800-673-8175

SCAN HERE

# aPHR

## Study Guide
## 2022-2023

Secrets Prep Book for the Associate
Professional in Human Resources
Certification

Full-Length Practice Test

Includes Detailed
Answer Explanations

Copyright © 2022 by Mometrix Media LLC

All rights reserved. This product, or parts thereof, may not be reproduced, stored in a retrieval system, or transmitted in any form or by any means—electronic, mechanical, photocopy, recording, scanning, or other—except for brief quotations in critical reviews or articles, without the prior written permission of the publisher.

Written and edited by the Mometrix Test Prep

Printed in the United States of America

This paper meets the requirements of ANSI/NISO Z39.48-1992 (Permanence of Paper).

Mometrix offers volume discount pricing to institutions. For more information or a price quote, please contact our sales department at sales@mometrix.com or 888-248-1219.

Mometrix Media LLC is not affiliated with or endorsed by any official testing organization. All organizational and test names are trademarks of their respective owners.

Paperback
ISBN 13: 978-1-5167-2013-2
ISBN 10: 1-5167-2013-X

# DEAR FUTURE EXAM SUCCESS STORY

First of all, **THANK YOU** for purchasing Mometrix study materials!

Second, congratulations! You are one of the few determined test-takers who are committed to doing whatever it takes to excel on your exam. **You have come to the right place.** We developed these study materials with one goal in mind: to deliver you the information you need in a format that's concise and easy to use.

In addition to optimizing your guide for the content of the test, we've outlined our recommended steps for breaking down the preparation process into small, attainable goals so you can make sure you stay on track.

We've also analyzed the entire test-taking process, identifying the most common pitfalls and showing how you can overcome them and be ready for any curveball the test throws you.

Standardized testing is one of the biggest obstacles on your road to success, which only increases the importance of doing well in the high-pressure, high-stakes environment of test day. Your results on this test could have a significant impact on your future, and this guide provides the information and practical advice to help you achieve your full potential on test day.

## Your success is our success

**We would love to hear from you!** If you would like to share the story of your exam success or if you have any questions or comments in regard to our products, please contact us at **800-673-8175** or **support@mometrix.com**.

Thanks again for your business and we wish you continued success!

Sincerely,
The Mometrix Test Preparation Team

> **Need more help? Check out our flashcards at:**
> http://mometrixflashcards.com/aPHR

Copyright © 2022 by Mometrix Media LLC. All rights reserved.
Written and edited by the Mometrix Exam Secrets Test Prep Team
Printed in the United States of America

# TABLE OF CONTENTS

# Introduction

**Thank you for purchasing this resource**! You have made the choice to prepare yourself for a test that could have a huge impact on your future, and this guide is designed to help you be fully ready for test day. Obviously, it's important to have a solid understanding of the test material, but you also need to be prepared for the unique environment and stressors of the test, so that you can perform to the best of your abilities.

For this purpose, the first section that appears in this guide is the **Secret Keys**. We've devoted countless hours to meticulously researching what works and what doesn't, and we've boiled down our findings to the five most impactful steps you can take to improve your performance on the test. We start at the beginning with study planning and move through the preparation process, all the way to the testing strategies that will help you get the most out of what you know when you're finally sitting in front of the test.

We recommend that you start preparing for your test as far in advance as possible. However, if you've bought this guide as a last-minute study resource and only have a few days before your test, we recommend that you skip over the first two Secret Keys since they address a long-term study plan.

If you struggle with **test anxiety**, we strongly encourage you to check out our recommendations for how you can overcome it. Test anxiety is a formidable foe, but it can be beaten, and we want to make sure you have the tools you need to defeat it.

Copyright © Mometrix Media. You have been licensed one copy of this document for personal use only. Any other reproduction or redistribution is strictly prohibited. All rights reserved.

# Secret Key #1 – Plan Big, Study Small

There's a lot riding on your performance. If you want to ace this test, you're going to need to keep your skills sharp and the material fresh in your mind. You need a plan that lets you review everything you need to know while still fitting in your schedule. We'll break this strategy down into three categories.

## Information Organization

Start with the information you already have: the official test outline. From this, you can make a complete list of all the concepts you need to cover before the test. Organize these concepts into groups that can be studied together, and create a list of any related vocabulary you need to learn so you can brush up on any difficult terms. You'll want to keep this vocabulary list handy once you actually start studying since you may need to add to it along the way.

## Time Management

Once you have your set of study concepts, decide how to spread them out over the time you have left before the test. Break your study plan into small, clear goals so you have a manageable task for each day and know exactly what you're doing. Then just focus on one small step at a time. When you manage your time this way, you don't need to spend hours at a time studying. Studying a small block of content for a short period each day helps you retain information better and avoid stressing over how much you have left to do. You can relax knowing that you have a plan to cover everything in time. In order for this strategy to be effective though, you have to start studying early and stick to your schedule. Avoid the exhaustion and futility that comes from last-minute cramming!

## Study Environment

The environment you study in has a big impact on your learning. Studying in a coffee shop, while probably more enjoyable, is not likely to be as fruitful as studying in a quiet room. It's important to keep distractions to a minimum. You're only planning to study for a short block of time, so make the most of it. Don't pause to check your phone or get up to find a snack. It's also important to **avoid multitasking**. Research has consistently shown that multitasking will make your studying dramatically less effective. Your study area should also be comfortable and well-lit so you don't have the distraction of straining your eyes or sitting on an uncomfortable chair.

The time of day you study is also important. You want to be rested and alert. Don't wait until just before bedtime. Study when you'll be most likely to comprehend and remember. Even better, if you know what time of day your test will be, set that time aside for study. That way your brain will be used to working on that subject at that specific time and you'll have a better chance of recalling information.

Finally, it can be helpful to team up with others who are studying for the same test. Your actual studying should be done in as isolated an environment as possible, but the work of organizing the information and setting up the study plan can be divided up. In between study sessions, you can discuss with your teammates the concepts that you're all studying and quiz each other on the details. Just be sure that your teammates are as serious about the test as you are. If you find that your study time is being replaced with social time, you might need to find a new team.

2

Copyright © Mometrix Media. You have been licensed one copy of this document for personal use only. Any other reproduction or redistribution is strictly prohibited. All rights reserved.

# Secret Key #2 – Make Your Studying Count

You're devoting a lot of time and effort to preparing for this test, so you want to be absolutely certain it will pay off. This means doing more than just reading the content and hoping you can remember it on test day. It's important to make every minute of study count. There are two main areas you can focus on to make your studying count:

## Retention

It doesn't matter how much time you study if you can't remember the material. You need to make sure you are retaining the concepts. To check your retention of the information you're learning, try recalling it at later times with minimal prompting. Try carrying around flashcards and glance at one or two from time to time or ask a friend who's also studying for the test to quiz you.

To enhance your retention, look for ways to put the information into practice so that you can apply it rather than simply recalling it. If you're using the information in practical ways, it will be much easier to remember. Similarly, it helps to solidify a concept in your mind if you're not only reading it to yourself but also explaining it to someone else. Ask a friend to let you teach them about a concept you're a little shaky on (or speak aloud to an imaginary audience if necessary). As you try to summarize, define, give examples, and answer your friend's questions, you'll understand the concepts better and they will stay with you longer. Finally, step back for a big picture view and ask yourself how each piece of information fits with the whole subject. When you link the different concepts together and see them working together as a whole, it's easier to remember the individual components.

Finally, practice showing your work on any multi-step problems, even if you're just studying. Writing out each step you take to solve a problem will help solidify the process in your mind, and you'll be more likely to remember it during the test.

## Modality

*Modality* simply refers to the means or method by which you study. Choosing a study modality that fits your own individual learning style is crucial. No two people learn best in exactly the same way, so it's important to know your strengths and use them to your advantage.

For example, if you learn best by visualization, focus on visualizing a concept in your mind and draw an image or a diagram. Try color-coding your notes, illustrating them, or creating symbols that will trigger your mind to recall a learned concept. If you learn best by hearing or discussing information, find a study partner who learns the same way or read aloud to yourself. Think about how to put the information in your own words. Imagine that you are giving a lecture on the topic and record yourself so you can listen to it later.

For any learning style, flashcards can be helpful. Organize the information so you can take advantage of spare moments to review. Underline key words or phrases. Use different colors for different categories. Mnemonic devices (such as creating a short list in which every item starts with the same letter) can also help with retention. Find what works best for you and use it to store the information in your mind most effectively and easily.

Copyright © Mometrix Media. You have been licensed one copy of this document for personal use only. Any other reproduction or redistribution is strictly prohibited. All rights reserved.

# Secret Key #3 – Practice the Right Way

Your success on test day depends not only on how many hours you put into preparing, but also on whether you prepared the right way. It's good to check along the way to see if your studying is paying off. One of the most effective ways to do this is by taking practice tests to evaluate your progress. Practice tests are useful because they show exactly where you need to improve. Every time you take a practice test, pay special attention to these three groups of questions:

- The questions you got wrong
- The questions you had to guess on, even if you guessed right
- The questions you found difficult or slow to work through

This will show you exactly what your weak areas are, and where you need to devote more study time. Ask yourself why each of these questions gave you trouble. Was it because you didn't understand the material? Was it because you didn't remember the vocabulary? Do you need more repetitions on this type of question to build speed and confidence? Dig into those questions and figure out how you can strengthen your weak areas as you go back to review the material.

Additionally, many practice tests have a section explaining the answer choices. It can be tempting to read the explanation and think that you now have a good understanding of the concept. However, an explanation likely only covers part of the question's broader context. Even if the explanation makes sense, **go back and investigate** every concept related to the question until you're positive you have a thorough understanding.

As you go along, keep in mind that the practice test is just that: practice. Memorizing these questions and answers will not be very helpful on the actual test because it is unlikely to have any of the same exact questions. If you only know the right answers to the sample questions, you won't be prepared for the real thing. **Study the concepts** until you understand them fully, and then you'll be able to answer any question that shows up on the test.

It's important to wait on the practice tests until you're ready. If you take a test on your first day of study, you may be overwhelmed by the amount of material covered and how much you need to learn. Work up to it gradually.

On test day, you'll need to be prepared for answering questions, managing your time, and using the test-taking strategies you've learned. It's a lot to balance, like a mental marathon that will have a big impact on your future. Like training for a marathon, you'll need to start slowly and work your way up. When test day arrives, you'll be ready.

Start with the strategies you've read in the first two Secret Keys—plan your course and study in the way that works best for you. If you have time, consider using multiple study resources to get different approaches to the same concepts. It can be helpful to see difficult concepts from more than one angle. Then find a good source for practice tests. Many times, the test website will suggest potential study resources or provide sample tests.

4

Copyright © Mometrix Media. You have been licensed one copy of this document for personal use only. Any other reproduction or redistribution is strictly prohibited. All rights reserved.

# Practice Test Strategy

When you're ready to start taking practice tests, follow this strategy:

## UNTIMED AND OPEN-BOOK PRACTICE

Take the first test with no time constraints and with your notes and study guide handy. Take your time and focus on applying the strategies you've learned.

## TIMED AND OPEN-BOOK PRACTICE

Take the second practice test open-book as well, but set a timer and practice pacing yourself to finish in time.

## TIMED AND CLOSED-BOOK PRACTICE

Take any other practice tests as if it were test day. Set a timer and put away your study materials. Sit at a table or desk in a quiet room, imagine yourself at the testing center, and answer questions as quickly and accurately as possible.

Keep repeating timed and closed-book tests on a regular basis until you run out of practice tests or it's time for the actual test. Your mind will be ready for the schedule and stress of test day, and you'll be able to focus on recalling the material you've learned.

Copyright © Mometrix Media. You have been licensed one copy of this document for personal use only. Any other reproduction or redistribution is strictly prohibited. All rights reserved.

# Secret Key #4 – Pace Yourself

Once you're fully prepared for the material on the test, your biggest challenge on test day will be managing your time. Just knowing that the clock is ticking can make you panic even if you have plenty of time left. Work on pacing yourself so you can build confidence against the time constraints of the exam. Pacing is a difficult skill to master, especially in a high-pressure environment, so **practice is vital**.

Set time expectations for your pace based on how much time is available. For example, if a section has 60 questions and the time limit is 30 minutes, you know you have to average 30 seconds or less per question in order to answer them all. Although 30 seconds is the hard limit, set 25 seconds per question as your goal, so you reserve extra time to spend on harder questions. When you budget extra time for the harder questions, you no longer have any reason to stress when those questions take longer to answer.

Don't let this time expectation distract you from working through the test at a calm, steady pace, but keep it in mind so you don't spend too much time on any one question. Recognize that taking extra time on one question you don't understand may keep you from answering two that you do understand later in the test. If your time limit for a question is up and you're still not sure of the answer, mark it and move on, and come back to it later if the time and the test format allow. If the testing format doesn't allow you to return to earlier questions, just make an educated guess; then put it out of your mind and move on.

On the easier questions, be careful not to rush. It may seem wise to hurry through them so you have more time for the challenging ones, but it's not worth missing one if you know the concept and just didn't take the time to read the question fully. Work efficiently but make sure you understand the question and have looked at all of the answer choices, since more than one may seem right at first.

Even if you're paying attention to the time, you may find yourself a little behind at some point. You should speed up to get back on track, but do so wisely. Don't panic; just take a few seconds less on each question until you're caught up. Don't guess without thinking, but do look through the answer choices and eliminate any you know are wrong. If you can get down to two choices, it is often worthwhile to guess from those. Once you've chosen an answer, move on and don't dwell on any that you skipped or had to hurry through. If a question was taking too long, chances are it was one of the harder ones, so you weren't as likely to get it right anyway.

On the other hand, if you find yourself getting ahead of schedule, it may be beneficial to slow down a little. The more quickly you work, the more likely you are to make a careless mistake that will affect your score. You've budgeted time for each question, so don't be afraid to spend that time. Practice an efficient but careful pace to get the most out of the time you have.

Copyright © Mometrix Media. You have been licensed one copy of this document for personal use only. Any other reproduction or redistribution is strictly prohibited. All rights reserved.

# Secret Key #5 – Have a Plan for Guessing

When you're taking the test, you may find yourself stuck on a question. Some of the answer choices seem better than others, but you don't see the one answer choice that is obviously correct. What do you do?

The scenario described above is very common, yet most test takers have not effectively prepared for it. Developing and practicing a plan for guessing may be one of the single most effective uses of your time as you get ready for the exam.

In developing your plan for guessing, there are three questions to address:

- When should you start the guessing process?
- How should you narrow down the choices?
- Which answer should you choose?

## When to Start the Guessing Process

Unless your plan for guessing is to select C every time (which, despite its merits, is not what we recommend), you need to leave yourself enough time to apply your answer elimination strategies. Since you have a limited amount of time for each question, that means that if you're going to give yourself the best shot at guessing correctly, you have to decide quickly whether or not you will guess.

Of course, the best-case scenario is that you don't have to guess at all, so first, see if you can answer the question based on your knowledge of the subject and basic reasoning skills. Focus on the key words in the question and try to jog your memory of related topics. Give yourself a chance to bring the knowledge to mind, but once you realize that you don't have (or you can't access) the knowledge you need to answer the question, it's time to start the guessing process.

It's almost always better to start the guessing process too early than too late. It only takes a few seconds to remember something and answer the question from knowledge. Carefully eliminating wrong answer choices takes longer. Plus, going through the process of eliminating answer choices can actually help jog your memory.

**Summary: Start the guessing process as soon as you decide that you can't answer the question based on your knowledge.**

7

Copyright © Mometrix Media. You have been licensed one copy of this document for personal use only. Any other reproduction or redistribution is strictly prohibited. All rights reserved.

# How to Narrow Down the Choices

The next chapter in this book (**Test-Taking Strategies**) includes a wide range of strategies for how to approach questions and how to look for answer choices to eliminate. You will definitely want to read those carefully, practice them, and figure out which ones work best for you. Here though, we're going to address a mindset rather than a particular strategy.

Your chances of guessing an answer correctly depend on how many options you are choosing from.

| How many choices you have | How likely you are to guess correctly |
| --- | --- |
| 5 | 20% |
| 4 | 25% |
| 3 | 33% |
| 2 | 50% |
| 1 | 100% |

You can see from this chart just how valuable it is to be able to eliminate incorrect answers and make an educated guess, but there are two things that many test takers do that cause them to miss out on the benefits of guessing:

- Accidentally eliminating the correct answer
- Selecting an answer based on an impression

We'll look at the first one here, and the second one in the next section.

To avoid accidentally eliminating the correct answer, we recommend a thought exercise called **the $5 challenge**. In this challenge, you only eliminate an answer choice from contention if you are willing to bet $5 on it being wrong. Why $5? Five dollars is a small but not insignificant amount of money. It's an amount you could afford to lose but wouldn't want to throw away. And while losing $5 once might not hurt too much, doing it twenty times will set you back $100. In the same way, each small decision you make—eliminating a choice here, guessing on a question there—won't by itself impact your score very much, but when you put them all together, they can make a big difference. By holding each answer choice elimination decision to a higher standard, you can reduce the risk of accidentally eliminating the correct answer.

The $5 challenge can also be applied in a positive sense: If you are willing to bet $5 that an answer choice *is* correct, go ahead and mark it as correct.

**Summary: Only eliminate an answer choice if you are willing to bet $5 that it is wrong.**

8

Copyright © Mometrix Media. You have been licensed one copy of this document for personal use only. Any other reproduction or redistribution is strictly prohibited. All rights reserved.

# Which Answer to Choose

You're taking the test. You've run into a hard question and decided you'll have to guess. You've eliminated all the answer choices you're willing to bet $5 on. Now you have to pick an answer. Why do we even need to talk about this? Why can't you just pick whichever one you feel like when the time comes?

The answer to these questions is that if you don't come into the test with a plan, you'll rely on your impression to select an answer choice, and if you do that, you risk falling into a trap. The test writers know that everyone who takes their test will be guessing on some of the questions, so they intentionally write wrong answer choices to seem plausible. You still have to pick an answer though, and if the wrong answer choices are designed to look right, how can you ever be sure that you're not falling for their trap? The best solution we've found to this dilemma is to take the decision out of your hands entirely. Here is the process we recommend:

**Once you've eliminated any choices that you are confident (willing to bet $5) are wrong, select the first remaining choice as your answer.**

Whether you choose to select the first remaining choice, the second, or the last, the important thing is that you use some preselected standard. Using this approach guarantees that you will not be enticed into selecting an answer choice that looks right, because you are not basing your decision on how the answer choices look.

This is not meant to make you question your knowledge. Instead, it is to help you recognize the difference between your knowledge and your impressions. There's a huge difference between thinking an answer is right because of what you know, and thinking an answer is right because it looks or sounds like it should be right.

**Summary: To ensure that your selection is appropriately random, make a predetermined selection from among all answer choices you have not eliminated.**

Copyright © Mometrix Media. You have been licensed one copy of this document for personal use only. Any other reproduction or redistribution is strictly prohibited. All rights reserved.

# Test-Taking Strategies

This section contains a list of test-taking strategies that you may find helpful as you work through the test. By taking what you know and applying logical thought, you can maximize your chances of answering any question correctly!

It is very important to realize that every question is different and every person is different: no single strategy will work on every question, and no single strategy will work for every person. That's why we've included all of them here, so you can try them out and determine which ones work best for different types of questions and which ones work best for you.

## Question Strategies

### READ CAREFULLY

Read the question and answer choices carefully. Don't miss the question because you misread the terms. You have plenty of time to read each question thoroughly and make sure you understand what is being asked. Yet a happy medium must be attained, so don't waste too much time. You must read carefully, but efficiently.

### CONTEXTUAL CLUES

Look for contextual clues. If the question includes a word you are not familiar with, look at the immediate context for some indication of what the word might mean. Contextual clues can often give you all the information you need to decipher the meaning of an unfamiliar word. Even if you can't determine the meaning, you may be able to narrow down the possibilities enough to make a solid guess at the answer to the question.

### PREFIXES

If you're having trouble with a word in the question or answer choices, try dissecting it. Take advantage of every clue that the word might include. Prefixes and suffixes can be a huge help. Usually they allow you to determine a basic meaning. Pre- means before, post- means after, pro - is positive, de- is negative. From prefixes and suffixes, you can get an idea of the general meaning of the word and try to put it into context.

### HEDGE WORDS

Watch out for critical hedge words, such as *likely, may, can, sometimes, often, almost, mostly, usually, generally, rarely,* and *sometimes.* Question writers insert these hedge phrases to cover every possibility. Often an answer choice will be wrong simply because it leaves no room for exception. Be on guard for answer choices that have definitive words such as *exactly* and *always.*

### SWITCHBACK WORDS

Stay alert for *switchbacks.* These are the words and phrases frequently used to alert you to shifts in thought. The most common switchback words are *but, although,* and *however.* Others include *nevertheless, on the other hand, even though, while, in spite of, despite, regardless of.* Switchback words are important to catch because they can change the direction of the question or an answer choice.

**10**

Copyright © Mometrix Media. You have been licensed one copy of this document for personal use only. Any other reproduction or redistribution is strictly prohibited. All rights reserved.

## FACE VALUE

When in doubt, use common sense. Accept the situation in the problem at face value. Don't read too much into it. These problems will not require you to make wild assumptions. If you have to go beyond creativity and warp time or space in order to have an answer choice fit the question, then you should move on and consider the other answer choices. These are normal problems rooted in reality. The applicable relationship or explanation may not be readily apparent, but it is there for you to figure out. Use your common sense to interpret anything that isn't clear.

# Answer Choice Strategies

## ANSWER SELECTION

The most thorough way to pick an answer choice is to identify and eliminate wrong answers until only one is left, then confirm it is the correct answer. Sometimes an answer choice may immediately seem right, but be careful. The test writers will usually put more than one reasonable answer choice on each question, so take a second to read all of them and make sure that the other choices are not equally obvious. As long as you have time left, it is better to read every answer choice than to pick the first one that looks right without checking the others.

## ANSWER CHOICE FAMILIES

An answer choice family consists of two (in rare cases, three) answer choices that are very similar in construction and cannot all be true at the same time. If you see two answer choices that are direct opposites or parallels, one of them is usually the correct answer. For instance, if one answer choice says that quantity $x$ increases and another either says that quantity $x$ decreases (opposite) or says that quantity $y$ increases (parallel), then those answer choices would fall into the same family. An answer choice that doesn't match the construction of the answer choice family is more likely to be incorrect. Most questions will not have answer choice families, but when they do appear, you should be prepared to recognize them.

## ELIMINATE ANSWERS

Eliminate answer choices as soon as you realize they are wrong, but make sure you consider all possibilities. If you are eliminating answer choices and realize that the last one you are left with is also wrong, don't panic. Start over and consider each choice again. There may be something you missed the first time that you will realize on the second pass.

## AVOID FACT TRAPS

Don't be distracted by an answer choice that is factually true but doesn't answer the question. You are looking for the choice that answers the question. Stay focused on what the question is asking for so you don't accidentally pick an answer that is true but incorrect. Always go back to the question and make sure the answer choice you've selected actually answers the question and is not merely a true statement.

## EXTREME STATEMENTS

In general, you should avoid answers that put forth extreme actions as standard practice or proclaim controversial ideas as established fact. An answer choice that states the "process should be used in certain situations, if..." is much more likely to be correct than one that states the "process should be discontinued completely." The first is a calm rational statement and doesn't even make a definitive, uncompromising stance, using a hedge word *if* to provide wiggle room, whereas the second choice is a radical idea and far more extreme.

11

Copyright © Mometrix Media. You have been licensed one copy of this document for personal use only. Any other reproduction or redistribution is strictly prohibited. All rights reserved.

## BENCHMARK

As you read through the answer choices and you come across one that seems to answer the question well, mentally select that answer choice. This is not your final answer, but it's the one that will help you evaluate the other answer choices. The one that you selected is your benchmark or standard for judging each of the other answer choices. Every other answer choice must be compared to your benchmark. That choice is correct until proven otherwise by another answer choice beating it. If you find a better answer, then that one becomes your new benchmark. Once you've decided that no other choice answers the question as well as your benchmark, you have your final answer.

## PREDICT THE ANSWER

Before you even start looking at the answer choices, it is often best to try to predict the answer. When you come up with the answer on your own, it is easier to avoid distractions and traps because you will know exactly what to look for. The right answer choice is unlikely to be word-for-word what you came up with, but it should be a close match. Even if you are confident that you have the right answer, you should still take the time to read each option before moving on.

# General Strategies

## TOUGH QUESTIONS

If you are stumped on a problem or it appears too hard or too difficult, don't waste time. Move on! Remember though, if you can quickly check for obviously incorrect answer choices, your chances of guessing correctly are greatly improved. Before you completely give up, at least try to knock out a couple of possible answers. Eliminate what you can and then guess at the remaining answer choices before moving on.

## CHECK YOUR WORK

Since you will probably not know every term listed and the answer to every question, it is important that you get credit for the ones that you do know. Don't miss any questions through careless mistakes. If at all possible, try to take a second to look back over your answer selection and make sure you've selected the correct answer choice and haven't made a costly careless mistake (such as marking an answer choice that you didn't mean to mark). This quick double check should more than pay for itself in caught mistakes for the time it costs.

## PACE YOURSELF

It's easy to be overwhelmed when you're looking at a page full of questions; your mind is confused and full of random thoughts, and the clock is ticking down faster than you would like. Calm down and maintain the pace that you have set for yourself. Especially as you get down to the last few minutes of the test, don't let the small numbers on the clock make you panic. As long as you are on track by monitoring your pace, you are guaranteed to have time for each question.

## DON'T RUSH

It is very easy to make errors when you are in a hurry. Maintaining a fast pace in answering questions is pointless if it makes you miss questions that you would have gotten right otherwise. Test writers like to include distracting information and wrong answers that seem right. Taking a little extra time to avoid careless mistakes can make all the difference in your test score. Find a pace that allows you to be confident in the answers that you select.

Copyright © Mometrix Media. You have been licensed one copy of this document for personal use only. Any other reproduction or redistribution is strictly prohibited. All rights reserved.

## KEEP MOVING

Panicking will not help you pass the test, so do your best to stay calm and keep moving. Taking deep breaths and going through the answer elimination steps you practiced can help to break through a stress barrier and keep your pace.

# Final Notes

The combination of a solid foundation of content knowledge and the confidence that comes from practicing your plan for applying that knowledge is the key to maximizing your performance on test day. As your foundation of content knowledge is built up and strengthened, you'll find that the strategies included in this chapter become more and more effective in helping you quickly sift through the distractions and traps of the test to isolate the correct answer.

Now it's time to move on to the test content chapters of this book, but be sure to keep your goal in mind. As you read, think about how you will be able to apply this information on the test. If you've already seen sample questions for the test and you have an idea of the question format and style, try to come up with questions of your own that you can answer based on what you're reading. This will give you valuable practice applying your knowledge in the same ways you can expect to on test day.

**Good luck and good studying!**

Copyright © Mometrix Media. You have been licensed one copy of this document for personal use only. Any other reproduction or redistribution is strictly prohibited. All rights reserved.

14

Copyright © Mometrix Media. You have been licensed one copy of this document for personal use only. Any other reproduction or redistribution is strictly prohibited. All rights reserved.

# HR Operations

## Organizational Strategy and Its Connection to Mission, Vision, Values, Business Goals, and Objectives

### LINK BETWEEN HR AND ORGANIZATIONAL STRATEGY

**Organizational strategy** is a dynamic plan detailing the necessary actions that will enable the organization to achieve its short- and long-term goals. HR plays a critical role in an organization's strategic plan. Understanding an organization's strategy and how the business operates allows HR to better serve the organization's needs and human asset-related issues. Human capital impacts many aspects of a business, including recruitment, performance management, compensation and training, and development. HR must ensure the correct people are aligned and performing in accordance with the organizational strategy adopted by the organization. There is a strong connection between HR, strategic planning, and implementation because HR must leverage human capital to optimize the success of an organization.

### VISION STATEMENT

A **vision statement** provides a concise assertion that captures what the leadership team foresees as the future of the organization. This long-term, result-driven declaration serves as a guiding, inspirational force for the organization. A vision statement is aspirational and usually contains several of the following key elements: it is inspirational, future-oriented, captures the organization's culture, and strives to articulate its benefits in the future. Disney's vision statement is "To make people happy," Ben & Jerry's is "Making the best ice cream in the nicest possible way," the Apple vision statement says "We believe that we are on the face of the earth to make great products and that's not changing," and TED's is "Spread ideas." A vision statement is vital for the planning and execution of organizational strategies. As an organization grows and evolves, a vision statement might be altered over time.

### MISSION STATEMENT

A **mission statement** describes an organization's purpose and the activities an organization will pursue to achieve its vision. This declaration is designed to answer three basic elements: (1) an overall description of who the company is, (2) a description of what the company does, and (3) an explanation of why the company exists. The statement also serves as a communication tool explaining, at a high-level, how an organization will achieve its goals with its customers, employees, and all other stakeholders. A mission statement also explains to suppliers, customers, and clients why they should want to do business with an organization. In fact, organizations frequently use their mission statement theme in advertising and marketing collateral. A mission statement could also be thought of as the guiding force of an organization's operating manual, helping employees and other stakeholders better understand its central purpose. A mission statement might be altered over time as an organization grows and evolves.

### VISION VS. MISSION STATEMENT

A vision statement and mission statement are essential components of an organization's strategic planning process. They both help the organization directionally prepare for the future and achieve its goals. However, a mission statement highlights what the organization is currently doing in the present, while a vision statement highlights what the organization strives to achieve in the future. As such, a mission statement is more short-term in nature, usually one to three years, detailing the organization's purpose and current activities. A vision statement, on the other hand, is a long-term

15

Copyright © Mometrix Media. You have been licensed one copy of this document for personal use only. Any other reproduction or redistribution is strictly prohibited. All rights reserved.

declaration that is more inspirational in nature, highlighting the organization's hope for the future. Additionally, a vision statement is directional and may or may not be crystal clear as to what the future state will look like. Alternatively, a mission statement is crystal clear in its goals, objectives, and desired performance for successful achievement. It should be noted that a vision statement can only be achieved if the mission statement is successfully implemented.

## ORGANIZATIONAL VALUES

Values are part of an organization's strategic plan and define what is important to a particular business. Organizational values are frequently referred to as the "heart" of the organization, helping form the culture and playing a significant role in directing employee behavior. Some organizations choose to document their values and include them with their vision and mission statements. Alternatively, in other organizations, values are more informal and/or unwritten. Organizational values help drive decision making in the organization and ultimately signify what it stands for. These values serve as a filter, defining how organizational tasks should be accomplished. When organizational values and employee behavior are not in sync, conflict can develop, causing negative consequences and possibly interfering with the achievement of strategic goals. Values should be understood by all employees and serve to enhance employee contribution and commitment to the organization.

## BUSINESS GOALS VS. OBJECTIVES

Goals and objectives help guide an organization. **Goals** broadly describe the general direction that an organization wants to go in the future. The primary purpose of having goals is to improve the effectiveness of a company, guiding it to a desired state. As such, goals should be linked to an organization's mission statement. On the other hand, **objectives** are the specific activities that need to be accomplished to achieve desired goals. Objectives are typically quantitative in nature, with numbers and dates set in advance as goals to achieve. For example, an organization might have the goal to become a more inclusive environment. One objective to achieve that goal might be to increase the hiring of women by 7 percent.

| Goal | Objective |
|---|---|
| Describes the general direction an organization wants to follow | Specific steps that must be taken to achieve a goal |
| Increases an organization's effectiveness to achieve a desired state | Support goals by specifying exactly what must be done for efficient goal achievement |
| Usually qualitative (words) | Usually quantitative (numbers and dates) |
| Linked to mission statement | Linked to a specific goal |

## CORPORATE SOCIAL RESPONSIBILITY (CSR)

**Corporate social responsibility** (CSR) refers to an organization's effort to improve its environmental and social impact on the community at large. This is based on the premise that organizations can make the community (and world) a better place. At the very least, the goal of CSR is to avoid causing damage that will ultimately do harm to the community. Typically, CSR programs can benefit the organization and its shareholders. Examples of CSR initiatives include, but are not limited to, donating to local charities such as food kitchens, job training or mentoring programs for disadvantaged populations, reducing its negative footprint on the environment, and helping in the event of natural or manmade disasters. There is evidence to support that CSR programs can positively benefit the organization financially, as well as establishing itself as a reliable, upstanding member of the community. From an HR perspective, CSR programs could assist in recruiting, as potential employees may seek to work for a socially responsible company. Additionally, they may

Copyright © Mometrix Media. You have been licensed one copy of this document for personal use only. Any other reproduction or redistribution is strictly prohibited. All rights reserved.

also improve customer relations, brand management, and public relations, which may lead to competitive advantages and the possibility of improved profits.

# Organizational Culture

## PURPOSE OF ORGANIZATIONAL CULTURE

Organizational culture is the way activities are accomplished. It is a tone set by leaders for everyone in the organization to share basic beliefs that support an overall direction and strategy. Employees play a pivotal role in achieving organizational goals by behaving in a certain way, knowing they will be rewarded for displaying the organization's values. Organizational culture is the foundation that drives how an organization operates. It is often referred to as the force behind an organization's mission attainment and success. There is no specific model or formula to develop a culture. A robust culture is grounded in shared beliefs and common goals and is supported by strategies and processes in an organization. However, it is often challenging to define an organization's specific culture. Following are some keywords that might capture an organization's culture: family-oriented, innovative, customer-focused, motivating, fast-paced, rewarding, ethical, fun, technology-driven, inclusive, etc.

## CONNECTION BETWEEN STRONG ORGANIZATIONAL CULTURE AND SUCCESS

In order to sustain a strong culture, an organization's values and beliefs must be shared and adhered to by every employee. Maintaining a strong sense of culture can lead to enhanced collaboration among employees, more efficient decision making, and can ultimately drive competitive advantage—all of which contribute to making an organization successful. In other words, behavior is supported or justified by the common denominator of a culture developed by organizational leaders and driven by leaders and employees into all aspects of work. All members in an organization have the framework of culture to guide their behavior and act as an informal control system. Oftentimes, an ineffective culture can lead to employee disengagement, high employee turnover, poor customer relationships, and loss of revenue and business. For some enterprises, culture has been a significant factor in their ability to implement strategies and successfully execute the mission statement.

## "CARETAKER" OF ORGANIZATIONAL CULTURE

One of the most important assets of an organization is its people. HR plays an essential role in ensuring that an organization's culture is built and cultivated in order to gain or maintain a competitive advantage. HR must work with leaders not only to understand strategic direction and monetary goals, but also to influence leaders by showing them how an organization's culture can drive the achievement of these priorities. HR can influence this by doing the following:

- Communicating and reinforcing an organization's values
- Building and maintaining communication and continuous feedback
- Ensuring ethical standards are defined, understood, and practiced.
- Providing professional development and training
- Defining roles and responsibilities for employees
- Developing and maintaining a recognition and/or rewards system
- Observing, recognizing, and facilitating organizational and specific employee relations problems
- Motivating employees in order to maintain job satisfaction
- Establishing external professional relationships that benefit the organization

Copyright © Mometrix Media. You have been licensed one copy of this document for personal use only. Any other reproduction or redistribution is strictly prohibited. All rights reserved.

## HOW CULTURE IS FREQUENTLY UNWRITTEN

Mission and vision statements are literally documented with specific words. However, an organization's culture is about behavior and what is observed, heard, and felt—in other words, it is unwritten. Culture is about the degree to which an organization subscribes to or pursues its mission, be it aggressively or slow-and-steady; the value placed on people and their work-life balance; or the hierarchy of the organizational structure. Some unwritten cultural clues could include dress code, size or location of offices, open doors, hallway or breakroom conversations, friendliness, laughter, facial expressions, etc. Unwritten rules are simply the way an organization operates and are deep-rooted in its culture. Other unwritten rules are operational and can easily be learned by observation. For example, in some organizations, employees feel it is in their best interest to always agree with the organization's leaders or else possibly face negative consequences. Other organizations may encourage open and honest feedback with company leaders and reward new or alternative ideas. Employees usually learn to adapt and alter their behavior based on observations.

## CONNECTION BETWEEN TRADITION AND ORGANIZATIONAL CULTURE

Usually, an organization's culture is based on factors that contributed to its success in the past, and thus became tradition. In its early stages, an organization's leaders play a significant role in establishing its culture, thereby planting the seeds of behavioral norms that are closely aligned with their values. These norms will blossom and grow over time to become tradition, shaping an organization's culture. Tradition, when embedded in an organization's culture, can take many forms. How conflicts are resolved, whether respectfully, quietly, privately, or perhaps in the open with raised voices, serves as an example of culture. Decision making is another example, such as one organization making all decisions in a hierarchical manner, while another organization has a more ad-hoc decision-making process. Culture is an all-encompassing term that includes beliefs and an organization's traditions that are passed down over time. HR should be aware of an organization's traditions and their positive or negative impacts on the organization.

## ENCOURAGING EMPLOYEE COMMUNICATION AND EMPLOYEE INVOLVEMENT

It is possible for a particular strategy to be used as both a communication strategy and an involvement strategy because the amount of employee involvement within an organization is closely related to the amount of employee communication. This is because strategies that encourage communication between an organization's employees and that organization's management will often allow employees to have more input in the organization's decision-making processes and ultimately allow employees to become more involved in the organization's operations as a whole. However, this does not necessarily mean that every strategy is both a communication strategy and an involvement strategy. In fact, a strategy that allows a manager to communicate important information to employees without allowing each employee to respond to or discuss the information may be considered a communication strategy, but it cannot be considered an involvement strategy. At the same time, a strategy that allows an individual to have more control over a particular task may be an involvement strategy without being a communication strategy because it does not encourage an individual to communicate.

## EMPLOYEE INVOLVEMENT STRATEGIES

- **Delegating authority** refers to an employee involvement strategy in which an organization grants an individual the power to make decisions related to his or her position. This strategy specifically allows an individual to become more involved in the organization by allowing the individual to make certain decisions without having to receive permission.

**18**

Copyright © Mometrix Media. You have been licensed one copy of this document for personal use only. Any other reproduction or redistribution is strictly prohibited. All rights reserved.

- An **employee survey**, also known as a climate survey, is an employee involvement strategy in which an organization gathers information about the priorities and concerns of the organization's employees by having each employee fill out and submit a form.
- A **suggestion program** is an employee involvement strategy whereby an organization can gather ideas for how to handle the concerns of the organization's employees and/or ideas for how to control or eliminate problems within the organization by allowing employees to submit anonymous ideas. Suggestion programs usually use suggestion boxes, voicemail, and other similar systems.
- An **employee-management committee** is a group of employees that work with the supervisors and managers of the organization to make decisions related to a particular concern of the organization or activity within the organization.
- A **task force** is a group of employees who work together in order to determine the cause of a particular problem and ultimately identify a solution to the problem. Employees are usually only assigned to a task force until the cause of a particular problem is identified and/or solved.

# Legal and Regulatory Environment

## STEPS OF A FEDERAL BILL TO BECOMING A FEDERAL LAW

There are approximately 12 steps for a federal bill to become a law:

1. The process of forming a new law begins with the bill being introduced by the Senate or the House of Representatives and given a number.
2. The bill is then referred to a committee that determines if the bill should be considered further by a subcommittee, considered further by the entire floor of the House or Senate, or if the bill should be ignored.
3. If the bill is deemed credible, it is referred to a subcommittee and hearings are held with experts or other public officials providing testimony.
4. After hearings are held, the bill is modified and amended.
5. After subcommittee review, the bill goes back to full committee where the members vote on whether it should proceed to the House or Senate in a process known as "ordering a bill reported."
6. A written report on the bill is produced.
7. The bill is given a date on the calendar for debate.
8. If the bill passes, it moves to the floor of the House or Senate, and the bill is debated.
9. A vote is taken to pass or defeat the bill.
10. If the bill is passed in the Senate, then the bill is passed on to the House to be considered in the same way and vice versa.
11. After both the House and Senate have approved a bill, the bill is sent to the president to be signed into law, vetoed, or returned to Congress.
12. It may become law automatically if it is ignored for 10 days while Congress is in session, or die automatically if it is ignored until after Congress is in session.

## KEY ANTIDISCRIMINATION LAWS GOVERNING HOW AN ORGANIZATION OPERATES

Employment laws and regulations detail the legal parameters under which an organization must operate. It should be noted that the application of laws may vary depending on the size of an organization, the type of organization, and many other factors. Additionally, laws can also vary based on local, state, and federal laws. A large percentage of employment laws are overseen by the

Copyright © Mometrix Media. You have been licensed one copy of this document for personal use only. Any other reproduction or redistribution is strictly prohibited. All rights reserved.

Equal Employment Opportunity Commission (EEOC), a federal government agency that interprets and enforces federal laws prohibiting discrimination.

- Equal Pay Act (EPA) of 1963 – Prohibits wage discrimination based on gender for anyone in the same organization, performing the same or similar job, in the same or similar conditions.
- Title VII of the Civil Rights Act of 1964 – Prohibits discrimination based on race, color, religion, gender, or national origin.
- Age Discrimination Employment Act (ADEA) of 1967– Prohibits discrimination of anyone 40 years of age or older as it relates to hiring, termination, promotion, compensation, and benefits.
- Uniform Guidelines on Employee Selection Procedures (1978) – Procedures that cover all aspects of employee selection decisions (recruiting, testing, interviewing, etc.) designed to achieve equal employment opportunities without any form of discrimination. Note that these are guidelines and not a law.
- Americans with Disabilities Act (ADA) of 1990 and the ADA Amendments Act (ADAAA) of 2008 – Prohibit discrimination against people with disabilities and guarantees people with disabilities have the same opportunities as those without disabilities.
- Lily Ledbetter Fair Pay Act of 2009 – Implements a somewhat flexible time frame for filing wage discrimination claims.

## LEGAL EMPLOYMENT REGULATIONS OVERSEEN BY THE U.S. DEPARTMENT OF LABOR

The US Department of Labor (DOL) established and actively enforces hundreds of employment laws and regulations. Following are three major acts administered by the DOL:

- Fair Labor Standards Act (FLSA) – An act administered by the DOL Wage and Labor Division. Establishes basic wage requirements for employment in the private sector such as wages, overtime pay, recordkeeping, and employment standards for children.
- Family Medical Leave Act (FMLA) – An act administered by the DOL Employment Standards Administration. Requires covered employers to provide employees with job protection and unpaid leave in the event of qualified medical and family reasons. Such reasons include pregnancy, adoption, foster care placement of a child, personal or family illness, or family military leave.
- Occupational Safety and Health Act (OSHA) – An act administered by the DOL Occupational and Health Administration. Ensures that employers provide safe and healthy working conditions for employees. Employers covered under the act must comply with legal safety and health standards, free from hazards.

## ASSISTING AN ORGANIZATION TO ABIDE BY LEGAL REGULATIONS IN THE WORKPLACE

Compliance with all laws and regulations is mandatory for all aspects of HR programs, practices, and policies. The HR professional must stay current with applicable federal, state, local, and possibly international laws impacting their organization. Basically, HR professionals work to ensure a safe and fair workplace at all times. At the same time, they should also be aware and ready to communicate the cost of non-compliance of legal regulations, including fines, possible lawsuits, and other liabilities. This means that it is necessary to coach managers and employees with regard to applicable laws in such matters as hiring, terminations, and employee relations issues. HR professionals can assist their employers in hanging in common areas legally required posters detailing Fair Labor Standards Act (FLSA) and Occupational Safety and Health Act (OSHA) information. The legal requirement for what should be displayed on these posters may differ based

Copyright © Mometrix Media. You have been licensed one copy of this document for personal use only. Any other reproduction or redistribution is strictly prohibited. All rights reserved.

on local, state, or federal guidelines. Understanding and complying with all local, state, and federal laws helps the organization and its employees do the right thing and reduce costly legal liability.

# Confidentiality and Privacy Rules That Apply to Employee Records, Company Data, and Individual Data

## WORKPLACE CONFIDENTIALITY

**Workplace confidentiality** is defined as the policies and procedures created by an organization to maintain confidential, private, sensitive, or compromising information related to the employer and its employees. Confidential or private information may include, but is not limited to, business planning and forecasting, client information and contracts, research and development studies, and employee records. HR plays a vital role in maintaining confidential and private information. There are laws for specific types of data and how they should be maintained, and other data types come with suggested procedures to securely protect an organization from legal risks. A general litmus test in the dissemination of private information is (1) is sharing the information legal? and (2) does the individual or group absolutely need to know because their input is mandatory in order to investigate, settle, or solve the issue? A breach in confidential or private information can result in a broad range of negative consequences legally, financially, and in the court of public opinion.

## IMPORTANCE OF CONFIDENTIALITY IN THE WORKPLACE

Confidentiality is vital in human resources practices. Maintaining the confidentiality of all employee records is imperative. Information to be safeguarded includes, but is not limited to, social security numbers, birth dates, addresses, phone numbers, personal emails, benefits enrollments, medical or other leave details, garnishments, bank account information, disciplinary actions, grievances, and employment eligibility data. When employee record information is requested for legitimate purposes, a written release signed by the employee should be obtained and kept on file. Examples of these requests include employment verification for bank loans and mortgage applications.

Further, human resources should internally disclose this sensitive data only to those who are authorized and have a need to know based on the scenario at hand. For example, a supervisor should have knowledge of employees' disciplinary histories so that they can manage them more effectively. However, that supervisor doesn't need to know what benefit plan the employee chose or that the employee has a tax lien.

However, human resources cannot always promise complete confidentiality. For example, if an employee makes a harassment allegation, human resources will move to investigate immediately. Human resources should inform the complainant and anyone involved in the investigation that the situation will be handled as discreetly as possible; the nature of an investigation dictates that information obtained during the process may be shared with those on a need-to-know basis, including the accused.

## CONFIDENTIALITY RULES PERTAINING TO EMPLOYEE RECORDS

An organization's HR department collects a substantial amount of employee paperwork: completed job application, resumes, contact information, completed benefit forms, performance evaluations, and possibly performance improvement plans and medical records. Some documents, whether in paper or electronic form, must remain private and thus protected. Medical records absolutely must be kept confidential, as release of this information in any form could be a violation of the Americans with Disabilities Act (ADA), the Genetic Information Nondiscrimination Act (GINA) and/or the Health Insurance Portability and Accountability Act (HIPAA). The rationale for confidentiality is that this type of information, if not held private, could result in possible discriminatory decisions by

Copyright © Mometrix Media. You have been licensed one copy of this document for personal use only. Any other reproduction or redistribution is strictly prohibited. All rights reserved.

an organization. For example, the ADA maintains that employee medical information must be kept separate—in a locked file cabinet or secured behind a firewall, for instance—from the employee's personnel record. This is a specific legal ruling. However, there are other documents that most organizations should keep secure and private because it is in everyone's best interest, including I-9 forms, background check results, performance evaluations, termination data, and investigative documents (harassment, complaints, etc.). These documents may include information that could potentially be utilized in a discrimination case against the employer if released and wrongdoing is suspected.

## WORKPLACE MONITORING PARAMETERS

Workplace monitoring is a documented policy and program that an employer can use to monitor and gather information related to suspicious activity by a person in their organization. This monitoring is conducted if the employer has reason to believe a person in their organization is engaged in some activity that might threaten the interests of the business. Monitoring methods might include reviewing internet content usage, wiretapping, GPS tracking, interviewing other employees, etc. Many of these surveillance methods are easier if the company requires employees to utilize company-issued phones and computers. Before any workplace monitoring activities are deployed, two actions must occur: (1) employers must be aware and adhere to all local, state, and federal laws regarding the desired method of workplace monitoring; and (2) employers must ensure that all employees have been made aware and given documentation of all company rules and regulations at the onset of employment and changes thereafter. Employees' knowledge of employer rules and regulations assist if there is unethical or illegal activity because, when such activity is committed, existing employee knowledge proves the activity was committed intentionally by the employee.

## CONFIDENTIALITY RULES PERTAINING TO COMPANY DATA

Company data must be kept private and only released to those who have been identified as needing to know the information in order to operate the organization. Typically, the following information is considered proprietary and confidential data: client names, sources of revenue, expenditures and losses, trade secrets, and all business processes and operations. Confidentiality applies to paper and electronic company data. Paper documents must be kept in a secure, locked location, and electronic data must have appropriate firewalls and password protection. Organizations will often have an employee sign a privacy or nondisclosure agreement that clearly documents what information is protected, and how and with whom proprietary information can be shared. This is an important step to avoid potentially negative legal repercussions, loss of business, or competitive advantage. For example, if an employee reveals trade secrets to a competitor, thus causing harm to their employer, they are in violation of their non-disclosure agreement and could face legal consequences. Additionally, some organizations have procedures in place for protecting intellectual property via trademark, patent, and copyright protocols.

Copyright © Mometrix Media. You have been licensed one copy of this document for personal use only. Any other reproduction or redistribution is strictly prohibited. All rights reserved.

# Business Functions

## IMPORTANCE OF UNDERSTANDING BUSINESS FUNCTIONS

HR professionals operate as both strategic partners and business partners, necessitating the need to understand the business from an operational perspective. When this understanding is gained, HR can then provide the necessary support to business units or functions to meet business goals.

- HR is usually the first area to listen to employee relations concerns that must be communicated to organizational managers in such a way that doesn't cause financial harm or loss of productivity—thus requiring knowledge of business functions.
- HR must understand business strategies so they can recruit the appropriate talent needed. Human capital must be leveraged for an organization to achieve its strategic goals.
- HR assists in managing the performance and training needs of an organization. For example, input from HR is vital when an employee is underperforming and requires intervention to achieve improvement, sometimes referred to as a performance improvement plan (PIP). Otherwise, there could be negative legal consequences if this documented plan is not written and implemented correctly.
- How an organization measures business functions (financial, efficiency rates, etc.) is essential to understanding both present and future goals. Within a dynamic, rapidly changing business environment, HR is typically at the forefront of change management initiatives, requiring redirection or re-education of employees for the future.

## FUNCTIONS OF AN ACCOUNTING DEPARTMENT

The accounting department manages the financial nuances of an organization: collecting and processing financial information through activities and reports. Accounting maintains a record of all monies spent, owed, received, or borrowed, in addition to assessing value of assets and liabilities, enabling the organization to report profits/loss.

- Accounts payable: A liability the organization owes others; a record of payment for goods or services.
- Accounts receivable: Assets that others owe the organization; monies earned from sales, payments from debtors, and other sources.
- Payroll: Wages and salaries earned by employees per pay period (gross earnings), calculated based on information in an employee's personnel file; earnings for a period of time and any applicable deductions (income tax, social security, etc.).
- Reporting: Usually generated from accounting software and used for budgeting, forecasting, or other financial business decisions; used to communicate financial status to stakeholders.
- Financial controls: Organizations typically follow Generally Accepted Accounting Principles (GAAP), reconciliations, and division of responsibilities which are all designed for compliance, fraud, and theft prevention.

## FUNCTIONS OF A FINANCE DEPARTMENT

The finance department manages the acquisition of funds, the management of existing funds, and plans for the future spending of funds. Working closely with organizational decision makers, the finance department assists in achieving the financial goals of the organization. The finance department evaluates the speed at which funds are being spent, how fast revenue is being produced, and analyzes financial patterns and trends. Generally, the finance department uses this information to distribute capital to longer term assets, balanced against risk considerations, in order to yield the greatest return. In turn, the finance department must determine when to sell assets that are underperforming and using those funds to acquire new, better-performing assets.

Copyright © Mometrix Media. You have been licensed one copy of this document for personal use only. Any other reproduction or redistribution is strictly prohibited. All rights reserved.

The constant balance of equity and debt must be managed effectively by the finance department. Sometimes riskier investments carry the potential for greater returns on equity, but also carry significant risk. The finance department's goal is usually to maximize return while minimizing risk. Lastly, how dividends or profits are distributed is a function of the finance department, whether that is balancing a payout to shareholders and/or distributing all or part back into the organization.

## ROLE OF BUSINESS OPERATIONS MANAGEMENT

**Business operations management** (OM) is responsible for managing the systems and processes that produce goods and services. Business operations management in an organization seeks to develop and/or maintain business practices that enable the organization to function as efficiently as possible. This primarily means utilizing people and materials to produce goods and services efficiently, yielding the maximum profit to the organization. Overall, OM aims to balance cost and revenue to maximize net operating profit. OM oversees an organization's processes, design, planning control, performance efficiency, and strategic alignment. OM typically interacts with finance, accounting, marketing, human resources, and information technology. Responsibilities for OM could include resourcing and financially reasonable acquisition of materials when needed, management of inventory, delivery of goods, quality standards, and engineering processes for the labor necessary to complete a function in the most cost-efficient and productive manner.

## FUNCTION OF SALES AND MARKETING IN AN ORGANIZATION

Sales and marketing are frequently grouped together in an organization because their functions complement one another. Typically, the two divisions share information and ideas to enhance and yield positive results for the organization. **Marketing** covers the processes and techniques of promoting and distributing an organization's product or service. It is usually responsible for raising awareness about a given product or service and developing potential customers or clients for the sales team. **Sales** covers the activities required in promoting and selling an organization's goods or services. Marketing and sales must communicate and collaborate together in order to develop qualified leads and other high value prospects. The better their communication and efforts, the better they both service their end goal, which is to attract and retain clients while increasing sales.

## CASH FLOW METRICS, RETURN ON INVESTMENT, AND RETURN ON EQUITY

**Cash flow metrics** is data that examines money coming into and going out of a business.

**Return on investment** (ROI) is a ratio or percentage comparing gains of an investment versus its initial price. In other words, this measures the return of an investment relative to the cost. For example, imagine John invested $1,000 in Company A in 2019 and sold his stock shares for $1,300 the following year. To calculate his ROI, he would divide his profits ($1,300 - $1,000 = $300) by the investment cost ($1,000), for an ROI of $300/$1,000, or 30%. Following is the formula for ROI:

$$\text{ROI} = \frac{Value\ Investment - Cost\ Investment}{Cost\ Investment}$$

**Return on equity** (ROE) is a ratio or percentage measuring the earnings of the organization during a period of time as compared to the amount of money invested in shareholder equity. ROE reveals if an organization is efficiently using investments to make profits by measuring the organization's rate of return on shareholder equity. In other words, it signals to shareholders if their investment is being used wisely. For example, suppose Company B has $1 million in net income and $10 million in shareholder equity. Dividing net income by shareholder equity reveals the ROE: $1million/$10

Copyright © Mometrix Media. You have been licensed one copy of this document for personal use only. Any other reproduction or redistribution is strictly prohibited. All rights reserved.

million = 10%. This is a 10% return on the shareholders' investment. Sometimes a company will compare their ROE with similar competitors in the field. Following is the basic formula for ROE:

$$ROE = \frac{Net\ Income}{Shareholder\ Equity}$$

## SALES METRICS USED TO ACQUIRE CUSTOMERS AND CLIENTS

The goal of marketing and sales metrics is to measure the effectiveness of an organization's promotional activities and campaigns. The first key measure is a **lead**, a potential customer or client that interacts with the organization. Leads can be measured by the total number acquired for a given period of time, often referred to as lead volume or **leads generated**. This total number will also prove if a given sales or marketing campaign or activity was successful in acquiring more leads. Generally, the number of sales leads is large and then becomes narrower as sales are nurtured or lost, often referred to as a **sales funnel**. This narrowing can also be called **lead conversion** and reveals the ratio or percentage of lead volume to actual new customers.

## SALES METRICS USED TO GAUGE CUSTOMER ACQUISITION SUCCESS

One way for an organization to measure customer activity is the **average transaction value**, meaning what one customer spends per transaction. An organization can use this to forecast its sales by multiplying the average transaction value by the anticipated number of customers for a given period of time, thereby adjusting campaigns and strategies to increase sales. Sales strategy can be measured by the gross profit margin (revenue minus cost of goods sold), which will indicate if a given set of sales strategies is profitable. Additionally, the customer acquisition cost (amount of money spent to acquire a new customer) must be calculated to determine if sales efforts are too costly.

Another measurement to gauge customer acquisition success is the **opportunity success rate**. This is similar to the point halfway down a sales funnel whereby success is uncertain but hope remains. This rate measures how many leads the sales department is able to convert into customers. An organization can use this information to evaluate sales strategies and overall business planning. If the rate is high, then the organization knows they can successfully acquire new customers; if the rate is low, then strategy and planning need to be adjusted.

# HR Policies and Procedures

## IMPORTANCE OF HR POLICIES AND PROCEDURES

An **HR policy** is a set of rules that all members of an organization are required to follow, whereas an **HR procedure** covers the steps necessary to implement a policy. Basically, policy states what rules must be followed in an organization, while procedures detail in writing how to adhere to organizational policies. For an organization to be successful, HR policies and procedures contain the following core elements: employee role descriptions that detail employee expectations specific to each position in an organization; rules and regulations that specify what employees can or cannot do, as well as behavior that is or is not acceptable; and a clear description of consequences for unethical or inappropriate behavior or actions. There are many reasons why an organization needs to have HR policies: (1) It gives people defined rules to achieve a respectful environment, (2) it reduces conflict and provides an organization with a certain standard to guide acceptable behavior, and (3) it assists an organization in forming an image in the community that is also helpful for recruiting.

Copyright © Mometrix Media. You have been licensed one copy of this document for personal use only. Any other reproduction or redistribution is strictly prohibited. All rights reserved.

## POLICIES AND PROCEDURES LEGALLY PROTECTING AN ORGANIZATION

Policies and procedures detail how an organization should function. Additionally, policies and procedures communicate an organization's internal values and specify best practices. These policies and procedures can also help protect an organization from legal risk, thereby reducing potential lawsuits. This is achieved in many ways as policies and procedures help employees maintain compliance with rules that are behavioral in nature. In a regulated industry, they assist in legal and regulatory compliance. In a situation with evolving issues, policies and procedures can be leveraged as a mechanism to alter company culture and forge change. HR policies primarily communicate a standard of expected behavior, and disciplinary action is a measured response in keeping with these established policies and procedures. The role of HR is to ensure these policies and procedures are in legal compliance with all federal, state, and local laws, as well as promote fairness, equity, and consistency in how they are implemented. Examples of HR policies and procedures might include anti-discrimination policies, termination procedures, disciplinary actions, etc.

## GUIDING PRINCIPLES WHEN APPROACHING EMPLOYEE DISCIPLINE

Discipline in the workplace is necessary, but should always be fair and within the legal constraints of federal, state, and local laws. To paraphrase an old proverb, "the punishment should fit the crime." All discipline should be applied consistently, or the organization is at risk for a legal violation. Additionally, it is a good practice to document a record of facts, including dates, leading to the disciplinary action and steps taken to remedy the situation. An HR professional should be in a position to support any disciplinary action(s). Asking questions to clarify when in doubt is an important step. An employee may not always agree with the action, but they must understand why corrective actions are needed. Being firm, consistent, and showing respect and empathy towards the employee is needed when discipline must be deployed.

## PROGRESSIVE DISCIPLINE

**Progressive discipline** is a method to inform an employee about behavior, conduct, or job performance that is unsatisfactory and to gradually implement actions designed to improve their behavior or performance. The goal is to give the employee the opportunity to correct the undesired behavior or poor performance through a gradual progression of disciplinary responses. The goal of this process is to get the employee back on track toward becoming a more productive member of the organization.

There is not a specific formula for implementing progressive discipline. Usually, the seriousness of the infraction and number of incidents factors into the implementation of progressive discipline. Progressive discipline is typically a five-step process consisting of (1) a verbal warning, or a one-on-one session with a manager reviewing the issues and the corrective action; (2) a written warning, in which a manager documents the issue and lack of improvement; (3) a performance improvement plan (PIP), which is a documented plan that is time-bound and details what will happen if corrective action is not achieved; (4) suspension, for when a corrective action is not met and the employee is given time away from work to reflect on the situation; and (5) termination, at which point the progressive discipline is labeled a failure and the employee is terminated. The overall rationale behind progressive disciple is to ensure employees are treated fairly and to help nurture a positive organizational culture.

## CENTRAL PURPOSE OF THE AMERICANS WITH DISABILITIES ACT (ADA)

The Americans with Disabilities Act (ADA) is a federal law that prohibits discrimination against people with disabilities and guarantees that people with disabilities have the same opportunities as those without disabilities. A disability is generally defined as having at least one of the following: a

Copyright © Mometrix Media. You have been licensed one copy of this document for personal use only. Any other reproduction or redistribution is strictly prohibited. All rights reserved.

physical or mental impairment that significantly limits one or more major life activities, a record of an impairment, or the individual is regarded as having such an impairment. As it relates to HR, this means it is not legal to discriminate in employment practices such as benefits, promotions, compensation, recruitment, hiring, firing, job assignments, training and development, and many other employee relations matters. The ADA was passed by Congress in 1990 and amended in 1994 to cover all businesses, employment agencies, or organized labor unions with 15 or more employees. This legislation requires employers to make reasonable accommodations so that disabled employees are able to adequately perform their jobs so long as the accommodations do not present undue hardship to the business. These modifications or accommodations may also mean physical adjustments to the building, such as access ramps outside and within the building, bathroom accessibility, etc.

## EQUAL EMPLOYMENT OPPORTUNITY COMMISSION (EEOC)

The **Equal Employment Opportunity Commission (EEOC)** was formed by Title VII of the Civil Rights Act to protect certain groups of individuals from unlawful discrimination. The EEOC is a federal agency designed to encourage equal employment opportunities; to train employers to avoid practices and policies that could cause unlawful discrimination; and to enforce the laws included in the Civil Rights Act, Age Discrimination in Employment Act, and laws included in other similar anti-discrimination legislation. Discriminatory practices by an employer are either intentional (like an employer advertisement saying they will not hire a certain race) or unintentional (such as banning hats for reasons unrelated to safety being discriminatory against those who wear a head covering for religious purposes). Regardless, equal opportunity laws prohibit both intentional and unintentional discrimination. The EEOC attempts to obtain settlements from employers for actions that the commission deems to be discriminatory. If the employer will not settle with the EEOC, the EEOC will continue their attempt to enforce the law by filing a lawsuit against the employer on behalf of the victim of the discrimination.

## EEO REPORTING

The **Equal Employment Opportunity Act** (EEO), passed by Congress in 1972, strives to ensure that any person in the U.S. may not be discriminated against when applying for a job based on age, gender, race, ethnicity, or religion. The Equal Employment Opportunity Commission (EEOC), which enforces the EEO Act, requires annual workforce reporting for any employer with 100 or more employees, and federal contractors who have 50 or more employees as well as contracts of at least $50,000. In addition to reporting, employers must post EEO posters in workplace common spaces in their offices. The reason for the reporting requirement is to calculate and capture the workforce composition and ensure there is no discrimination against a protected class. There are various EEO reports that must be completed if an employer meets the EEO reporting criteria, and none of it is voluntary. EEO reports capture information in nine categories:

1. Senior-level officials and managers – Highest level workers who set strategy, develop policies, and direct.
2. Professionals – Not always, but usually requires degrees. Includes engineers, accountants, and teachers.
3. Technicians – This requires very specialized skills for a specific form of work. Includes emergency medical technicians and dental hygienists.
4. Sales workers – A worker who lists sales as their primary function. Includes retail, real-estate agents, and telemarketers.
5. Administrative support – Office and clerical workers. Includes secretaries and payroll clerks.

27

Copyright © Mometrix Media. You have been licensed one copy of this document for personal use only. Any other reproduction or redistribution is strictly prohibited. All rights reserved.

6. Craft workers – Specific skill with advanced knowledge or skills. Includes carpenters, plumbers, and auto mechanics.
7. Operatives – Jobs that require minimal training. Operatives are sometimes called semi-skilled. Includes bakers and butchers.
8. Laborers – Jobs that require a marginal amount of training. Laborers are referred to as unskilled. Includes assistants and freight movers.
9. Service workers – This ranking does not imply this is the lowest level of work and some make more money than other categories. Includes janitors, hairstylists, and police.

## EEO-1 REPORTING

Private employers with 100 or more employees and federal contractors with 50 or more employees as well as contracts of at least $50,000 must complete and submit an EEO-1 report each year. This report organizes employee-specific data by race, gender, and job category for an employer. The completed report is submitted to the EEOC and the Office of Federal Contract Compliance Programs (OFCCP) for adherence to federal laws against employment discrimination. This is a mandatory report. If it is not filed, if false information is provided, or if an employer discriminated against an employee, then there are monetary as well as legal consequences and/or penalties. While there are other EEO reports (EEO-3, EEO-4, EEO-5) that apply to unions, governmental entities, public schools, etc., the EEO-1 report is the most utilized reporting mechanism by the EEOC.

# HR Metrics

## COST-BENEFIT ANALYSIS

**Cost benefit analysis** is presented as a ratio that helps an organization determine how certain activities and related costs impact its profitability. The following formula calculates cost-benefit ratio:

$$\text{Cost-benefit ratio} = \frac{Value\ of\ projected\ benefits}{Cost}$$

For example, if an HR department made the decision to participate in an employee program that resulted in a cost savings of $10,000 and the cost of the program was $2,000, then the cost-benefit ratio would be 5:1. HR typically performs cost-benefit analyses on a regular basis to justify continuing or ending a particular program or activity.

## COST PER HIRE

**Cost per hire** is an HR recruitment metric that measures the total money invested to hire someone divided by the number of hires in a given time period. Internal costs might include employee referral awards, recruiter salaries, cost of internal recruiting systems, etc. External costs might include advertising, events, job fairs, background checks, assessments, etc. If an organization's total annual internal and external recruiting costs were $2.25 million and 500 employees were hired, then the cost per hire would be $4,500. The formula to calculate cost per hire is:

$$\text{Cost per Hire} = \frac{(Total\ Internal + External\ Recruiting\ Costs)}{Total\ Number\ of\ Hires\ in\ Given\ Time\ Frame}$$

Continuing the example, if the same organization wants to hire 400 employees next year and its average cost per hire is $4,500, and assuming nothing else changes, then the organization can anticipate spending $1.8 million for recruiting. This is a strategic metric used to assess the

Copyright © Mometrix Media. You have been licensed one copy of this document for personal use only. Any other reproduction or redistribution is strictly prohibited. All rights reserved.

efficiency and effectiveness in an organization's recruiting process, and is frequently benchmarked against similar organizations and industry peers.

## SELECTION RATIOS

**Selection ratio** is used in the HR recruiting process to assess and evaluate sourcing for job positions. It is a ratio obtained by taking the number of candidates the business desires to hire and dividing it by the total number of candidates for the open jobs. A low ratio means the organization can be more selective, while a high selection ratio indicates the organization need not be as selective. Following is the formula for selection ratio:

$$\text{Selection Ratio} = \frac{Number\ of\ Hired\ Candidates}{Total\ Number\ of\ Candidates}$$

Selection ratios can be applied in many ways. For example, it can be used to evaluate applicant acceptance of offers via dividing the number of offers accepted by those that were extended. Additionally, the percentage of minority applicants can be determined by number of minority applicants divided by total number of applicants for that same position in the same time period.

## TURNOVER AND TURNOVER STATISTICS

**Turnover** refers to when an employee permanently leaves an organization. Turnover is typically captured as a rate or percentage on a monthly or yearly basis and is useful in predicting the number of new employees that must be hired to replace those that have permanently left the organization. More often, turnover statistics are analyzed on a monthly basis to also highlight at what point in the year employees tend to exit the organization. Following is the formula to calculate monthly employee turnover:

$$\text{Monthly Turnover Rate} = \frac{Number\ of\ Separations\ During\ Month}{Average\ Number\ of\ Employees\ During\ Month} \times 100$$

For example, if 30 employees leave the organization in the month of January, and there was an average of 200 employees in the month of January, then the turnover rate is 15%. Turnover statistics are more than just a number or percentage. This rate gives an organization a starting point to analyze why employees are leaving and take corrective actions, if needed, to maintain a healthy organization. Some of the reasons for turnover might include poor performance, better pay, personal reasons, career advancement, etc.

## INNOVATION RATE

Innovation in an organization usually includes new or improved products or services. **Innovation rate** measures if new ideas, products, and services are profitable. To determine the innovation rate, divide revenue generated by new products and services by total revenue from all products and services over a defined time period. If the innovation rate is equal to or higher than competitors' rates, then the current innovation strategy is appropriate and the focus should be on designing products and services similar to those recently placed on the market. On the other hand, if the innovation rate is significantly lower than competitors' rates, a new innovation strategy should be implemented that focuses on developing products and services not similar to those recently placed on the market. The innovation rate is not a measure of how innovative a company is, but rather a measure of how profitable each group of new innovations has been for the firm.

Copyright © Mometrix Media. You have been licensed one copy of this document for personal use only. Any other reproduction or redistribution is strictly prohibited. All rights reserved.

## IMPORTANCE OF TRACKING EMPLOYEE GRIEVANCES

A **grievance** is a complaint of some type of unfair treatment by an employee to an employer regarding a violation. An employee grievance can be formal, like a written report; or informal, like a verbal discussion. Generally, a grievance can be from an employee against an employer or management official, an employee against another employee, or any combination thereof. Some examples of grievances might include harassment, discrimination, safety, workplace relationships, organizational changes, etc. HR often is involved and tracks grievances for awareness and to determine if there are trends in grievances pointing to a bigger issue in an organization, such as a large number of grievances against one manager. Tracking grievances based on subject matter can assist in implementing quicker corrective actions. Measuring the time that it takes to close a grievance could also impact employee satisfaction with the organization. If the problem is quickly addressed and resolved in a fair and expedient time frame, then the employee will feel more valued and satisfied. Tracking grievances also provides the organization a picture as to whether employee complaints and grievances are rising or falling, which is another measure of organizational health.

# Tools to Compile Data

## NEED OF TECHNOLOGY-BASED TOOLS

HR utilizes large volumes of data about the organization and the people it employs for the purpose of recruitment, performance management and evaluations, payroll, EEO, etc. Tools to compile data make organizational functions more efficient and productive. Some tools are unique to HR management, such as a human resources information system (HRIS), and others are more commonplace, like Microsoft Office with Excel, Word, PowerPoint, etc. HR specifically compiles data to include types of employees, employee specifics, compensation, training, open jobs, etc. This type of data is vital to HR for many reasons, such as budgeting, succession planning, salary surveys and reviews, ensuring EEO compliance, applicant presentations, etc. It is important to remember that different tools or software are used for different purposes. Therefore, the key is to understand available HR tools and software and use those that best suit the functions needed for a specific project. Frequently, it is necessary to filter and download data from one source or tool and bring it into another to optimize data manipulation or present information. An example of this would be using data from an HRIS to complete an Excel file.

## SPREADSHEETS

A **spreadsheet** is a computer application used to store, analyze, and organize data in a tabular format of horizontal rows and vertical columns. Data, both numeric and in text form, is entered into cells that can be used to calculate and display information. For example, a spreadsheet could contain information such as employee names, job titles, locations, and compensation that could be used to calculate compensation information by title or location. This information can also be referred to as a database. One of the most popular spreadsheet programs is Microsoft Excel. Following are some key functions performed in Excel for HR analysis:

- Query – A request of data that filters and formats information from a spreadsheet or database.
- Sorting – The process of arranging data in a specific order, whether alphabetical, lowest to highest, etc.
- Filter – A condition that qualifies data to be revealed or hidden, such as data from a certain location or department.
- VLOOKUP – Filters a high volume of data based on conditions and reveals specific information from two columns and displays it as one.

Copyright © Mometrix Media. You have been licensed one copy of this document for personal use only. Any other reproduction or redistribution is strictly prohibited. All rights reserved.

- Pivot table – Permits data to be summarized using interactive fields and filter buttons. The benefit is that it enables easy retrieval of specific data from a large amount of data.

## STATISTICAL TOOLS

Statistics usage in HR is a data–driven approach to managing people and other variables in an organization. Statistics can help people understand a situation, forecast future possibilities based on previously obtained data, and can sometimes help an organization mitigate risk. For example, statistics might help an organization better gauge when people will leave, discover possible bias in the hiring process, and help guide benefit decisions. There are many tools and software applications available to organizations for statistical analysis. The following are some commonly used HR statistical tools:

- R – A programming language that is a powerful statistical tool for data analysis and visualization, designed to manipulate enormous datasets.
- Python – Similar to R, offers less visualization and statistical analysis features, but is easier to learn.
- Power BI (business intelligence) – Statistical software that can aggregate large amounts of data as well as perform analysis and offer visualization benefits. Useful when multiple data sources need to be combined.
- Tableau – Similar to BI, good for aggregation of data and considered to be outstanding at visualization.
- Excel – The most basic statistical software for smaller sets of data and the easiest-to-use statistical package.

## CONNECTION BETWEEN HR DATA AND EVIDENCE-BASED DECISION MAKING

**Evidence-based decision making** refers to identifying strategies and solutions to HR problems that utilize strong, reliable empirical data. Using such data to support decisions gives HR more credibility and logic in support of a given path or decision. Sometimes it gives an organization proof that a concept or practice will work, whereas other times it assists by using proven information to mitigate risk in a particular endeavor. The source of the data gathered can vary depending on the decision that needs to be made. Some examples of sources include empirical studies published in reputable journals, data from within an organization, opinions of experts in a given field of study, and the opinions of stakeholders who might be impacted by the decision. Evidence-based decision making is regarded as a collaborative process between HR, managers, and stakeholders, thereby increasing transparency, cooperation, and communication.

## HUMAN RESOURCE INFORMATION SYSTEM (HRIS)

A **human resource information system** (HRIS) is a computer system designed to help human resource professionals carry out the day-to-day human resource functions necessary for an organization to continue functioning normally. Most HRISs are designed to collect and store data related to the use of employee benefits, hiring, placement, training and evaluations of employees, payroll, and information about the work performed by the employee during a given period of time. An HRIS is designed to help a human resource professional carry out all primary functions associated with human resource needs, which include benefits administration, payroll, time and labor management, and human resources management. An HRIS not only aids the human resources department, but also helps the entire organization function effectively.

Copyright © Mometrix Media. You have been licensed one copy of this document for personal use only. Any other reproduction or redistribution is strictly prohibited. All rights reserved.

# Methods to Collect Data

### RELIABILITY AND VALIDITY

**Reliability** refers to the consistency of a particular measure. A research tool is said to be reliable if it produces consistent and repeatable measures every time. For example, measuring tapes and stopwatches provide consistent and reliable measures. Surveys should be reliable if the questions are clear and straightforward, but ambiguous questions might return unreliable results.

**Validity** refers to whether an instrument accurately measures what it is supposed to be measuring. The validity of a survey may be more difficult to interpret. For example, can a survey accurately measure company commitment or employee satisfaction? For an instrument to be deemed as valid, it needs to pass a rigorous statistical testing routine.

### QUALITATIVE VS. QUANTITATIVE DATA

Data interpretation involves drawing conclusions from data sets with the goal of answering a question and spurring meaningful action. Data can be qualitative or quantitative. **Qualitative** data is descriptive and focuses on categorizing concepts based on making observations, conducting interviews, or reviewing documents. **Quantitative** data, on the other hand, involves a numerical, statistics-driven approach in which data is derived from surveys and other quantifiable media.

### DESCRIPTIVE VS. INFERENTIAL STATISTICS

Statistics is used in the quantitative analysis of numeric data. **Descriptive statistics** tell a story about a large set of data in a graph, chart, or table format. This format summarizes a large volume of data quicker than looking at hundreds (or more) of rows and columns. For example, if someone wanted to determine the average salary for a particular job in multiple locations, they might summarize the average salary by location in a chart. In this example, a measure of tendency was to group data by a certain characteristic, salary in this case, and described the center of the data set. Measures of central tendency include (1) mean, or the average value; (2) mode, the value that occurs most often; and (3) median, the middle point in a data set. Also included are measures of dispersion, or the data's range, variance, and standard deviation. **Inferential statistics** involve complex calculations that enable a person to infer information about a large population based on studying a sampling from the larger population. It helps to identify relationships between variables in a small sampling and then predict how those variables relate to the larger population. Additionally, population is not typically a single number but a range of potential numbers rated with a degree of confidence.

### DATA COLLECTION FOR AN EMPLOYEE ENGAGEMENT SURVEY

An **employee engagement survey** is an empirical method for capturing what is in the hearts and minds of employees. It is usually conducted once a year. The survey is designed to measure aspects of employee engagement and is used as a tool to analyze the employee experience and drive change. An employee engagement survey can be administered on paper or electronically, depending on the environment and employee access to technology. Employee engagement surveys typically range from 20 to 40 questions. There is no exact number of desired questions because that depends on the organization and what information is trying to be extracted. A balance needs to be achieved between too few questions, which may not yield enough data; or too many questions, which might create an overabundance of data too complicated to summarize in reports. Usually, questions are written to measure engagement, determine what drives engagement, and provide the opportunity for open-ended questions and comments. Except for comments, responses can be indicated on a Likert scale of five ranking points that measures the degree to which an employee agrees or disagrees with a statement.

Copyright © Mometrix Media. You have been licensed one copy of this document for personal use only. Any other reproduction or redistribution is strictly prohibited. All rights reserved.

## ELEMENTS OF A PULSE SURVEY

A **pulse survey** is an employee feedback measurement tool that empirically measures very specific topics for an organization. The pulse survey is usually only a few questions, typically under 10, and can be conducted more frequently than an employee engagement survey. A pulse survey can be an effective tool to supplement an annual employee engagement survey and/or stand alone to measure specific aspects of progress. Additionally, the questions can change from department to department and can be modified over time to measure progress in a specific area. For example, how likely is an employee to recommend the company as a place to work for friends and colleagues? A pulse survey enables an organization to achieve the check-in more regularly with employees and better understand changes in opinions and trends over time. This information helps an organization continuously grow and improve in a positive manner.

## INTERVIEWS

The basic purpose of an interview is to obtain a certain amount of information from the interviewee concerning defined questions and issues. This give-and-take process is not merely words. Sometimes, information can be gathered from gestures, body language, facial expressions, posture, and other nonverbal communication. Communication with words can be further dissected when tone, speech speed, and inflection are taken into consideration. An interview is a purposeful exchange between the interviewer and the interviewee that can be one-on-one, in groups, or any combination thereof. Additionally, there are many types of interviews, including structured, patterned, stress, directive, nondirective, etc. The type of interview conducted also depends on many factors and situations, such as job selection interview, qualitative interview to obtain more in-depth information on an issue, exit interview, etc. Generally, interviews tend to be more personal than surveys and allow the interviewer to probe further with follow-up questions and additional clarification if needed.

## TYPES OF INTERVIEWS

Types of interviews depend on the situation and the preference of the interviewer. These are the most commonly-used types of interviews:

- **Structured** interview – Every interviewee is asked the same questions. Similar information from interviewees can then be fairly compared to others.
- **Patterned** interview – Interviewees are asked different questions, but all questioning the same body of knowledge, skill, or ability.
- **Stress** interview – The interviewer is aggressive in approach to see how an interviewee might respond. Stress interviews are frequently used in law enforcement.
- **Directive** interview – A structured interview whereby the interviewer asks very specific questions in a calm, controlled manner.
- **Nondirective** interview – The interviewer asks more open-ended questions in a particular direction, but the interviewees can drive the direction of questions. These are frequently used in counseling.
- **Behavioral** interview – The interviewer asks specific questions about past behavior, performance, and examples as a way to gauge interviewee skill set and knowledge. Typically, past performance can be a good indicator of future performance.
- **Situational** interview – The interviewer asks questions that require the interviewee to consider hypothetical situations he or she may have experienced in a certain role and how it was handled, thereby gauging an interviewee's knowledge and skills.

Copyright © Mometrix Media. You have been licensed one copy of this document for personal use only. Any other reproduction or redistribution is strictly prohibited. All rights reserved.

### STRUCTURE AND BEST PRACTICES OF EMPLOYEE FOCUS GROUPS

Focus groups can be used to investigate ideas, opinions, and concerns. Focus groups can be beneficial for clarifying supplemental research because they are relatively timely and inexpensive. The topic and objectives of the group should be clearly defined before potential participants are identified. Participants should be notified that their identities will be anonymous and that all information will be confidential. Once a pool of participants has been selected and separated into groups, a trained facilitator should be chosen and a guide of discussion questions should be constructed. Most studies will contain three to 10 focus groups, each with five to 12 voluntary participants. A private location is ideal, and many discussions will last approximately 90 minutes. Finally, all collected information will be analyzed and reported.

### MANAGEMENT BY WALKING AROUND STRATEGY

The **management by walking around** (MBWA) strategy is simply a communication and involvement method in which an organization encourages employee communication and employee involvement by making managers and supervisors readily available. Under this strategy, an organization makes its managers and supervisors more readily available by encouraging managers and supervisors to traverse the workspace so they can check on the progress of each employee, discuss questions or concerns, and ultimately handle any problems that the employee or the manager identifies. This particular strategy may appear to be extremely straightforward and relatively obvious because most organizations attempt to make sure that managers and supervisors are actually monitoring the progress of the employees under their supervision. However, it is an important qualitative methodology for informally collecting information about what employees might be thinking. This is extremely useful during times of rapid changes when observing and listening captures the essence or tone of an issue(s) that other methods of data collection might miss. This form of data collection usually requires active listening training for the manager and the ability to direct or redirect conversations in a non-confrontational format to reveal the root of a problem or trends.

## Reporting and Presentation Techniques

### COLUMN CHART, BAR CHART, LINE CHART, AND AREA CHART

A simple **column chart** will usually display categories along the horizontal axis and values along the vertical axis. If a column chart is laid on its side, it would be a bar chart. In a **bar chart**, the horizontal axis displays the value and the vertical axis displays the category. Utilization of a column chart versus a bar chart is usually a matter of preference and a judgment call as to which one looks better. Generally, bar charts are more effective when displaying and comparing categorical data, or groupings. A **line chart** is similar to a column chart, except it displays data over a given period of time on an axis that is evenly scaled on both the horizontal and vertical axes. Line charts are frequently used at periodic intervals, such as months and quarters, to illustrate trends. An **area chart** is similar to a line chart except that instead of a single line, the entire area is a solid color. It is

Copyright © Mometrix Media. You have been licensed one copy of this document for personal use only. Any other reproduction or redistribution is strictly prohibited. All rights reserved.

better at revealing the magnitude of change and displaying parts of a whole. Area charts, like line charts, are typically used to illustrate trends over time.

**Column Chart:** Number of Vacancies by Position

**Bar Chart**: Number of Vacancies by Position

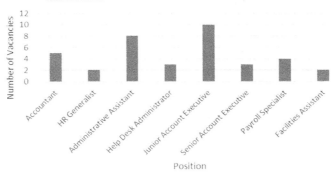

**Line Chart**: Number of New Hires in a Year

35

Copyright © Mometrix Media. You have been licensed one copy of this document for personal use only. Any other reproduction or redistribution is strictly prohibited. All rights reserved.

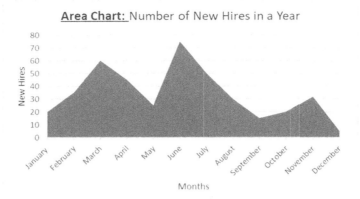

**Area Chart:** Number of New Hires in a Year

## HISTOGRAM, SCATTER PLOT, AND PIE CHART

A **histogram** offers an illustration of data by organizing and grouping the data points that fall within a range of values. These values are referred to as bins. The frequency of numbers that are within the defined bins is graphically represented as a bar on the chart. This chart is used to show the frequency distribution of numeric data and values, which is great for understanding the spread of data. A **scatter plot**, sometimes called an XY scatter plot, illustrates the correlation between two sets of values. For example, it may be used to demonstrate the connection between salary and years of education. A **pie chart** represents the distribution of data over a total. Proportions are usually represented as percentages. Pie charts are so named because they are circular, with data divided into what looks like different-sized slices of a pie. Pie charts are useful when there are fewer categories.

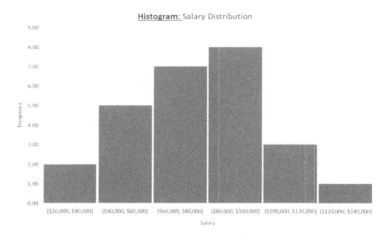

**Histogram:** Salary Distribution

Copyright © Mometrix Media. You have been licensed one copy of this document for personal use only. Any other reproduction or redistribution is strictly prohibited. All rights reserved.

**Scatter Plot**: Correlation between Average Salary and Years of Education

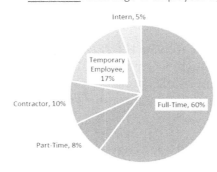

**Pie Chart:** Percentage of Employees by Status

## FORECASTING

**Forecasting** in business is the ability to predict or estimate, based on past data, the likelihood of a particular event becoming a reality. In HR, forecasting is used to predict the staffing needs of an organization as well as the financial impact of all costs related to labor (benefits, training, etc.). HR forecasting can be short- or long-term and is dependent on many factors in an organization, such as revenue, growth, attrition, etc. Forecasting assists the HR plan for the number and types of employees the organization will need and related costs. Forecasting enables the organization to plan for growth based on educated, quantitative information and also permits the organization to make decisions in the event of downsizing. In addition to using forecasting for direct staffing needs, an organization also uses it for budgeting. For example, forecasting may reveal that an organization needs more employees in the months of November and December. HR must examine its budget and determine if it makes more sense to pay overtime to existing workers, hire temporary workers, or have a small staff of part-time employees.

## OBJECTIVITY IN DATA ANALYSIS

Objectivity is critical in the analysis, interpretation, and presentation of data. Compiling and analyzing data requires converting data, frequently in large volumes, into information an organization can use to drive decisions. Sometimes the research and/or presentation of data has a confirmation bias—a tendency to interpret information that favors one's existing beliefs, values, or opinions. Confirmation bias can skew or invalidate data. This might happen if researchers discover the data does not reflect their opinion and/or does not support what the organization would like it to reveal. Other times, researchers may overlay an emotional approach instead of an objective one.

37

Copyright © Mometrix Media. You have been licensed one copy of this document for personal use only. Any other reproduction or redistribution is strictly prohibited. All rights reserved.

This is more likely to occur during the collection of qualitative data such as interviews. Researchers must be ready to reconsider or reevaluate data and/or respondent answers to maintain objectivity.

# Impact of Technology on HR

## USE OF SOCIAL MEDIA IN HR

Social media is playing a greater role in everyday life than ever before. Social media is extremely popular and growing with platforms like Facebook, Twitter, and Instagram. Additionally, professional social media sites like LinkedIn continue to experience growth. HR utilizes social media to assist an organization in many ways. Recruiting leverages social media platforms to reach a wider pool of job candidates, both those seeking a new position and those who are passive job candidates, thereby increasing the ease and efficiency with which positions can be filled. For example, LinkedIn enables recruiters to post job opportunities on their company page. This makes it easier for job applicants to find positions based on their specific skill and/or experience in a given industry, and is especially useful with hard-to-fill positions. On the flip side, LinkedIn also enables recruiters to quickly vet candidates and find exactly what they are looking for in a job applicant.

Social media is a powerful communication tool for HR. An organization's presence on numerous platforms helps capture and communicate their culture, which is another means to attract top job applicants. HR should consider an organization's presence on social media and how it influences a prospective job candidate's impression of the organization's values and cultural fit.

## ROLE OF BIOMETRICS IN HR

**Biometric technology** measures a personal body characteristic that is used in computer science as identification. These biometric measurements can include, but are not limited to, a person's hand, finger, iris, voice pattern, and face. The purpose of biometrics is to verify a person's unique identity efficiently and without the use of more traditional security methods such as punch cards, memorized passwords, and special code combinations. In HR, biometrics is usually utilized for employee timekeeping and access to sensitive information. Its usage permits an organization, especially one with multiple sites, to quickly gather time and attendance information. This information can be derived in real-time and used to detect irregularities and predict employee work patterns. Typically, information from the biometric system interfaces with the payroll application an organization uses. Additional benefits of biometrics for HR might include transparency, meaning that an organization knows where their employees are and when; cost savings, which eliminate having a dedicated resource to manage attendance; or improved punctuality and more efficient attendance management for scheduling and to track absences. While utilizing biometrics offers many efficiencies to an organization, it can also be a liability because this information can be hacked or stolen. An organization needs to abide by all federal, state, and local laws before implementing the use of biometrics and must have an extensive written policy whereby employees must be made knowledgeable about its usage, how their personal information is stored and for how long, and all security measures that are in place.

## PRIVACY PRINCIPLES AND IMPACT IN THE WORKFORCE

With technology now a part of every business transaction, it is essential that companies and employees adhere to strict confidentiality practices and **privacy principles**. From employee monitoring to asking interview questions, employers need to carefully avoid invading personal privacy. Legal regulations that inform best practices and internal privacy policies should be consulted regularly for guidance. On the other hand, companies should consider implementing confidentiality or nondisclosure agreements so employees are aware that databases, client lists, and

Copyright © Mometrix Media. You have been licensed one copy of this document for personal use only. Any other reproduction or redistribution is strictly prohibited. All rights reserved.

other proprietary information must be protected and that the sharing of these records externally is strictly prohibited.

## EMPLOYEE MONITORING SOFTWARE

An organization may choose to utilize **employee monitoring software** to gain information on how employees are using their time at work. Usually, monitoring software allows the employer to see internet activity and software usage. It can also save random screenshots and track keystrokes. This monitoring is typically done from a central location, but can also capture information from local and remote computers. The rationale behind employee monitoring software is to understand how an employee spends their time while working because it can directly and indirectly impact the organization's productivity and security. Best practices for the deployment of employee monitoring software includes clearly communicating to employees, usually in an HR handbook or company policy manual, what is and is not appropriate computer usage in a given organization and possible repercussions for violating such a policy. It is important that the employee know from the beginning of their employment that the organization has the right to monitor all technology use from company-procured or sponsored equipment. The goal is to effectively design and communicate a technology policy that protects the organization from threats such as viruses, hacking, unethical activity, etc. while at the same time providing employees some balance in internet and/or software usage.

## USE OF PREDICTIVE ANALYTICS

**Predictive analytics** refers to a type of technology that uses reliable current or historical data to forecast future behavior. These analytics technologically apply the old adage that "past behavior is the best indicator of future behavior." However, predictive analytics use science and technology to make predictions that are usually very specific. Predictive analytics use many different statistical techniques that will scrutinize reliable current or historical data and related outcomes. The goal is to generate a formula or algorithm that best replicates the outcomes. This information can then be leveraged to forecast reliable future outcomes.

HR captures a tremendous amount of data about employees, and the data is usually stored in its human resource information system (HRIS). This data could be used to generate predictive models for HR professionals to enable better organizational decision making instead of relying on an unquantifiable feeling or some other non-science-based metric. HR analytics are being used more frequently to help an organization predict and respond accordingly to a variety of people policies. Some of the areas to which predictive analytics are being applied include improving employee turnover, predicting revenue through employee engagement measures, improving hiring decisions, evaluating employment risk, and many more.

## ADVANTAGES AND DISADVANTAGES OF TECHNOLOGY SYSTEMS

**Human resource information systems** (HRIS) enable employees to have greater and more expedient access to their personal HR-related data. Some advanced HRIS programs allow employees to immediately request time off, change their mailing address, adjust 401(k) contributions, etc. In this respect, HR technology has automated very labor-intensive paperwork, thereby creating more organizational efficiencies and possibly enabling HR professionals to expand into more strategic roles.

**Applicant tracking systems** (ATS) automate the application process from the beginning through the hiring of an employee. This has many benefits for realizing efficiencies, but could also overwhelm recruiters with unqualified candidates they must weed through.

Copyright © Mometrix Media. You have been licensed one copy of this document for personal use only. Any other reproduction or redistribution is strictly prohibited. All rights reserved.

An HR **knowledge management system** (KMS) is a central repository for HR information that can be quickly accessed by employees, usually considered a 24/7 self-service portal. Frequently, it may provide access to onboarding information, benefit selection and policy information, requests for time off and historical attendance information, general HR policy information, etc. The main benefits of a KMS include the increased ability for an employee to quickly access information, that the information can be updated easily and thus reduce misinformation, and that it reduces the administrative workload for HR. However, the system needs to be maintained and permissions must be managed so that employees have access only to information that is pertinent to them.

**Integration of technology tools** – HR now has many technological tools to manage employees. Access to too much data and sometimes irrelevant data can be a consideration in effective data usage. Also, the integration of various technology platforms can be challenging.

## CONFIDENTIALITY DISCLOSURES IN TECHNOLOGY

Confidentiality disclosures should include definitions and exclusions of confidential information while outlining individual responsibilities. Confidentiality disclosures are used to keep private or secure information available only to those who are authorized to access it. It is important to ensure that only the proper individuals have access to the information needed to perform their jobs. Moreover, legislation mandates due diligence to protect the confidential information of employees and customers. Technology breaches in confidentiality could happen via phone, fax, computer, email, and electronic records. For this reason, some businesses might utilize encryption software, limit the communications that can be sent via email, and include a statement notifying the reader what to do if it is inadvertently sent to the wrong person.

## INFORMATION TECHNOLOGY (IT) SECURITY

**Information technology (IT) security** is becoming a more serious topic and rapidly gaining more attention. It is important for human resource practitioners to be conscientious of controls to mitigate organizational exposure and risk. Some companies may have IT security policies and acknowledgements in place to reduce liability. Multiple layers of corporate IT security might include the encryption of data files, firewalls, access controls or logins, systems monitoring, detection processes, antivirus software, cyber insurance, and so on. Implementing stronger IT security can provide companies with benefits such as mitigating lost revenue, protecting brand reputation, and supporting mobilization.

# Employee Records Management

## ELEMENTS OF WORKPLACE RECORDS RETENTION MANAGEMENT AND ACCESS

Workplace employee-related records should have organizational policies that might be regulated by federal, state, and local laws as well as operational necessity. It is sometimes easier to think of a record as the complete, final version of a document so that there is no need to keep every draft or note. Following are key elements of workplace records retention management and access:

- How long to **retain** records – First, all records that are regulated by law should be kept for the prescribed time period according to federal, state, and/or local laws. This can be confusing because certain records might be regulated by more than one law or the time period may vary. In these cases, records should be kept for the longest period required.

Copyright © Mometrix Media. You have been licensed one copy of this document for personal use only. Any other reproduction or redistribution is strictly prohibited. All rights reserved.

- Who should have **access** to records – Access should be provisioned only to those people with (1) a legitimate business need; and (2) where federal, state, and local laws permit such access. For example, the Health Insurance Portability and Accountability Act (HIPAA) and many data privacy regulations specify not only who may have access, but how the information may be used.

## STORAGE OF RECORDS AND SECURITY NEEDED

Workplace policy should describe specifically where records will be stored and in what format—paper or electronic. Records should be held in a secure, locked location or electronically maintained with necessary technological protections. There is no specific law that dictates how records must be stored, whether paper or electronic, but the law does dictate that an organization must have the ability to quickly retrieve information and supply paper copies if necessary. It is imperative for HR to always protect employee records and the privacy of the information, regardless of the format. Frequently, an organization will have a documented employee records confidentiality policy to protect all employee information and maintain confidentiality. Furthermore, if an employee feels there has been a breach in confidentiality, then HR needs to investigate the allegation immediately. Alternatively, if an organization feels there was a breach in confidentially, regardless of how it occurred, the organization usually has an obligation to share the breach and offer corrective actions.

## CONCERNS BEFORE DESTRUCTION OF HR RECORDS

Employee records management is critical to comply with federal, state, and local requirements and to reduce legal liabilities. If an organization prematurely destroys HR records, that organization could face criminal liabilities and possible legal penalties or litigation. Additionally, the organization may not be able to adequately defend itself in employment-related litigation due to spoliation of evidence. It is important to remember an organization should only retain the legal HR records that are required to comply with federal, state, and local laws or operational necessity. For example, holding onto every scrap of paper an employee writes on is not necessary, only legally mandated documents are necessary. In some cases, keeping every scrap could turn into a liability for the organization. The end goal for HR is to keep what is legally mandated and to properly, legally dispose of the rest. Disposal of confidential, personal, or financial information after the legally dictated retention period is over should comply with all federal, state, and/or local regulations. For example, the Fair and Accurate Credit Transaction Act (FACTA) has specific rules for how to dispose of background check documentation. Usually, if it is paper, this means shredding on site or hiring a professional vendor that specializes in shredding. In the case of electronic records, the organization must follow protocols so that the information is erased and not able to be read or reconstructed.

## PRE-EMPLOYMENT RECORDS RETAINED

The pre-employment phase of a job is comprised of activities that occur before a candidate is chosen for and has accepted a position at an organization. During this phase, HR posts a job for employment, resumes are submitted, applications are completed, reference checks and/or background checks may be conducted, and interviews may be held. All of these documents should be retained for EEO purposes demonstrating non-discriminatory hiring, equal opportunity, and overall fairness and equity. Organizations must retain the following information for all applicants: job posting; resumes; and completed applications, including interview notes related to the decision to hire or not hire an applicant. Based on federal regulations in the Age Discrimination in Employment Act (ADEA), Americans with Disabilities Act (ADA), and Civil Rights Act of 1964 (Title VII), these documents are retained one year after creation of the documents or hire/no hire decision, whichever is later. In the case of federal contractors, document retention is two years. If the contractor has less than 150 employees or a government contract is less than $150,000, then

Copyright © Mometrix Media. You have been licensed one copy of this document for personal use only. Any other reproduction or redistribution is strictly prohibited. All rights reserved.

the retention is, again, one year. These are the federal retention regulations, but retention rates could vary slightly depending on state and local laws.

## EMPLOYMENT RECORDS RETAINED

Employee records, whether they are paper or electronic, have specific retention requirements. Retention of employee records could vary according to federal, state, and local laws. Therefore, it is important to understand the legal requirements as well as the system that an organization utilizes. Following is a summary of federal guidelines for the most common HR records.

- **I-9 forms** – Securely retained for three years beginning from the hire date, or one year after separation of employment.
- **Payroll records** – These records, which contain personal information such as name, address, social security number, and compensation should be retained for three years according to federal laws. There are many federal laws that regulate payroll records, including the Age Discrimination Employment Act (ADEA), Fair Labor Standards Act (FLSA), Service Contract Act, Davis-Bacon Act, Walsh-Healey Act (for federal contractors), and Family Medical Leave Act (FMLA). However, it is recommended for the purposes of the Lily Ledbetter Fair Pay Act to retain these documents for at least five years after the end of employment. Additionally, under the Equal Pay Act (EPA), employers must retain two years of all payroll records in case they need to justify the pay wage differential between different sexes.
- **Employment benefits** – These records should be retained for six years and are carefully regulated, requiring employer reporting based on the Employee Retirement Income Security Act (ERISA).
- **Background checks** – These are retained for a minimum of one year based on the Equal Employment Opportunity Commission (EEOC) requirements and Title VII of the Civil Rights Act of 1964 to possibly report hiring and selection records. However, it is often recommended to save background check documents for five years after the date of the consumer report is accessed because the statute of limitations in the Fair Credit Reporting Act is five years.
- **Tax records** – All related tax records should be retained by the employer for four years after the fourth quarter of the year in order to be in compliance with the Federal Insurance Contribution Act (FICA), Federal Unemployment Tax Act, and the Internal Revenue Code.
- **Safety records** – This data, and related reports, should be retained for five years after the year that the record pertains to, based on the Occupational Safety and Health Act (OSHA) and the Walsh-Healy Act (for federal contractors).
- **Family Medical Leave Act (FMLA) records** – Based on the requirements in the FMLA, these records should be retained for three years.
- **Disability accommodations** – All employee disability and accommodations documentation should be retained for one year from the date of the record or last date of an action. However, for contractors and public employees, the records should be retained for two years. There are many laws that require compliance with disability issues, such as American Disabilities Act as Amended (ADAAA), Executive Order 11246, and Vietnam Era Veterans Readjustment Assistance Act (VEVRAA).

Record retention can be a complex process. However, it is a critical HR function to support and protect an organization.

Copyright © Mometrix Media. You have been licensed one copy of this document for personal use only. Any other reproduction or redistribution is strictly prohibited. All rights reserved.

## SEPARATING PERSONNEL FILES INTO TWO CATEGORIES

Not every record in a personnel file should be treated the same. Specific records regarding an employee and their employment history should be kept in their personnel file, while other documents, because of their confidential nature, might need to be protected differently.

- **Personnel file** – This file should include job description, application resume, offer letter, acknowledgement of organization handbook, emergency contact information, job performance, promotions, transfers, appraisals, awards, training, any disciplinary actions, and all documents related to separation from the organization.
- **Confidential personnel information** – These records should have an added layer of protection because of the employee's privacy rights and, if breached, to protect the employer from liability. These records usually include any medical information such as ADA accommodations, workers' compensation, drug tests, disability information, Family Medical Leave Act (FMLA), health insurance, COBRA, all employee credit information, I-9 form, and any documents related to a complaint or investigation.

# Statutory Reporting Requirements

## EMPLOYMENT RETIREMENT INCOME SECURITY ACT (ERISA)

The Employment Retirement Income Security Act (ERISA) outlines the standards for private health and pension plans offered by an employer. This act specifies what an employer must do, what they are not permitted to do, and what they might be able to do as it relates to private health and pension plans. This is a complicated statute, but the goal is for employees to receive the benefits promised and outlined by the employer, and are protected against any type of funds mismanagement. The employer has three primary regulatory obligations as it relates to ERISA:

1. The Internal Revenue Service (IRS), Department of Labor, and the Pension Benefit Guaranty Corp. developed a form titled **Form 5500** that contains reported financial conditions, investments, and operations. This form must be completed annually and filed by an employer to satisfy reporting requirements outlined under ERISA and the IRS.
2. **Dissemination and disclosure information** for all participants in the employer sponsored plan.
   a. Must have an easily accessible, documented plan.
   b. Must annually receive a summary plan description (SPD) within 90 days for new participants and 120 days for new plans.
   c. Must receive (in a timely fashion) a summary material modification (SMM) if the plan is altered no later than 210 days after changes and no later than 60 days if there is a material reduction in coverage.
   d. Must be given a summary annual report (SAR).
3. **Standard of conduct obligation** that requires fiduciaries (trusted individuals) to conduct activities for the sole benefit of the participants and beneficiaries, not in their own self-interest.

If an employer fails to comply with any or all requirements of this mandate, they could face severe civil and criminal penalties.

## AFFORDABLE CARE ACT (ACA)

The Affordable Care Act (ACA) requires employers of 50 or more employees to offer healthcare options providing minimum essential coverage that is both affordable and gives minimum value.

43

Copyright © Mometrix Media. You have been licensed one copy of this document for personal use only. Any other reproduction or redistribution is strictly prohibited. All rights reserved.

This act requires employers with a self-insured health plan to annually complete the following Internal Revenue Service (IRS) forms:

- **Form 1094-C** - Employer information, including number of full-time employees and total number of employees by month, minimal coverage offered to 95 percent of eligible employees for each month and if a 4980H safe harbor (line 16) was used each month.
- **Form 1095-B** - Employee proof of insurance – Employees' share of the lowest cost monthly premium and if a 4980H safe harbor was used each month.

Additionally, employers are required to give a copy of form 1095-B to all employees. Included on this form is information for the IRS and for employees who are covered by the ACA-mandated essential health benefit. Reporting is mandatory for employers with 50 or more (on average) full-time employees. Employers who fail to comply with all ACA requirements and deadlines could be subject to substantial penalties and steep fines.

## OCCUPATIONAL SAFETY AND HEALTH ACT (OSHA) REPORTING

The Occupational Safety and Health Act (OSHA) of 1970 set safety and related recordkeeping standards for the workplace. Safety records could include a log of occupational injuries and illnesses related to work while performing a job, a record and summaries of illnesses and injuries, and a record of any toxic exposures for employees. OSHA regulations require compliance by an organization that is engaged in commerce with one or more employees. OSHA also protects employees who may work in substandard conditions by informing them of their rights and providing training to remedy the situation. An employee can reach out to OSHA to investigate possible substandard conditions without legal fear of retaliation. Following are the OSHA forms that an organization may have to complete, depending on the situation.

- **Form 300** – Used by an employer to record and keep information about an injury or illness an employee experienced. There are three parts to this form: (1) identification, including name of the person, maybe a case number, job title, and department; (2) description of event, with date, location, and summary of event; and (3) classification of injury or illness, its type, number of days off from work, and any restrictions.
- **Form 301** – Used if the injury or illness event has supplemental material that needs to be documented. For example, it may contain information about events leading up to the occurrence, if an object or substance was involved, etc.
- **Form 300A** – A summary of illnesses and injuries that occurred throughout the year. It should be noted that 300A does not contain any of the personal information that is on Form 300. The primary purpose of this form is to calculate incident rates.

> **Review Video: What is OSHA (Occupational Safety and Health Administration)**
> Visit mometrix.com/academy and enter code: 913559

## EEO-1 REPORTING

All private employers with 100 or more employees and federal contractors with both 50 or more employees and contracts of at least $50,000 must complete and submit an EEO-1 report each year. This report organizes employee-specific data by race, gender, and job category for an employer. The completed report is submitted to the EEOC and the Office of Federal Contract Compliance Programs (OFCCP) for adherence to federal laws against employment discrimination. This is a mandatory report. If it is not filed, if false information is provided, or if an employer discriminated against an employee, then there are monetary as well as legal consequences and/or penalties. While there are

Copyright © Mometrix Media. You have been licensed one copy of this document for personal use only. Any other reproduction or redistribution is strictly prohibited. All rights reserved.

other EEO reports (EEO-3, EEO-4, EEO-5) that apply to unions, governmental entities, public schools, etc., the EEO-1 report is the most utilized reporting mechanism by the EEOC.

# Purpose and function of Human Resources Information Systems (HRIS)

## HUMAN RESOURCE INFORMATION SYSTEM

A **human resource information system** (HRIS) is a database, either software-based or online, that electronically stores all critical employee data that the HR department may need for the organization's operational efficiency and legal compliance. It allows for data entry, tracking, and reporting on a variety of HR-related matters. It is important to note that every HRIS is different, with varying functions and capabilities depending on the needs of the business. Some of the HRIS functions could include the following:

- **Basic employee information** – May include name, address, salary, emergency contact information, etc.
- **Company documentation** – May include items such as employee handbooks, emergency procedures, and safety guidelines.
- **Benefit administration** – Could include enrollment capabilities, insurance changes, attendance and time off, and the ability for employees to look up and track information.
- **Payroll integration** – Reduces duplication of efforts with payroll and increases efficiencies.
- **Applicant tracking** – Allows recruiters to manage an applicant's information, then move the applicant to employee status and retain information.
- **Performance management** – Could include performance evaluations; possible improvement plans can follow the employee throughout the organization.
- **Disciplinary issues** – May include the recording of demotions, suspension, or other negative actions taken, all of which may be important to retain even after an employee leaves the organization.
- **Training** – Retains records of required certifications, licenses, and/or other compliance training.

## BENEFITS

There are many benefits afforded by an HRIS:

- **Productivity** – The primary purpose of an HRIS is to improve HR productivity. An HRIS enables HR to quickly access information, thereby increasing the speed of decision-making.
- **Reduced errors** – Whenever the manipulation of data occurs, the opportunity for error can increase, which in HR could lead to financial loss, unwanted legal issues, and/or possible damage to the brand or image.
- **Metric analysis** – Analyzing employee-related metrics such as recruiting costs, attendance, and benefit usage, is an essential HR function. As such, an HRIS allows for the proper storage and retrieval of needed data for calculations and statistical analysis impacting the organization.
- **Attendance management** – Tracking employee time off, whether for illness, PTO, or vacation. This reduces the need for HR to manually capture and track all time-off situations.
- **Payroll management** – Capturing payroll-related information such as time-off or certain benefit selections, thereby making it easier to keep accurate records and expediently retrieve information for analysis.

Copyright © Mometrix Media. You have been licensed one copy of this document for personal use only. Any other reproduction or redistribution is strictly prohibited. All rights reserved.

- **Benefit administration** – Keeping records of health insurance, pension information, bonuses, and any other benefits, enabling HR to not only quickly retrieve data, but to also efficiently analyze trends.
- **Training management** – Storing relevant training information for an organization. Employees, depending on their occupation or position, may be required to have current training credentials, training may be legally required, or training may enhance an employee's skill set, thereby increasing an organization's competitive advantage.
- **Communication** – Some HRIS software enables an organization to quickly distribute information or changes to everyone or segments of a population, such as procedural changes, handbook updates, weather-related closings, warnings, and policies. Some HRIS programs are even designed to distribute and analyze surveys.
- **Self-service** – Some HRIS programs have the capability to respond to employee questions about things like benefits, time off, and policies, thereby reducing the amount of time HR professionals spend answering simple questions.
- **E-signature capabilities** – As information and communication have become more digitized, so has the need for electronic signatures—e-signatures—on contracts, forms, etc. Many HRIS products have a feature whereby an electronic signature can be stored, which reduces a tremendous amount of paperwork.

## DISADVANTAGES

The purpose of an HRIS is to safely store employee-related information, retrieve it efficiently, and analyze the data, allowing for more expedient organizational decision making. In other words, it is a system that is used to enhance the quality and efficiencies of management's decision making. Sometimes these advantages come at a cost and could become a disadvantage. Following are some of the possible disadvantages of an HRIS:

- **Human error** – There is an old adage: "garbage in, garbage out." If there is a human error made in data input, then there will be an error in the output, putting the organization at risk of making a decision based on false information.
- **Expensive** – An HRIS can be costly to purchase, maintain, and update. Additionally, depending on the system, it could require an organization to hire an HRIS specialist to efficiently administer and maintain it. Additionally, new systems and updates require training. The time spent on training needs to show a positive return on investment (ROI) for the HRIS to be cost effective.
- **Technical malfunctions** – System downtime can occur and takes time and effort to resolve, possibly costing the organization time and money.
- **Unauthorized access** – As with any technology system, necessary precautions such as encryption and firewalls need to be made so that only those with a "need to know" have access to HRIS information.

# Job Classifications

## FLSA

The **FLSA of 1938,** also known as the Wagner-Connery Wages and Hours Act, or the Wage Hour Bill, sets minimum wage standards, overtime pay standards, and child labor restrictions. The act is administered by the Wage and Hour Division of the Department of Labor. FLSA carefully separates employees as exempt or nonexempt from provisions, requires that employers calculate overtime for covered employees at one-and-one-half times the regular rate of pay for all hours worked in excess of 40 hours during a week, and defines how a workweek should be measured. The purpose

Copyright © Mometrix Media. You have been licensed one copy of this document for personal use only. Any other reproduction or redistribution is strictly prohibited. All rights reserved.

of minimum wage standards is to ensure a living wage and to reduce poverty for low-income families, minority workers, and women. The child labor provisions protect minors from positions that may be harmful or detrimental to their health or well-being and regulates the hours minors can legally work. The act also outlines requirements for employers to keep records of hours, wages, and related payroll items.

## EXEMPT EMPLOYEES

An **exempt employee** is not entitled to minimum wage or overtime pay as defined by the Fair Labor Standards Act (FLSA). Exempt employees do not comply with FLSA regulations. It is usually decided by the employer if they wish to compensate an employee for working more than 40 hours and is usually achieved through bonuses or extra benefits; it is not mandatory. Additionally, exempt employees must meet certain tests based on job duties performed and earn no less than $684 per week. It is important to note that it is not a job title alone that determines an exempt status, but rather the tasks performed on the job. An exempt employee is paid by salary, not hourly, and spends more than 50 percent of their time performing bona fide exempt functions, usually falling into three general categories:

1. Executive employees – Responsibilities include directing the work of two or more full-time employees. The primary focus of their job is management and having direct input into the hiring, ongoing management, and firing of employees.
2. Professional employee – This category is most often associated with learned professionals; it requires knowledge and education in a specific field such as doctors, engineers, accountants, etc. This category also includes more creative fields that rely on invention, creation, imagination, or artistic talent such as writers, actors, graphic design, etc.
3. Administrative employees – Duties include utilizing judgment and discretion with regard to the management of an organization and/or handling high-level interactions with customers.

These three categories are not an all-inclusive list. In fact, there are many other types of jobs that may be classified as exempt, such as outside sales or computer systems management. Another exempt category could be highly compensated employees if they do non-manual work and whose salary is $107,432 or higher and also performs one of the three main categories. State and local wage and hourly rate laws may have their own requirements in addition to FLSA.

## NONEXEMPT EMPLOYEES

Nonexempt employees fall under the regulation of the Fair Labor Standards Act (FLSA). Nonexempt employees are hourly workers who earn wages less than $684 a week or $35,568 annually. Nonexempt workers are required to receive at least minimum wage up to 40 hours a week and must receive overtime pay for any time above 40 hours of work. Overtime pay requires employers to pay at a rate of time-and-one-half the employees' regular rate of pay. Generally, nonexempt positions do not require special education, independent judgment or discretion, and/or supervising others and could work in almost any field. Typically, nonexempt workers have work that is routine and utilizes their body or skills, such as carpenters, plumbers, craftsman, mechanics, first responders, park rangers, emergency medical technicians, correctional officers, etc. It is important to note that some states have nonexempt regulations in addition to FLSA.

## CHARACTERISTICS OF INDEPENDENT CONTRACTORS

An **independent contractor** is not covered by the Fair Labor Standards Act (FLSA) and hence not eligible for minimum wage or overtime pay. Moreover, the most important distinction between an employee and a contractor is if the worker is dependent on the employer, meaning they are an employee; or conducting business for the sole benefit of him or herself, making them an

Copyright © Mometrix Media. You have been licensed one copy of this document for personal use only. Any other reproduction or redistribution is strictly prohibited. All rights reserved.

independent contractor. The United States Department of Labor refers to this as an "economic reality test," which takes five factors into consideration:

1. Workers' control over the nature of their work, be it schedule, projects, etc.
2. Workers' control over profit or loss
3. Worker skill needed for the work performed, particularly specialized skills that require training
4. Worker relationship with the employer with regards to permanent status
5. Worker is part of an existing unit within the organization

The first two factors above carry the most weight and must be examined first. If the answer to questions one and two is affirmative, then there is a substantial likelihood that the worker is an independent contractor. These first two questions are often called "core factors." However, if there is ambiguity, then the next three factors must be examined for clarification. Employers must also remember to comply with all federal, state, and local laws with regard to worker classification, as they may vary.

# Job Analysis Methods and Job Descriptions

## JOB ANALYSIS

**Job analysis** involves the systematic evaluation of activities and responsibilities in a specific job. The three main products of a job analysis include job competencies, job specifications, and job descriptions. **Job competencies** are a detailed list of all broad skills and traits needed for a particular position. **Job specifications** are detailed descriptions of all specific qualifications an individual must have to perform the role. A **job description** is a detailed, written breakdown of all tasks that a worker in that role must complete, as well as the job competencies and job specifications required to be qualified for that role. Some of the major uses of job analysis include the following:

- Human resources planning to develop job categories
- Recruiting to describe and advertise job openings
- Selection to identify skills and criteria for choosing candidates
- Orientation to describe activities and expectations to employees
- Evaluation to identify standards and performance objectives
- Compensation to evaluate job worth and develop pay structures
- Training to conduct needs assessments
- Discipline to correct subpar performance
- Safety to identify working procedures and ensure workers can safely perform duties
- Job redesign to analyze job characteristics that periodically need updating
- Legal protection to identify essential functions that must be performed and safeguard the organization against claims

## CONDUCTING JOB ANALYSIS

A job analysis is an essential part of any workforce planning process because it identifies specific skills and knowledge required to meet staffing goals and objectives. It also identifies the specific skills and qualifications required to meet the strategic goals and objectives set for the organization as a whole. A job analysis allows the organization to not only identify which tasks need to be performed, but also breaks those tasks into specific skills, traits, and knowledge that would qualify an individual to perform each task appropriately.

Copyright © Mometrix Media. You have been licensed one copy of this document for personal use only. Any other reproduction or redistribution is strictly prohibited. All rights reserved.

## INFORMATION COLLECTION FOR USE IN JOB ANALYSIS

Job analysis begins with the collection of pertinent information about a particular job. This information can best be described as job characteristics that differentiate a specific job from other jobs. These characteristics may include the following:

- Level of supervision, whether provided or received
- Computer, machine, or other technical equipment used
- External and/or internal interaction
- Specific work activities and behaviors needed
- Knowledge or education needed, sometimes referred to as "knowledge, skills and abilities" or KSAs
- Performance standards
- Working conditions

Grouping jobs by similar function is usually advantageous during the job analysis process. This is frequently accomplished by defining the overall job family and drilling down to job responsibilities and then specific details about work performed. Following is an example:

- Job family: HR service center
  o Job: HR call center representative
    ❖ Task: Provides support by phone and/or email for customer inquires

## COMMON JOB ANALYSIS METHODS

Collecting information for job analysis can be tricky and there is no specific formula because it depends on the job and information available. As a general rule, direct observation of the job and work performed, in conjunction with information obtained from previous job incumbents, is the most useful. However, this information might not always be available or there may be other circumstances whereby it is not possible to collect the data or the data might not be reliable. Following are some of the most common job analysis methods that can be deployed, depending on a variety of circumstances:

- **Observation** – After literally observing the job, a record of job tasks is documented and categorized into the knowledge, skills, and abilities (KSAs) needed to perform the job. This method is best suited for production jobs or short-cycle processes.
- **Interview** – The interviewer asks pre-scripted questions to qualified people in the job or job incumbents with the goal to obtain KSAs for the given job. This method works well with most professional jobs.
- **Behavioral event interview** – This method is called a "competency-based" form of job analysis because it is designed to get behavioral descriptions about how a person performs a given job instead of KSAs. The goal is for the interviewer to get the interviewee to talk about specific stories or occurrences that happened on the job and gather information about their behaviors, thoughts, and actions in real-life situations. This method is used in jobs that may be considered high-stress.
- **Structured questionnaire** – These questionnaires only permit very specific responses to obtain information about the frequency of particular tasks and the importance of the skills required to perform those tasks. This finite data set helps clarify jobs that are challenging to understand and the data generated from this type of questionnaire lends itself to being easily used for computer modeling analysis.

Copyright © Mometrix Media. You have been licensed one copy of this document for personal use only. Any other reproduction or redistribution is strictly prohibited. All rights reserved.

- **Open-ended questionnaire** – This type of questionnaire is completed by job incumbents and/or manager(s) to determine the KSAs needed for a particular job. This information is then compiled into a summary document of job requirements. This method is useful for most jobs where the information is available.
- **Work diary** – This method involves an employee keeping a record, typically over a period of weeks or months, of the frequency and timing of tasks. The information recorded is analyzed and compiled for the purpose of identifying duties, responsibilities, and trends. It should be noted that this method involves sifting through a tremendous amount of data that may or may not be useful and/or difficult to interpret and keep current.

## JOB DESCRIPTION

A **job description** documents the duties, tasks, and responsibilities for a particular position based on information obtained in a job analysis. More specifically, it provides detailed information about who does a particular job, how the work is to be performed and completed, and link the work performed to the organization's mission and goals. There are many explanations for why an organization should have job descriptions for all of their positions, including calculating salary levels, performance reviews, initially setting job titles and grades of pay, measure for reasonable accommodations, recruiting purposes, etc. Job descriptions are also needed for operational purposes such as training, legal compliance obligations, and possibly in the situation when an employee's performance is in question and may need improvement.

## ESSENTIAL FUNCTIONS OF A JOB DESCRIPTION

Essential functions are documented within a job description, detailing what a job applicant unquestionably must be able to do—it is essential to the job. The reason that capturing all essential functions in a job description is so important is they are used to determine the legal rights of an employee with a disability under the American with Disabilities Act (ADA). If an employee cannot perform the essential function, even with reasonable accommodations, then that employee is not qualified for the job and cannot be safeguarded from discrimination as outlined in the ADA. In other words, a person cannot bring a disability lawsuit against an employer if the person, due to a disability, could not perform the essential functions as documented in the job description. A job analysis is significant in determining essential functions because if an essential function is not honestly an essential function, then the employer cannot exclude a person with a disability from the given position because they cannot perform the function. Following are some guidelines to consider when documenting essential functions for every task:

- Ensure the task is truly a requirement to perform the job.
- Evaluate and determine frequency and time spent performing a task.
- Evaluate if not performing the task would be detrimental to the employer.
- Determine if the task could be redesigned, conducted in a different manner, or altered in a way that doesn't severely compromise the end product or service.
- Decide if the task could be given to a similar employee to be accomplished.

After drafting a job's essential functions, the employer should carefully consider whether the functions are truly essential or marginal. The actual words "essential function" are part of a typical job description and should clearly state those functions are essential to perform the job.

## COMPONENTS OF A JOB DESCRIPTION

A **job description** is a documented summary of the scope, responsibilities, skills, qualifications and working conditions for a particular job. Job descriptions are usually obtained through job analyses. They are used in the recruitment process as well as in the performance management process to

Copyright © Mometrix Media. You have been licensed one copy of this document for personal use only. Any other reproduction or redistribution is strictly prohibited. All rights reserved.

evaluate performance against expectations. As such, there is not a specific template for any job description because it is dependent on the particulars of the job and the organization. However, a job description is usually standardized in appearance in most organizations. Following are some of the most important elements that should be included in a job description:

- Job title
- Classification (exempt, nonexempt, contractor)
- Date when the job description was written
- Summary of the job and key objectives
- Listing of all essential functions, knowledge, skills, and abilities (KSAs). KSAs may or may not be included in essential functions. If not, there should be a separate section for competencies.
- Level of supervision – Number of direct reports or an individual contributor with no supervisory responsibilities
- Work environment conditions such as temperature and noise, and physical demands such as bending, sitting, lifting, etc.
- Hours – On-site; remote; and/or percentage of travel required, if applicable
- Education and/or experience required, including college, certifications, and/or number of years of experience in a specific industry or environment
- Salary range for the position
- Affirmative action plan and/or equal employment opportunity statement. These are especially necessary if the position is a federal contractor, but is usually common practice.

# Reporting Structure

## ORGANIZATION'S REPORTING STRUCTURE

Organizational structure allows organizations to carry out their goals in the most efficient and productive manner possible. Basically, organizational structure is the way work flows through an organization. There is no such thing as a one-size-fits-all organizational structure; it is dependent on the work that needs to be accomplished and by whom. Organizational structure can be formal or less formal and considered more loose or flexible depending on the organizational goals. Typically, organizational structure is aligned with the organization's strategy. Interdependencies between business functions and output need to be carefully examined. This requires looking closely at the relationship between leadership, which is responsible for strategy and results; the organization, which determines how processes and operations strategy is implemented; the jobs and the responsibilities needed to perform key organizational roles; and the people whose experience is needed to execute operations and achieve strategic goals. Understanding and maintaining the sync between these interdependencies is what drives the type of organizational structure that will work best for a business.

The creation of an organization reporting structure is based on several factors:

- Job departmentalization - How jobs are grouped together to complete work
- Span of control - Number of people who report to a supervisor or manager
- Centralization - Decision making that is conducted by upper-level management
- Decentralization - Decision making that is conducted by lower- or middle-level management

Copyright © Mometrix Media. You have been licensed one copy of this document for personal use only. Any other reproduction or redistribution is strictly prohibited. All rights reserved.

## ELEMENTS OF A FLAT ORGANIZATIONAL STRUCTURE

A **flat organizational structure** is a list of company employees, usually managers and supervisors, who report to a single leader. It is sometimes called a horizontal organizational structure because the list is usually arranged horizontally along a single line below the leader. This type of organization chart is most often used by small or startup companies. Also typical of this structure is that middle management is eliminated, thereby allowing employees to more easily make independent decisions and change direction quickly. This structure also provides employees with more responsibility, which increases employee involvement and leads to a freer exchange of ideas and communication. Alternatively, this type of structure can also make it challenging for employees because supervision is sometimes not so clear. Overall, a flat organizational structure is very difficult to maintain as a company grows larger.

# Flat (Horizontal) Organization Chart

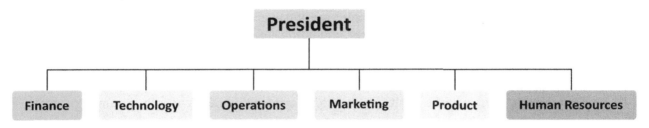

## HIERARCHY ORGANIZATION STRUCTURE

A **hierarchy organization chart** looks like a tall pyramid and is sometimes also referred to as a functional or functional hierarchical organizational chart. The top portion of the chart is almost always a single person, usually the president or CEO. The chart widens slightly on the second level with employees who report directly to the leader, possibly vice presidents. It widens further at the next level for employees who report to vice presidents, possibly directors. This pattern continues, with the chart widening as it includes more employees, until it reaches the bottom level with the lowest title designations. Each level is subordinate to the levels above it. This organization structure is best suited for large organizations, whereby supervision and responsibility are clearly established. Typically, the hierarchical environment utilizes specialists or positions with expertise in a specific area that tend to have a strong allegiance to their area or department within the business. This quality can be good for the individual department, but it makes horizontal communication across the other areas of the business very challenging, especially when decision making may be a benefit for one department and not necessarily for another. Sometimes a hierarchical structure is considered very bureaucratic in nature, thereby possibly causing a slow

Copyright © Mometrix Media. You have been licensed one copy of this document for personal use only. Any other reproduction or redistribution is strictly prohibited. All rights reserved.

response to changing market conditions or customer needs, and making the entire structure generally less flexible.

# Hierarchy Structure

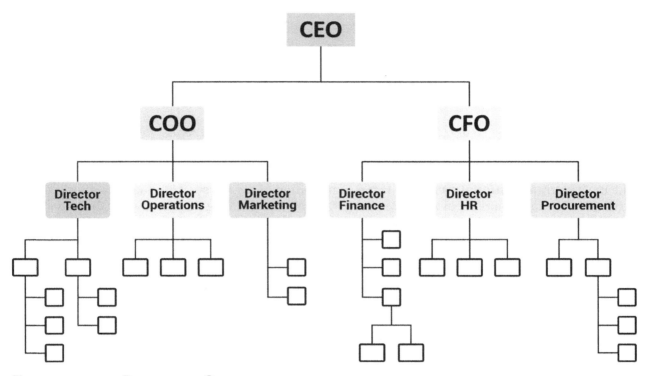

## ELEMENTS OF A DIVISIONAL STRUCTURE

A **divisional structure** basically separates an organization into parts. This could mean organizing a business by product or service and output. Divisions could also be further divided by geographical region. Each division is then responsible for everything related to that product, service, or region, depending upon how the business is structured. For example, a large beverage company might have three divisions: soda, water, and flavored seltzer. Each division would have its own department, such as finance, marketing, and research and development. In other words, there could be identical departments in each division. Continuing with this example, soda would have separate departments for finance, marketing, and research and development. Water would also have separate departments for finance, marketing, and research and development, as would the flavored seltzer division. This structure allows for intense focus and attention on each of the specialized services or products a company has and easy coordination within each specialized division, especially when compared with a hierarchical structure. Decision making is also faster in each functional area. On the other hand, the main disadvantage of divisional structure is that there is a duplication of effort and some efficiencies could be lost between duplicated departments. From a financial perspective, different divisions might be competing against each other for the same customers, and procurement of supplies might cost more than if the divisions purchased together. Additionally, a

Copyright © Mometrix Media. You have been licensed one copy of this document for personal use only. Any other reproduction or redistribution is strictly prohibited. All rights reserved.

divisional structure reduces the ability for employees in a certain department to benefit from the knowledge and continuing education from another identical department in a different division.

## Divisional Organization Chart

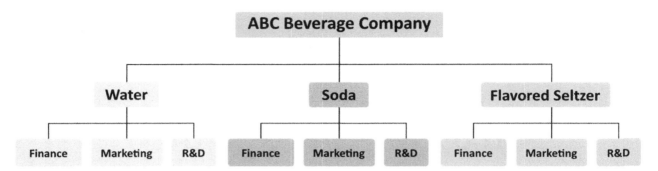

### MATRIX ORGANIZATIONAL STRUCTURE

The **matrix organizational structure** is the combination of the flat structure and the divisional structure. Basically, employees are supervised by at least two managers who are usually equally responsible for the employee performance depending on which function they perform. For example, an employee might work in a specialized area in a business division dedicated to a product, service, geographical region, or customer. This structure is useful when a product or service is complex in nature or is rapidly expanding. Businesses might choose this structure when the silos that exist within divisions no longer make the organization efficient. Furthermore, it is an optimal structure if rapid change is needed for a business to achieve a competitive advantage, whether that change requires more resources or additional expertise. In this manner, the business can focus more on the work that needs to be completed and a little less on the people in their silos. As a result, cost is typically minimized through the sharing of people and/or resources. There are also disadvantages to this structure. For instance, reporting to more than one manager can be challenging as responsibilities may be unclear or complicated. The matrix structure requires constant awareness, communication, and coordination between two or more managers to figure out an employee's work assignments and priorities. This could sometimes lead to conflicting messaging and demands causing the employee's stress level to rise, resulting in a loss of efficiencies as the work assignments moving forward are agreed upon. Matrix structures are common in project-driven organizations or circumstances whereby employees from different specialties form a team until the completion of the project, after which they return to their standard functions. From

Copyright © Mometrix Media. You have been licensed one copy of this document for personal use only. Any other reproduction or redistribution is strictly prohibited. All rights reserved.

an HR perspective, ensuring fairness and equity can sometimes be tricky in a matrix structure because there are many reporting levels for employees.

## Matrix Organization Chart

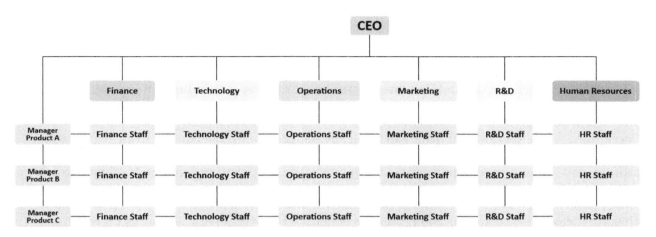

## OPEN BOUNDARY STRUCTURE

An organization with an **open boundary structure** is established without traditional boundaries or divisions. In other words, there are none of the boxes or solid lines found in a typical organization chart. Instead, all units or functions are fluid and flexible. Traditional departments are more team-like and the business, including suppliers, work closely together as one. This means that everyone can participate in decision making, as organizational hierarchy is almost nonexistent. The most important characteristic of an open boundary structure is the organization's ability to quickly adapt and be flexible in order to be as innovative as possible. Additionally, organizations with this structure are usually tech savvy, utilizing the latest and greatest technology; and have flexible working schedules that rely heavily on all forms of electronic communication. The primary advantage of this structure is it fully leverages everyone's talent, eliminates bureaucratic bottlenecks, and can adapt and change to market forces quickly. Alternatively, this type of structure needs strong leadership and vision because efficiencies based on specialty knowledge may not always be achieved and could be time-consuming to maintain.

# Types of External Providers of HR Services

### NECESSITY OF EXTERNAL HR SERVICE PROVIDERS

An **external HR service provider** is a contracted vendor that provides a service not otherwise available or limited in capacity within the organization. Sometimes it is less expensive and more efficient to utilize outside vendors rather than internally employ the particular service or expertise within the organization. External vendors offer many different HR support services such as recruitment, benefits, training, employee relations, temporary staffing, and compensation. There are many different HR considerations to think about as they relate to external vendors such as cost, level of expertise, ethical practices, and more. The idea of using an external vendor for a specialized function also allows an HR organization to focus on core business functions. Additionally, some projects may require an expertise not available in an organization, such as training or benefits.

Copyright © Mometrix Media. You have been licensed one copy of this document for personal use only. Any other reproduction or redistribution is strictly prohibited. All rights reserved.

## RECRUITMENT FIRMS

A **recruitment firm** is an external vendor that supplements an organization's internal recruiting effort, primarily helping an organization hire full-time, permanent employees. A recruiting firm usually has a network of potential candidates with whom they have fostered a relationship. Other times, a recruitment firm may be utilized for a specialized role that internal recruiters may not have experience hiring. This type of specialized recruiting is sometimes referred to as "niche recruiting." Similarly, a recruitment firm could also specialize in executive recruiting through their network of pre-identified, qualified candidates; these firms are sometimes called "headhunters." In many cases, regardless of the position, the recruiter will handle the initial screenings by sifting through resumes, phone screenings, and first interviews so that they can present qualified candidates to the organization. Some organizations, especially startups, smaller companies, and those with infrequent staffing needs may not have an internal recruiter and may find it more efficient to use a recruitment firm. Recruitment firms can be an advantageous external partner to an organization, but there are a few drawbacks. For example, they are not fully immersed in an organization's culture, and thereby are not always able to represent the organization completely. They also may not be totally aware of the exact skills an organization is seeking in a candidate, and a bit slower to understand small nuances to changing candidate requirements. Overall, external recruitment firms that are measurably recruiting good hires are beneficial to partner with, as long as there is open communication.

## BENEFIT BROKERS

A **benefit broker** is an external vendor that assists an organization in navigating employee benefit options which are cost-effective and tailored to an organization's needs. Benefit options may include health, dental, vision, financial, and more. It should be noted that not all brokers are the same. For example, some might work for a large provider and therefore only offer choices that particular providers offer—think of a large insurance company with only four options for medical insurance to choose from. Others still may only specialize in one type of benefit, such as vision. Additionally, some may have a sizable amount of different benefit options in a variety of specialties, but may or may not have extensive knowledge across all benefit offerings. Generally, benefit brokers supply expertise on some or all of the following common offerings:

- Forms of insurance – Most benefit brokers offer some form of insurance such as medical, dental, vision, disability, and life.
- Compliance expertise – Counsel organizations on benefits to stay in compliance with federal laws, including the Employee Retirement Income Security Act (ERISA), Affordable Care Act (ACA), and specific state and local laws and regulations.
- Overall benefit analysis – This could include cost efficiencies, examination of potential changes based on laws or changing environments, and analysis of existing benefits and related claims.
- Direct employee assistance – This assistance could include direct communication with employees about benefits regarding coverage, claim questions, etc. Additionally, they could provide assistance with enrollment and offer training sessions about benefit options.

Benefit broker fees are usually contingent on the type of coverages and services offered. However, there are others that charge a flat fee based on specific services and offerings.

## STAFFING AGENCIES

A **staffing agency** is an external vendor that offers employees for an organization to hire, usually for temporary assignments. Staffing agencies can be industry-focused, specialized, or broader-based across industries and specialties. The most important distinction is that the staffing agency

Copyright © Mometrix Media. You have been licensed one copy of this document for personal use only. Any other reproduction or redistribution is strictly prohibited. All rights reserved.

hires the worker. Therefore, the agency is the employer of record and not the organization. Hence, it is the staffing agency and not the organization that payrolls the worker and offers benefits. Typically, staffing agencies work with candidates that might be considered more entry-to-mid-level management. Frequently, staffing agencies are utilized during a company's busiest season, special projects, or possibly replacing someone on leave. Additionally, most staffing agencies interview, test, and prepare workers for placement instead of the organization.

## PROFESSIONAL EMPLOYER ORGANIZATION (PEO)

A **professional employer organization** (PEO) is an external vendor that is contracted by a business to perform a variety of HR functions and services. These may include, but are not limited to, payroll processing, benefit administration and management, workers' compensation administration, regulatory compliance advice and management, risk management, talent acquisition, and employee relations consulting. This contract is considered a co-employment agreement, whereby liability is shared between the client and PEO. Actually, the PEO usually becomes the employer of record as a legal necessity in order for the PEO to conduct financial transactions such as payroll and taxes. A PEO relationship occurs more often in small to mid-sized companies that lack the expertise, or may find it too costly to accurately manage regulatory compliance, benefit administration, or any other service function offered by a PEO. Additionally, a client has the option to purchase which specific services best suit the needs of a particular business. For example, a small business may be able to manage talent acquisition, but finds it too costly to have a subject matter expert to administer payroll or maintain regulatory compliance. Hence, a business may choose to have only those functions managed by a PEO. There are several important factors for a business to consider before entering into a contract with a PEO, including the loss of control, security access to company systems and sensitive information, and influence on the business's culture.

# Communication Techniques

## WHY COMMUNICATION IS CRITICAL IN THE WORKPLACE

Workplace communication is the exchange of information and ideas in an organization. Good workplace communication is necessary in order to have a high-performing organizational culture and operate with maximum efficiencies. The most important aspect of communication is not simply saying or technically communicating information, but rather that the information is received accurately and correctly understood by the intended audience. Effective communication is critical in order for an organization to achieve its goals. The goal of effective workplace communication is to avoid confusion or ambiguity, build collaboration among employees, shape a positive culture, and create accountability. Frequently, the best measure of effective communication is to observe what works and what doesn't work. Additionally, workplace communication is a strong mechanism for all members of an organization to provide input and come away feeling that their thoughts were heard and valued.

## CHANNELS OF COMMUNICATION

Communication can be transmitted through a wide variety of channels or media, such as phone, email, face-to-face, reports, presentations, or social media. The chosen method should fit both the audience and the type of communication. **Information-rich communication channels** include phone, videoconferencing, and face-to-face meetings or presentations. **Information-lean communication channels** include email, fliers, newsletters, or reports. When trying to sell a product or service, a salesman might use a series of phone calls, face-to-face meetings, and presentations. This is because information-rich media are more interactive, which is more

Copyright © Mometrix Media. You have been licensed one copy of this document for personal use only. Any other reproduction or redistribution is strictly prohibited. All rights reserved.

appropriate for complex messages that may need clarification. Rich and verbal communications should be used when there is time urgency, immediate feedback is required, ideas can be simplified with explanations, or emotions may be affected. Lean and written communications should be used when the communicator is simply stating facts or needs information permanently recorded.

## IMPORTANCE OF ORAL COMMUNICATION IN THE WORKPLACE

Oral communication is the art of using speech to deliver information about ideas, feelings, and opinions. Good communication skills are not only a necessity in personal life, but extremely important in the workplace. In fact, most job offers require or at least prefer applicants with "excellent written and oral communication skills." Oral communication is how relationships and trust are formed among employees. Poor oral communication can lead to misunderstandings, conflict, and result in a loss of workplace productivity. Oral communication is a combination of what words a person chooses to use and how those words are communicated. The marriage of what and how a person communicates while speaking allows for the smooth flow of communication among employees and a more productive work environment. Additionally, this marriage of "what and how" is significant in human resources as critical information is frequently communicated by speaking, such as job offers, performance improvement, compensation changes, and layoffs. Usually, if information that is more emotional in nature needs to be communicated, then oral communication is the preferred method, although sometimes the same information is contained in a written follow-up. The right words, tone, and speed of oral communication impact how something is understood. Furthermore, another critical component of good oral communication is active listening, as the workplace is more successful if opinions are heard and employees feel engaged.

## USING EMAIL, TEXT, OR INSTANT MESSAGING (IM) AS A FORM OF COMMUNICATION

Emailing, texting, and instant messaging (IM) are becoming increasingly popular forms of workplace communication because they are simple and efficient. The workplace is becoming more technology-driven and many companies have implemented written communication policies that dictate what types of workplace communication are allowed via text and email versus phone and face-to-face. These policies vary by company, but they frequently outline or offer guidelines as to which form of communication is appropriate situationally. As a general rule, email, texting, and IM are excellent forms of communication for information that is clear, brief, and actionable. Examples include asking a coworker if they can attend a meeting on a particular date and time, requesting someone to review the following information and respond back, or asking for specific information. When writing via any form of technological communication, consideration must be evaluated as to whether the communication is necessary and if it is appropriate. Writing through technological systems is only one channel of communication and a determination should be made if it is the best method. For instance, a phone call might be more efficient if there is going to be a lot of dialogue. Additionally, email, texting, IM, or really any form of writing might not be appropriate if sensitive or bad news needs to be communicated because it can be challenging to communicate compassion, empathy, and tone. Information shared in this format could be misinterpreted, causing further harm. Similarly, anything put in an email, text, or IM could inadvertently be shared, potentially causing harm or embarrassment.

## PASSIVE AND AGGRESSIVE COMMUNICATION STYLES

Communication styles vary by individual, and there is not one communication style that is correct because so much is dependent on the situation and individual preference. Someone with a **passive communication** style frequently acts indifferent, may not express their feelings, and prefers to listen to others as opposed to objecting or disagreeing. A passive communicator usually wants to avoid causing any conflict, even to the point of remaining silent when they should speak out. In fact, sometimes their silence causes a misunderstanding. In the workplace, a person with this style of

Copyright © Mometrix Media. You have been licensed one copy of this document for personal use only. Any other reproduction or redistribution is strictly prohibited. All rights reserved.

easygoing, patient communication can be effective at calming nerves and putting others before themselves. They almost never complain and rarely object to work. Alternatively, someone with an **aggressive communication** style has no problem voicing their opinion at every opportunity they get, and frequently is rude and hurtful when speaking. The key for an aggressive communicator is to get their opinion heard and listened to, no matter the consequences. The old adage, "I'm right, you're wrong" could be the motto of an aggressive communicator. They put their needs ahead of others. Despite these often-unwanted characteristics, aggressive communicators who can temper or control their more negative tendencies often make excellent leaders because of their ability to attract attention and convince others to follow them.

## PASSIVE-AGGRESSIVE COMMUNICATION STYLE

A **passive-aggressive communication** style is challenging to describe, but easy to recognize when presented. While the passive-aggressive communicator doesn't literally state their feelings of anger, disagreement, or dissatisfaction, they will communicate their true thoughts in very subtle ways. This communication style is covert because the passive-aggressive person desires to suggest their discontent without the other person overtly knowing they are upset or in disagreement about something. Examples of this communication style in the workplace might include blaming others for personal issues or problems, starting rumors or gossip to distract or undermine leadership, facially expressing their opinion instead of using words, being quick to embarrass others, perhaps using words like "whatever" or sarcastically saying "fine," or verbally agreeing to something with absolutely no intention of doing whatever was agreed to. Frequently the end goal of a passive-aggressive communicator is to cause others to convey the feelings that the passive-aggressive person is feeling. This enables the passive-aggressive person the satisfaction of exerting their power over someone else.

## ASSERTIVE COMMUNICATION STYLE

An **assertive communication** style is defined by honest, direct verbalization about one's thoughts or opinions without judging others for their beliefs. The premise of an assertive communicator is to communicate in a polite manner while demonstrating respect for one's own beliefs or ideas as well as the opinions of others. When others deal with an assertive communicator, they feel comfortable and welcome to express their feelings because they know civility and consideration for all is an objective that will be met. An assertive communicator will try to find a solution that benefits all parties, allowing everyone to benefit or at least letting them feel as though their opinion was heard and valued. For example, an assertive communicator might respond with, "I really think this is the way to proceed, but I'm genuinely open to hearing your opinion." Those with an assertive communication style frequently use I-statements when conversing. An I-statement allows someone to be assertive without putting the listener on the defensive. It permits communicators to take ownership of their feelings without implying they are the cause of the problem. For example, instead of saying, "You never listen to me and probably aren't listening now," one could say, "I feel my concerns are not being heard." In the workplace, an assertive communicator is excellent at building and maintaining productive teams and collaboratively solving conflict.

## DELIVERING CLEAR MESSAGES

Delivering messages can be difficult, especially if the context is serious in nature. The message content should be tailored to fit the audience. This requires understanding the roles, expectations, and perspective of recipients. First, focus on eliminating any barriers or vague wording that may interfere with interpreting the message. Once the proper channel for delivery is selected, it may be important to focus on nonverbal signals and ensure that they coincide with the mood of the message content. Finally, messages should allow for feedback that will lead to follow-up discussions. If a message is complex in nature, such as a business change or new benefits offering, it

Copyright © Mometrix Media. You have been licensed one copy of this document for personal use only. Any other reproduction or redistribution is strictly prohibited. All rights reserved.

may be critical to share repeated reminders and have open lines of communication to reduce confusion and ensure success.

## CHARACTERISTICS OF AN ACTIVE LISTENER

**Active listening** is an important component of communication that requires paying close attention to what is being said. It often involves making eye contact and appropriately nodding to show engagement. To gain a better understanding, listeners should try to understand things from the speaker's point of view, or visualize what they are saying. It is important to be considerate, avoid distractions or interruptions, and respond appropriately. Additionally, listeners should try to pick up on emotional cues beyond the literal words that are used. Even if the message differs from the active listener's own opinion, the listener will try to focus on accepting what the other person has to say rather than being critical. Active listeners should make sure to fully hear what the other person is saying before formulating their own response. When compared to passive listeners, it has been noted that active listeners are more connected and conscientious.

Copyright © Mometrix Media. You have been licensed one copy of this document for personal use only. Any other reproduction or redistribution is strictly prohibited. All rights reserved.

# Recruitment and Selection

## Applicable laws and regulations related to recruitment and selection, such as non-discrimination, accommodation, and work authorization

### TITLE VII OF THE CIVIL RIGHTS ACT OF 1964

Title VII of the Civil Rights Act, which was originally passed in 1964 and amended in 1972, 1978, and 1991, is designed to prevent unlawful discrimination in the workplace. This section of the Civil Rights Act makes it unlawful to discriminate or segregate any aspect of an individual's employment based on the following:

- Race
- Color
- National origin
- Religion
- Gender

In other words, Title VII legislation prevents an employer from discriminating with regard to any condition of employment based on these criteria, including recruiting, hiring, and firing. Furthermore, Title VII prohibits an employer from limiting the opportunities for an employee with regard to compensation, career promotions, training, and other employment avenues for advancement or progress. Title VII also makes it unlawful for an employer to discriminate against individuals who are pregnant, about to give birth, or who have any similar medical condition. Title VII of the Civil Rights Act applies to any employer who has more than 15 employees. Exceptions include religious organizations, which can choose to hire only individuals within that religion or to consider individuals of that religion for employment before individuals of other religions; and Indian reservations, which can choose to hire or consider Indians living on or near a reservation for employment before other individuals.

### EEOC

The **Equal Opportunity Employment Commission** (EEOC) was formed by Title VII of the Civil Rights Act to protect certain groups of individuals from unlawful discrimination. The EEOC is a federal agency designed to encourage equal employment opportunities, to train employers to avoid practices and policies that could cause unlawful discrimination, and to enforce the laws included in the Civil Rights Act, Age Discrimination in Employment Act, and laws included in other similar anti-discrimination legislation. The EEOC attempts to obtain settlements from employers for actions that the commission deems discriminatory. If the employer will not settle with the EEOC, the EEOC will continue their attempt to enforce the law by filing a lawsuit against the employer on behalf of the victim of the discrimination. As such, employers need to be cognizant of EEOC regulations when writing job descriptions and in all recruitment activities. For example, an employer that does not want anyone over the age of 45 cannot document "any applicant over the age of 45 need not apply" because it would clearly be an EEOC violation on the grounds of age discrimination. Similarly, an employer could not state that only males should apply because the employer is fearful that someone female might have child care issues, as that too would be a case of gender discrimination under EEOC regulations.

Copyright © Mometrix Media. You have been licensed one copy of this document for personal use only. Any other reproduction or redistribution is strictly prohibited. All rights reserved.

## CIVIL RIGHTS ACT OF 1991

The Civil Rights Act (CRA) of 1991 made the Civil Rights Act of 1964 stronger, but it did not replace the Act. The CRA of 1991 primarily made the burden of proof (supplied by the victim) and liability for the employer difficult to circumvent, making it easier for employees to sue employers for unlawful discrimination. For example, if an employer is found guilty of intentional unlawful discrimination, the damages awarded to victims could be both compensatory for emotional distress and punitive for breaking the law. It should be noted there is a limit on how much juries can award per person. If there are four individuals suing, then the amount awarded increases four-fold. Moreover, the CRA of 1991 offers plaintiffs a jury option in alleged cases of intentional employment discrimination. Prior to the CRA of 1991, the only option was a judge's decision. The CRA of 1991 clarified statutory guidelines for disparate impact cases (nondiscriminatory actions at face value, but negatively impact a member of a protected class under Title VII). Additionally, the CRA of 1991 enhanced the strength of civil rights that were, at the time, losing power by unfavorable Supreme Court decisions, thereby increasing protection for employees from discriminatory treatment.

## CHANGES THE CIVIL RIGHTS ACT OF 1991 MADE TO TITLE VII OF THE CIVIL RIGHTS ACT OF 1964

The Civil Rights Act of 1991 made a number of changes to Title VII of the Civil Rights Act of 1964 including expanding the protection offered by Title VII to cover congressional employees, expanding the protection offered by Title VII to cover foreign locations owned and/or operated by American businesses, and creating a sliding scale for the maximum amount of damages for which a victim of discrimination could sue. The Civil Rights Act of 1991 also granted individuals or organizations accused of discrimination the right to a jury trial if a civil suit is brought against that individual or organization, placed the burden of proof for disparate impact cases on the victim of discrimination, and granted individuals or organizations accused of discrimination the right to prove that a specific action or policy was necessary to the operation of the business and use that proof as a legal defense against accusations of disparate impact. The Civil Rights Act of 1991 also set guidelines defining specific actions that should be considered unlawful discrimination.

## AGE DISCRIMINATION IN EMPLOYMENT ACT (ADEA)

The Age Discrimination in Employment Act (ADEA), which was originally passed in 1967 and then later amended in 1991, is designed to prevent discrimination against individuals over the age of 39. This act makes it unlawful to base decisions related to an individual's employment, such as pay or benefits, on the age of the individual if that individual is at least 40 years old. This act applies to any business, employment agency, labor organization, and state or local government agency with more than 20 employees. Exceptions include individuals age 40 or over who do not meet the occupational qualifications required to perform the tasks reasonably necessary to the business' operations, termination due to reasonable cause, employment of firefighters or police officers, retirement of employees with executive positions, or tenured educators under certain conditions. Pre-employment inquiries about an individual's age are not recommended because it could deter an older worker from applying for a position and indicate discriminatory intent on behalf of the employer on the basis of age. Someone's age can be determined after the employee is hired.

## REHABILITATION ACT OF 1973

The **Rehabilitation Act** of 1973 is similar to the Americans with Disabilities Act (ADA) in that the Rehabilitation Act is designed to prevent discrimination against individuals with disabilities. However, the ADA expands the protections granted by the Rehabilitation Act, which was only designed to prevent discrimination against individuals with disabilities if those individuals were seeking employment in federal agencies or with federal contractors that earned more than $10,000

Copyright © Mometrix Media. You have been licensed one copy of this document for personal use only. Any other reproduction or redistribution is strictly prohibited. All rights reserved.

a year from government contracts. Employers were not required under the Rehabilitation Act to make the organization's facilities accessible to individuals with disabilities, so there was no legal remedy for individuals who were employed but unable to access their place of employment.

## PREGNANCY DISCRIMINATION ACT OF 1978

There are two main clauses of the **Pregnancy Discrimination Act** (PDA) of 1978. The first clause applies to Title VII's prohibition against sex discrimination, which also directly applies to prejudice on the basis of childbirth, pregnancy, or related medical conditions. The second clause requires that employers treat pregnant women the same as others for all employment-related reasons and similarly in their ability or inability to work. In short, the Pregnancy Discrimination Act makes it illegal to fire or refuse to hire or promote a woman because she is pregnant, force a pregnancy leave on women who are willing and able to perform the job, and stop accruing seniority for a woman because she is out of work to give birth. If a pregnant woman is not able to perform her job because of a medical condition related to the pregnancy, the employer must treat the pregnant woman the same way it treats all other temporary disabilities, including providing reasonable accommodations. In addition to the PDA of 1978, employers should be aware of any other state regulations that may afford pregnant women more protections.

## AMERICAN DISABILITIES ACT (ADA)

The **Americans with Disabilities Act** (ADA), which was passed in 1990, is designed to prevent discrimination against individuals with disabilities. A disability, as defined by the ADA, is a mental or physical impairment that impedes one or more life activities. Examples might include, but are not limited to, mobility and personal hygiene. A qualified person with a disability should be able to perform the essential functions of a job with or without reasonable accommodations. This act makes it unlawful to base decisions related to aspects of an individual's employment (such as pay or benefits) on whether the individual is disabled. This act also requires the business, employment agency, or labor organization to ensure the disabled individual has access to his or her place of employment unless making these changes will cause the business significant harm.

## AREAS THE ADAAA OF 2008 AMENDS THE ADA OF 1990

The **ADA Amendments Act** (ADAAA) of 2008 amends the American Disabilities Act of 1990 (ADA) in areas that further clarify protections and definitions of a disability. The following modifications were made in the ADAAA of 2008:

- Prohibits the display of so-called "mitigating measures" in assessing if a person has a disability. Basically, a person will be assessed without certain measures used to manage their impairment such as prosthetic devices, hearing aids, etc. taken into consideration. Notable exceptions to these measures include eyeglasses and contact lenses.
- Further clarifies the ADA wording of "regarded as" having a disability if employees can prove that they have been discriminated against because of actual or perceived disability. In other words, if employees feel they have been discriminated against for being "regarded as" having a disability and were discriminated against by an employer, the organization could be in violation of the ADAAA of 2008. Note there could be a true disability or a perceived disability. Examples of discrimination include being denied training or not receiving a promotion.
- Expands the definition of "disability" to include a listing of life activities and conditions, including physical movement, cognitive functions, and medical conditions. It should be noted that the act states that "homosexuality, bisexuality, transvestitism and compulsive gambling" are not considered impairments. In general, most disabling conditions that are temporary in nature are also not included under this act.

Copyright © Mometrix Media. You have been licensed one copy of this document for personal use only. Any other reproduction or redistribution is strictly prohibited. All rights reserved.

## VIETNAM ERA VETERAN'S READJUSTMENT ASSISTANCE ACT (VEVRAA)

The Vietnam Era Veteran's Readjustment Assistance Act (VEVRAA) is designed to prevent discrimination against veterans. This act makes it unlawful for federal contractors or subcontractors with $25,000 or more in federal contracts or subcontracts to base employment decisions on the fact that the individual is a veteran. It also requires federal contractors or subcontractors meeting these requirements to list open positions with state employment agencies and requires these employers to institute affirmative action plans for veterans. However, in order for this act to apply, the veteran must have served for more than 180 days with at least part of that time occurring between August 5, 1964 and May 7, 1975; have a disability or group of disabilities that are rated at 10-30 percent or more, depending on the severity or circumstances of their disability, and be eligible for compensation from the Department of Veteran Affairs; or have served on active duty for a conflict with an authorized campaign badge.

## AREAS JVA OF 2007 ALTERED COVERAGE FOR THE VEVRAA OF 1974

The **Jobs for Veterans Act** (JVA) of 2007 amended the VEVRAA by raising the amount of a federal employer contract from $25,000 to $100,000 and further clarifying the categories of protected veterans. The JVA of 2007 applies to a contractor with contracts that began before December 1, 2003. The following categories were changed:

- Eliminated the category of Vietnam-era veterans, but still provided coverage under a new category titled "campaign veterans."
- Added a new category of "Armed Forces Service Medal" veterans.
- Expanded disability-related coverage to include all veterans with "service-connected disabilities."
- Changed coverage from one-year post-discharge from active duty to three years.

It should be noted that federal contractors and subcontractors are still required to post open positions (except top management jobs) on state and local job databases.

## PRACTICES PROHIBITED BY THE IMMIGRATION REFORM AND CONTROL ACT

The **Immigration Reform and Control Act** (IRCA) is designed to prevent discrimination based on nationality. This act makes it unlawful for an employer to base employment decisions such as pay or benefits on that individual's country of origin or citizenship status as long as the individual can legally work within the United States. This act also makes it unlawful for an organization to intentionally hire individuals that cannot legally work in the United States and requires the completion of the I-9 form for all new employees. This act specifically requires the employer to obtain proof of the employee's eligibility to work in the United States for the I-9 form, but the employee must be allowed to provide any document or combination of documents considered acceptable by the IRCA.

## VOCATIONAL REHABILITATION ACT

The **Vocational Rehabilitation Act** was intended to increase occupational opportunities for disabled individuals and to prohibit discrimination against qualified individuals with disabilities. In this case, "qualified" means that the person applying for the job can perform the essential function with or without reasonable accommodations. The act applies to federal government contractors and subcontractors holding contracts or subcontracts of $10,000 or more. Contractors and subcontractors with greater than $50,000 in contracts and more than 50 employees must develop written affirmative action plans that address hiring and promoting persons with disabilities. Although there are regulations that protect those engaged in addiction treatment, this act does not protect against individuals who currently suffer with substance abuse that prevents them from

Copyright © Mometrix Media. You have been licensed one copy of this document for personal use only. Any other reproduction or redistribution is strictly prohibited. All rights reserved.

performing the duties of the job or whose employment would constitute a direct threat to the safety and property of others. The primary focus of the act is to extend grants to states for vocational rehabilitation services with a heightened emphasis on those individuals with severe disabilities.

## UNIFORM GUIDELINES ON EMPLOYEE SELECTION PROCEDURES

The **Uniform Guidelines on Employee Selection Procedures** (UGESP), which were passed in 1978, is a procedural document that assists employers to comply with several federal anti-discrimination laws, such as EEO, with an emphasis on Title VII. The primary purpose of these guidelines is to define the specific types of procedures that may cause disparate impact and are considered illegal. These guidelines apply to all aspects of the selection and hiring process: recruiting, interviewing, testing, performance appraisals, and any other factor of consideration used to make employment decisions. The UGESP relates to unfair procedures that make it much less likely that an individual belonging to a protected class would be able to receive a particular position.

## GENETIC INFORMATION NON-DISCRIMINATION ACT (GINA)

The **Genetic Information Nondiscrimination Act** (GINA), passed in May 2008, protects people from discrimination based on their genetic information. The act specifically offers protection in two areas: (1) it prohibits discrimination with regard to healthcare coverage based on genetic information, and (2) it protects against discrimination based on genetic information in employment. Employers, under GINA, are not permitted to request any type of genetic information about prospective job candidates or employees, except for a few extreme situations. For example, an employer cannot ask a prospective job candidate about their family medical history. In fact, employers are strongly encouraged to ask healthcare providers not to collect genetic information in the case where an employee needs a medical exam for employment or ADA-related leaves of absence and possible accommodations. Additionally, GINA forbids any type of harassment based on genetic information.

## EXECUTIVE ORDERS

An **executive order** is a written declaration made by the President of the United States establishing a policy for enforcing existing legislation. Executive orders are legally binding and are treated as law if the order remains in the Federal Registry for more than 30 days. Executive Order 11246, which was published to the Federal Registry in 1965, states that federal contractors are not only required to avoid employment discrimination but are also required to take steps to ensure equal opportunities are available to individuals belonging to protected classes. This executive order established the concept of affirmative action and required federal contractors with more than $10,000 in government contracts during a single year to implement affirmative action plans, and federal contractors with $50,000 or more in contracts and 50 or more employees to file written affirmative action plans with the Office of Federal Contract Compliance Programs (OFCCP.)

### EXECUTIVE ORDER 11246

Originally, Executive Order (EO) 11246 applied only to employment discrimination based on an individual's color, national origin, race, or religion. However, EO 11375, EO 11478, EO 13152, and EO 13279 amended the policy and changed the groups that were covered. EO 11375 made it unlawful to discriminate based on gender, EO 11478 made it unlawful to discriminate based on disabilities or age if that individual is over age 40, EO 13152 made it unlawful to discriminate based on parental status, and EO 13279 excluded federal contractors who were religious or community organizations providing services to the community from the need to adhere to the policies.

Copyright © Mometrix Media. You have been licensed one copy of this document for personal use only. Any other reproduction or redistribution is strictly prohibited. All rights reserved.

## AFFIRMATIVE ACTION AND AFFIRMATIVE ACTION PLAN (AAP)

Affirmative action is a set of written procedures designed to correct discriminatory practices from the past and prevent the continuation of such practices now and in the future. Affirmative action plans (AAP) were first established by Executive Order 11246 and are required for those entities doing business with the federal government to have AAPs in compliance with equal employment opportunity laws. In other words, an AAP is supposed to help make sure that every person has equal opportunities when it comes to recruitment, selection, promotion, and training. Moreover, organizations with an AAP must prioritize a quantifiable grouping of qualified candidates who are disabled, minorities, female, and/or covered veterans. An AAP includes a list of action-oriented programs, an availability analysis of employees from protected classes, a section that designates the individual responsible for the organization's AAP, a job group analysis, an organizational profile, placement goals, a system for internal audits and reports related to analyzing barriers to equal employment opportunities, and a utilization analysis of the number of protected individuals employed by the company compared to the number of protected individuals available. The Office of Federal Contract Compliance Programs (OFCCP) oversees and enforces regulations for those organizations that comply with AAPs. Organizations with AAPs must file their AAP document and report related metrics with the OFCCP annually.

# Applicant Databases

## APPLICANT TRACKING SYSTEMS

An **applicant tracking system** (ATS) is a computer database used by employers to automate and manage all or some aspects of the job application and hiring process. Other names used for ATS programs include talent acquisition software, recruitment software, hiring database, or hiring platform. The primary purpose of an ATS is to efficiently manage information in the job application process. An ATS captures everything an applicant submits for a job posting, including name, resume, education, experience, contact information, and cover letter. In response, the ATS can be programmed by a recruiter to filter resumes for keywords or experiences, give online tests, schedule interviews, mail rejection letters (if applicable), and much more. An ATS allows multiple people to view job candidate information, including interview notes and evaluations. After a candidate is selected, the information obtained in the ATS can oftentimes be seamlessly transitioned to other software, such as a payroll system. An ATS creates efficiencies that allow an employer to optimize the hiring process.

> **Review Video: Applicant Tracking System**
> Visit mometrix.com/academy and enter code: 532324

## APPLICANT FLOW DATA REPORTING

**Applicant flow tracking** is required by the EEOC and necessary for any employer to complete if they have a federal contract. The information should detail the gender and race of every applicant that applies for an open position. The objective is to analyze source data and identify the selection rate among groupings by race and gender for a position to ensure a fair grouping of people are being sourced for the open job. Organizations with a federal contract are supposed to make a reasonable effort to collect and maintain this information. Typically, this information is voluntarily self-reported by the job candidate or casually observed by an HR representative in an interview situation. An applicant tracking system (ATS) assists in the recordkeeping of this information as well as the ability to generate reports needed to analyze the data. It is extremely important to note this information cannot be used in hiring decisions. During the application process, the job applicant is also made aware, in writing, that the hiring decision will not be based on self-reported

Copyright © Mometrix Media. You have been licensed one copy of this document for personal use only. Any other reproduction or redistribution is strictly prohibited. All rights reserved.

EEOC-related personal information. In fact, HR is to secure that information, either electronically or in paper format, and keep it separate from the employee's application. An ATS makes collecting and reporting this type of data more accurate and efficient.

## ADVANTAGES

There are many specific benefits an employer can derive from utilizing an applicant tracking system (ATS):

- **Job posting** - Post job requisitions across multiple third-party job boards as well as a company job posting
- **Easier application process for candidates** - Job candidates can more expediently apply for jobs via an ATS, allowing an employer to be seen as more favorable.
- **More efficient resume filtering** - Due to specialized keyword searches across resumes, recruiters can eliminate resumes more quickly.
- **Everything is in one spot** - Manage everything about a job applicant in one place, with no need for spreadsheets or computer folders
- **Increases overall administrative efficiency** - More efficiently complete administrative tasks associated with recruiting and hiring job candidates, including resume filtering, phone screenings, evaluations, interview scheduling, and tests
- **Captures and tracks job applicant data for reporting** - Efficiently and accurately capture job applicant information that may need to be tracked and reported to comply with Equal Employment Opportunity (EEO) and Office of Federal Contract Compliance Programs (OFFCP) regulations. Allows an employer to analyze the database of applicants for specific EEO categories and job classifications. Additionally, an employer can use the database for recruiting analytics.
- **Assists in the onboarding process** - Streamlines the onboarding of a selected job candidate as the information captured in the ATS can usually be transferred to other systems an employer might utilize such as payroll, information technology, etc. This may also eliminate a significant amount of paperwork.

## SAFEGUARDS

Overall, applicant tracking systems (ATS) make the recruitment process more efficient, but there are some limitations an employer should consider and address. Frequently an ATS is used to filter out resumes if the candidate does not have a certain skill or experience. This filter is based on a pattern of keywords. If applicants have the desired skill or experience, and they use synonyms or words not close enough to the keyword filters, then they might be eliminated from consideration. Furthermore, an ATS sometimes has character-restricted fields whereby a candidate might be qualified, but the character restriction did not allow them to provide enough information. Occasionally, an ATS might scan a resume incorrectly; this could occur if there is something in the resume that the system is not programmed to recognize. Usually, an ATS can be modified, and recruiters usually make an effort to ensure qualified candidates do not slip through the cracks.

# Recruitment Sources

## RECRUITING

**Recruiting** refers to the strategies and procedures used to identify qualified people for potential employment by an organization, including analyzing job responsibilities, sourcing or finding applicants, and finding the most qualified candidates. In short, recruiting adds new qualified people

Copyright © Mometrix Media. You have been licensed one copy of this document for personal use only. Any other reproduction or redistribution is strictly prohibited. All rights reserved.

to an organization in order to fill vacancies for open positions. Most often there are three types of recruiting:

- **Internal** – Identifying qualified candidates within an organization for a lateral position, transfer, or promotion to fill a job vacancy. Some of the benefits of internal recruiting include the person already being familiar with the organization's culture and procedures, the motivation for employees to work harder for a promotion, and reducing organization cost and recruiting efforts.
- **External** – Identifying and locating qualified job applicants outside an organization. There are many benefits to external hiring, including a large applicant pool to select from, new talent with different perspectives or ideas, a larger pool of possible candidates, and the possibility of increasing diversity within an organization.
- **Alternative or other** – This type of recruiting is primarily derived from volunteers, internships, or temporary workers. Sometimes a temporary worker can be promoted to a full-time employee in an organization.

## RECRUITMENT SOURCING OF ACTIVE, SEMI-ACTIVE, AND PASSIVE CANDIDATES

Recruiting candidates can be categorized into three primary groupings, depending on the level of candidate interest:

- **Active** – Candidates that are fully engaged in the search for a new job. This type of individual could be employed or unemployed, but energetically seeking new employment.
- **Semi-active** – While not fully engaged in the process of obtaining new employment, a semi-active candidate is open to the idea of a new job if it presents itself and is a better fit than their current position.
- **Passive** - This type of candidate is not looking for new employment. However, a passive candidate might have a particular skill set or experience that is sought by an employer. If a recruiter identifies such an individual, the burden is on the recruiter to convince the individual of the benefits of a new employment opportunity.

## EMPLOYEE REFERRALS

An **employee referral** is a recruiting method within an organization whereby existing employees identify and recommend friends or colleagues in their network for job openings. This is usually a documented program that encourages employees to recommend qualified people they know for job openings. These formal programs usually specify how long the referred person needs to remain employed and who is eligible to participate in a referral program. Additionally, the employee who made the referral is frequently monetarily rewarded or recognized for placing a qualified person within the organization. There are many benefits for an organization to have an employee referral program:

- Employees know their organization and who would or would not be a good cultural fit
- A win-win for the applicant because sourcing through an employee referral program could enable a job applicant to stand out more, placing the applicant in a better position for an interview or other type of screening
- Costs significantly less than most other forms of recruiting and saves time sourcing a candidate
- One of the ways recruiters can reach qualified passive candidates, especially for hard-to-find jobs

Copyright © Mometrix Media. You have been licensed one copy of this document for personal use only. Any other reproduction or redistribution is strictly prohibited. All rights reserved.

## SOCIAL NETWORKING

**Social networking** is the term used to capture the concept of making connections with individuals through the usage of social media sites like LinkedIn, Facebook, Twitter, etc. Although the channel of networking is through social media sites, the practice of networking is largely the same as it has been for years. The idea is that through connections with other people, and their connections with other people, one can widen their span of possibilities and goals. The concept of six degrees of separation, coined in the late 1920s, maintains that on average, people are only six or fewer social connections from each other. This means that if someone leverages their connections, they can expand their network to include more people. This concept is especially useful in recruiting and the usage of social media because social media enables people to more efficiently increase their network of contacts. By increasing the network of contacts on social media, recruiters are better positioned to identify qualified job candidates and candidates are more likely to find new employment. Social media has exponentially expanded the means by which people connect with others and collaborate together professionally.

### ROLE OF SOCIAL MEDIA

Social media is an external form of recruiting that has dramatically altered how organizations source job openings. There are many forms of social media. LinkedIn, Facebook, and Twitter are very popular for the purposes of recruiting because they are cost effective, efficient, and quick to reach a large audience of potential job candidates. More specifically, the breadth of candidates is literally worldwide, which may be important if candidates are needed in different or remote areas of the world. The breadth of social media sites further extends to interested candidates, both now and in the future, even if a candidate is not selected for the job. Simply posting the job may create more traffic for the organization's page on the site. Recruiting over social media also allows the recruiter to examine the potential job candidate in further depth by viewing the candidate's social media presence and learning more information about the candidate such as interests, goals, personal preferences, etc. Additionally, utilizing social media for sourcing is an excellent way for recruiters to identify and reach candidates not actively looking for new employment based on search criteria and matches.

# Recruitment Methods

## ADVANTAGES OF JOB FAIR RECRUITING

Job fairs are used as a recruitment tool to reach a large audience of job seekers in one location. Job fairs can be narrow in scope and size, such as on a college campus; or broader and larger, like in a large convention center. Larger job fairs can be expected to attract a larger variety of potential job candidates. Some job fairs can also be industry-specific. Generally, job fairs tend to be excellent recruiting opportunities for entry-level positions, college graduates, and veterans. Furthermore, they can also be a great opportunity to showcase an organization to different audiences and other professionals in attendance. Before deciding to attend and recruit at a job fair, an organization should make sure it is an appropriate job fair for their hiring needs. For example, it would not make sense for a company to attend a college job fair if the hiring needs were for professionals with five years of management experience. Similarly, the costs, time, and effort needed to prepare for a job fair should be taken into consideration. There needs be a good return on this recruiting method for the organization. In other words, a significant amount of potential job applicants should be identified as a result of the job fair.

Copyright © Mometrix Media. You have been licensed one copy of this document for personal use only. Any other reproduction or redistribution is strictly prohibited. All rights reserved.

## RECRUITMENT ADVERTISING

**Recruitment advertising** is a method used by organizations to attract candidates for the purpose of talent acquisition, both for the present and the future. Recruitment advertising can help an organization of any size reach potential candidates across almost all industries and levels of experience. This method of advertising can reach active job seekers as well as passive candidates whose interest in an organization may have been piqued by an advertisement. Traditional advertising for recruitment on TV, radio, and newspapers is still being utilized, but is severely limited in its ability to reach a larger audience when compared with web-based recruitment advertising. Online web-based advertising on general job boards, niche job boards, social networks, and more are usually the preferred method for organizations to recruit candidates for immediate job openings, and they motivate candidates to learn more about the company, thereby developing a potential talent pipeline. Remember, while recruitment advertising is a method most organizations deploy to attract talent, it is rarely the only tool an organization will utilize for talent acquisition.

## FORMATS FOR ONLINE RECRUITMENT ADVERTISING

**Online recruitment advertising** is a method used by organizations to attract potential job candidates via various forms of web-based media outlets. It is available in many different formats and for different strategic hiring objectives. However, it is not a one-size-fits-all recruitment method because the choice depends on an organization's desired audience, timing, related costs, and marketing plan. Following is an overview of several formats for recruitment advertising:

- **Job boards** – Websites used by employers to advertise their job openings and where job seekers search for open positions. There are many job boards for employment such as Indeed, Glassdoor, etc. Deciding upon which job board(s) to advertise the job openings depends on the position, size of potential audience, cost of advertising, and possibly integration with an organization's applicant tracking system. Additionally, job boards are considered to be user-friendly, making it easy for a candidate to apply.
- **Niche job sites** – These sites specialize in posting jobs specific to a certain industry, position, or for a specified job seeker. These could be sponsored by clubs; professional organizations; or really any grouping such as accountants, medical assistants, virtual employment, etc.
- **Social networks** – Most social networks such as Facebook and LinkedIn provide job-posting capabilities. Also, technologies like artificial intelligence and machine learning utilized by these networks have the potential to display targeted job ads for a specific audience.

## WORD OF MOUTH

Word of mouth is a tried-and-true method of recruitment. Basically, it means that current employees, or those familiar with the hiring needs of an organization, talk with their friends, associates, and people in their network about job openings. This type of advertising is usually a reliable supplement to more traditional recruiting methods and can also be quite effective and cost-efficient. Word of mouth is particularly useful with employers of choice, usually large, well-known brands or multinational companies, because they are frequently approached by job seekers for employment in their company. These jobs are viewed as coveted positions. Alternatively, very small companies or businesses that are the main employer in a given location also benefit by communicating to as many people as possible that there are open positions in their organization.

## INTERNAL PROMOTIONS, TRANSFERS, AND FORMER EMPLOYEES

**Internal recruiting**, defined as identifying and selecting a candidate within an organization, is sometimes used when it is not optimal or possible to find the desired requirements from external

Copyright © Mometrix Media. You have been licensed one copy of this document for personal use only. Any other reproduction or redistribution is strictly prohibited. All rights reserved.

candidates. There may be open positions that require certain knowledge or skills that can be easily obtained from an individual already within an organization. Therefore, organizations may prefer internal hires for many reasons, including a motivational incentive for employees to work harder, an increase in company morale, or knowledge of an employee's pre-existing skill set and past performance evaluations. Internal hiring is an efficient recruiting methodology for large and small organizations across a wide variety of industries. One of the common methods for internal recruiting is **promotions,** whereby an individual is selected for a hierarchically higher position that usually includes an increase in compensation and responsibilities. A promotion is sometimes seen as a reward for previously displaying talent in a particular area. Similar to a promotion, a **transfer** involves moving an employee from one job to another job that is comparable in some way. A transfer can be referred to as a lateral movement within an organization because it is a shift that is usually without substantiative changes in responsibilities or compensation. A transfer may occur for a variety of reasons: it gives an employee a wider experience within the organization, it may improve any conflicts that arise in the current situation, or a slight change in position may improve employee boredom. Alternatively, a different method for internal recruiting is through **former employees**, those who left the organization on good terms for any number of different reasons. Former employees understand the company, and the organization is familiar with the former employees. This method could also reduce cost per hire.

## Alternative Staffing Practices

### OUTSOURCING

**Outsourcing** is the practice of hiring a separate third-party business to perform services that were previously performed internally by employees within the organization. The rationale for outsourcing is almost always a cost-cutting measure, but also an avenue to hire expertise that is not within the company or not financially feasible to hire. Additionally, the decision on behalf of a company to outsource allows the company to focus on more critical aspects of the business, thereby improving their competitive advantage. There are three different types of outsourcing:

- **Onshore** – The outsourcing vendor is located in the same country as the parent business.
- **Nearshore** – The outsourcing vendor is in a neighboring country to the parent business.
- **Offshore** – The outsourcing vendor is in a country that is usually not near the parent company.

While outsourcing in general has many advantages as a staffing alternative, it also has some disadvantages, such as difficulty managing the third-party vendor and their employees, loss of control and confidentiality, and negative impact on morale (existing employees may worry about job security).

### JOB SHARING

**Job sharing** is when two or more employees share the job responsibilities of one full-time job, meaning each employee works part-time, with specific work hours differing slightly between those sharing the single job. Most often there are two types of job-sharing scenarios: (1) the twins model, in which two or more employees work seamlessly together on the same project or service; and (2) the island model, in which two or more employees share a job but work independently from one another. Job sharing is an arrangement designed by the employer and employee, and therefore not specifically addressed under the Fair Labor Standards Act (FLSA). Usually, an organization will enter into this type of arrangement with employees to assist in the retention of good employees who need flexibility in their work schedule and attract job candidates for other positions by maintaining a workplace that supports a work-life balance. This may help an organization become

71

Copyright © Mometrix Media. You have been licensed one copy of this document for personal use only. Any other reproduction or redistribution is strictly prohibited. All rights reserved.

an employer of choice or achieve a competitive advantage in the marketplace. Job sharing requires excellent communication between those in a twin model scenario because they must be able to function as one. Depending on an employer's benefits policy and federal, state, and local laws, job sharing could decrease benefits costs because neither employee is full-time.

## PHASED RETIREMENT

**Phased retirement** is a process that enables an employee to incrementally decrease their full-time working hours and at the same time draw upon retirement benefits like social security or a pension. Depending on the situations and applicable laws, this could mean an employee near retirement could possibly work part-time, job share, or use some other method to reduce their working hours. There are several benefits to phased retirement: it helps slowly transition full-time older workers into retirement, provides adequate time to transfer knowledge to remaining employees, and gives HR time to recruit new talent or strategize new talent acquisition. Alternatively, there are also several disadvantages. An employee switching from full-time to part-time can negatively impact their benefits received in the future. For example, if an employee chooses phased retirement and their salary is significantly reduced for a few years before retirement, it could reduce the social security benefits the retiree could receive once fully retired. Additionally, there are many federal, state, and local laws and also legal compliance issues that vary substantially from state to state that must be taken into consideration before an employer can devise a plan for phased retirement.

## GIG ECONOMY AND GIG WORKERS

A **gig economy** is based on the premise that independent freelancers, contractors, or short-term workers can provide services that are less expensive and more efficient for business in a free market system. This is a drastic contrast to more traditional employees in a business that works standard hours with benefits. The term "gig" actually is a word often used by musicians or others in the field of performing arts to describe a short-term job. Hence, a **gig worker** is an independent contractor that provides specific services to businesses, enabling the business to achieve cost savings for performing a specialized service efficiently and thereby reducing cost for the business. A variety of gig workers, such as food deliverers, drivers, shoppers, musicians, IT service technicians, digital sales personnel, and tutors are utilized to perform assignments. The propagation of gig workers was driven by several forces, including technology unburdening work from a physical location, businesses reacting more quickly to market forces without the financial burden of traditional employment, and workers desiring work flexibility and independence. However, gig workers must also contend with modest pay, thereby forcing the workers to perhaps seek multiple jobs; having no benefits; and not being legally classified as employees, meaning income and social security taxes are not withheld. Gig workers must buy and maintain whatever is necessary to sustain their particular area of expertise, and must manage the stress of constantly looking for their next gig. Businesses utilizing gig workers should adhere to any federal, state, or local laws regarding compensation and work classification.

# Interviewing Techniques

## STRUCTURED VS. UNSTRUCTURED INTERVIEWS

A **structured interview** is when the interviewer has a predetermined set of questions that are asked of each interviewee. In other words, each interviewee is asked the same questions so that their responses can be fairly compared to one another. Alternatively, an **unstructured interview** is when the interviewer may have a few questions beforehand, but the majority of the interview is more spontaneous or unplanned. Basically, each interviewee may be asked different questions depending on the direction of the question and follow-up questions. A structured interview is

Copyright © Mometrix Media. You have been licensed one copy of this document for personal use only. Any other reproduction or redistribution is strictly prohibited. All rights reserved.

considered to be measurable in the sense that the questions are the same and the responses could be judged against one another with a quantitative component. An unstructured interview is more qualitative in that the information gathered is not equally comparable, but more insight into the applicant may be obtained. A structured interview is frequently used when there is a large candidate pool that needs to be compared to one another in order to judge who may or may not be a better fit. On the other hand, an unstructured interview might be more useful when there are fewer candidates with qualifications that are almost identical, but the hiring manager needs to have a better feel for their thoughts and personality.

## BEHAVIORAL INTERVIEWS

A **behavioral interview** is a common interview technique designed to assess how an interviewee reacted to past job-related situations. The rationale is that future behavior can be predicted based on past behavior, especially behavior in the workplace. In a behavioral interview, the interviewer will not ask about certain desired skills; instead, they will ask the interviewee to speak about an occasion or circumstance where they displayed knowledge of a certain skill. An interviewer is trying to assess how an applicant behaved in the past versus how they will behave in the future. Common questions in a behavioral interview include, "Tell me about a time when you had to handle a difficult situation with a co-worker," or "Can you think of an occasion when you had a hard deadline for a project and simultaneously were constantly interrupted with unrelated matters?" The interviewer will often ask follow-up questions looking for details—asking specifically what was said, felt, or why or why not the applicant said something or reacted the way they did. Throughout the interview, the interviewer is assessing the applicant's behavioral responses to workplace scenarios. The best way for an interviewee to prepare for this type of interview is to try and remember stories they feel may be related to the job description. A useful method to accomplish this for the interviewee is the STAR technique: recall a **specific** situation, identify the **tasks** needed to be accomplished, the **actions** taken, and the end **result**.

## SITUATIONAL INTERVIEWS

During a **situational interview**, the interviewee is usually provided a given scenario and then asked how he or she would respond to the circumstances. The objective of a situational interview is for the interviewer to gauge the interviewee's reaction to any number of conditions, including their behavior and how a problem is solved. These responses are then used to evaluate how the interviewee would perform when faced with similar situations on the job. It could be said that behavioral interviews look at the past and situational interviews look at the future. For example, the questions in a situational interview are frequently hypothetical, such as, "If you know your boss is making a wrong decision, how would you handle it?" or "What would you do in the following situation...?" The questions are usually related to actual problems encountered in the workplace. The interviewer is interested in hearing if the interviewee has the basic knowledge to answer the question and solve the problem, exhibiting expertise in their given profession or job. At the same time, the interviewer may also listen to his or her ability to quickly assess the situation and the logic behind decisions.

## PANEL INTERVIEWS

A **panel interview** is when a group of people interview a prospective job candidate at the same time. The panel of interviewers are typically brought together in order to get different perspectives about whether or not a candidate is a good fit for a given position. Panel members tend to be those who will interact with the hired individual and have a good understanding of the organization and its culture. However, an effective panel interview should have a diverse assortment of personalities and viewpoints to accurately assess candidates. Everyone on the panel should also be allowed to freely offer their honest opinion. The goal of a panel interview is for the panelists to offer their

Copyright © Mometrix Media. You have been licensed one copy of this document for personal use only. Any other reproduction or redistribution is strictly prohibited. All rights reserved.

insights and collectively reduce the risk in hiring a candidate that will not be a good fit. Usually, the hiring manager leads the panel, but individuals on the panel often have opening questions and possibly follow-up questions that can be asked by anyone on the panel. Typically, this type of interview is longer than a traditional interview—about 90 minutes to two hours. Panel interviews can be conducted in many industries and for a variety of positions, but are most often used in senior executive positions, public sector government organizations or agencies, academic institutions, and large not-for-profit organizations.

### GROUP INTERVIEWS

A **group interview** consists of one or more interviewers who interview several interviewees at the same time. Group interview situations are more likely to occur in the hospitality industry, meaning hotel employment, rental agents, food service, and retail. Interviewing many people at once is time-efficient. Additionally, group interviews give the interviewer an opportunity to actually see and hear how well the interviewees interact with one another and behave under stress. Social interaction and stress under pressure are the two key characteristics of those who work in the industries noted above. Typically, interviewees are informed of the group interview format ahead of time so they are not surprised. The person(s) doing the interview will usually prepare questions ahead of time, and also be able to pivot and change direction if follow-up or clarification is needed. Group interviews usually begin with the interviewer(s) making the candidates comfortable and asking each one to say a little about himself or herself. Ground rules for courtesy and respect are outlined, and then the interviewer(s) begins asking questions.

### STRESS INTERVIEWS

A **stress interview** creates a scenario whereby the interviewee is placed under some form of psychological (not physical) pressure and then evaluated on how well the individual operates under stress. It should be noted that most other types of interviews try to put the interviewee at ease and garner information by engaging in a respectful communication exchange. Stress interviews are usually only used by certain industries and for specific positions that will encounter a tremendous amount of stress on the job. For example, stress interviews are sometimes used by law enforcement, sales agencies, airlines, etc. Again, these are positions that may encounter conflict and rudeness on a daily basis. Stress interviews can be conducted any number of ways, but generally the interviewer could use words to deliberately intimidate the interviewee, make the interviewee wait a long period of time, interrupt frequently, ask the same questions multiple times, act aggressively, walk around while asking questions, raise their voice, speak very softly, etc. The goal for the interviewer is to evaluate how calm the interviewee remains or if the individual buckles under the pressure. It is extremely important to note that stress interviews are controversial and reserved only for special positions. Legal counsel should be consulted before designing and implementing a stress interview.

# Post-Offer Activities

### CAUTIONARY MEASURES WHEN DESIGNING DRUG TESTING PROGRAMS

Many employers utilize drug testing to screen applicants and, in some cases, current employees. Generally speaking, employers can legally require applicants to pass a **drug test** as a condition of employment or adopt programs that test active employees as long as the programs are not discriminatory. Due to the controversial nature of drug testing, employers must be meticulously cautious when designing these programs to ensure practices will be upheld if brought to court. In addition, employers should make sure their drug testing program and related policies are in compliance with all state and local laws. For example, employers in some states can document they

Copyright © Mometrix Media. You have been licensed one copy of this document for personal use only. Any other reproduction or redistribution is strictly prohibited. All rights reserved.

have a zero-tolerance policy for drug usage, such as repercussions including employee termination; while employers in other states need to promote assistance programs for drug use. It is important to remember that the drug test results received from the testing company are confidential and should be filed and secured separately from the hired employee's personnel file. *Wilkinson v. Times Mirror Corporation* established the following elements for testing programs:

1. Samples are collected at a medical facility by persons unrelated to the employer.
2. Applicants are unobserved by others when they furnish samples.
3. Results are kept confidential.
4. Employers are notified only if the applicant was passed or failed by a medical lab.
5. Applicants are notified by the medical lab of the portion they failed—some instances will provide applicants an opportunity to present medical documentation prior to the employer receiving results.
6. There is a defined method for applicants to question or challenge test results.
7. Applicants must be eligible to reapply after a reasonable time.

## CONSIDERATIONS REGARDING PRE-EMPLOYMENT BACKGROUND CHECKS

Many employers will conduct pre-employment background checks on candidates to ensure that employees have sound judgment and are unlikely to engage in improper conduct and/or do not have a criminal record. Human resource departments often order credit checks or criminal record searches through online service providers and then review results. The Fair Credit Reporting Act, like many legal regulations, requires that employers not only notify applicants that they administer background checks, but applicants must also sign a written release consenting that the employer may receive their personal information. Furthermore, when implementing a pre-employment background check, employers must consider if doing so may be discriminatory and, as such, must validate the business necessity. Many states have joined the Ban the Box movement, which prohibits employers from asking about an applicant's criminal history at the time of application. If an offense is found, employers are urged to consider the severity of the offense, the amount of time elapsed since the offense, and if the offense is related to the nature of the job. Applicants must also have the opportunity to contest or explain adverse results before officially being turned down for employment. The prospective employer must furnish a copy of the report to the applicant. The Federal Trade Commission advises employers to give the applicant five days to respond before sending them an official letter of rejection.

## POST-OFFER MEDICAL EXAMS

A post-offer medical exam is usually requested by an employer to evaluate if the selected person can safely perform the essential functions of the job in such a manner as to not risk injury to themself or anyone else. The medical exam findings can also help determine if the individual will need accommodations in order to safely perform the job. The decision to institute a medical exam is based on detailed job requirements that clearly document which positions specifically require a medical exam. An employer usually has a written policy about which applicants need exams, procedures, and advanced notification to the candidate of this requirement. Employer planning is necessary to set up a cost-effective medical examination program with a third-party doctor performing the medical exam. The doctor must be completely familiar with the job requirements and necessary good health needed to perform those duties. The doctor's summary report back to the employer is only supposed to contain information that will impact the individual's ability to perform the job and nothing else in order to maintain the examinee's privacy. It is important to remember that the file received from the doctor is confidential and should be filed and secured separately from the hired employee's personnel file.

Copyright © Mometrix Media. You have been licensed one copy of this document for personal use only. Any other reproduction or redistribution is strictly prohibited. All rights reserved.

# Orientation and Onboarding

### ONBOARDING VS. ORIENTATION

The terms onboarding and orientation are sometimes used interchangeably, but there is a difference. **Onboarding** is the overall strategic process of acclimating a new hire into the business and its culture. This process can last anywhere from one month to a couple years. Meanwhile, **orientation** is part of the onboarding process designed to introduce new employees to their specific job, including colleagues and others they may interact with on the job. Orientations are one-time events but, depending on the organization and the job, can last anywhere from one hour to a few days. During an orientation, the new hire will be instructed about their specific job and the tools, methodologies, interactions, and instructions needed to perform the job. An orientation is critical in the onboarding process because it helps the new hire understand how their position contributes to overall organizational goals.

### BASICS OF THE ONBOARDING PROCESS

**Onboarding,** sometimes called organizational socialization, is a strategically choreographed process that enables a new employee to holistically understand an organization, its culture, and how the individual fits into the business. Onboarding varies depending on the organization and the position. There is not one particular correct format because it is dependent on many factors. However, the overall goal is to assist the employee with being a productive contributor. The onboarding process can be a few months to a couple years, although one year is more common. Typically, the following is covered during the onboarding process, though not necessarily in this order, and delivery methods could include virtual, in-person classroom, self-directed learning, one-on-one instruction, and meet-and-greets:

- An overview of **policies and benefits** – This may include paperwork that needs to be completed, such as benefit selection, payroll, proof of citizenship, emergency contact information, and an instructional overview of company policies and procedures including the employee handbook and the organization's diversity policy. This portion of onboarding could also be called "orientation."
- Understanding how the **role fits into the organization** – Information about an employee's job expectations and related interactions with other areas of the organization
- Customized **role-specific training** – Training can be conducted with the employee's supervisor or any other person knowledgeable in the position. Many organizations have a continuous learning environment to maintain a competitive advantage, making it an ongoing process.
- Organizational **culture training** – This can be a formal or more casual process whereby an employee learns company values and engages in activities related to visions and mission, such as team building events, dinners, and classroom trainings.
- **Facilitated social connections** – This could be simple meet-and-greet facilitated by the employee's manager, a formal "buddy system" whereby another more-tenured employee is assigned to help facilitate social connections, or many other scenarios.

### ASPECTS OF AN EMPLOYEE ORIENTATION

**Orientation** is the first step in the onboarding process and the beginning of the employer-employee relationship. Orientation tends to be more administrative in nature, as it is usually a series of tasks that need to be completed before an employee can proceed into their specific role. For example, it may include a tour of the work facilities, I-9 verification, benefit selection, payroll forms and processing information. Additionally, orientation also covers company policies and where to go for various types of information. An overview of the organization and introductions

76

Copyright © Mometrix Media. You have been licensed one copy of this document for personal use only. Any other reproduction or redistribution is strictly prohibited. All rights reserved.

may also take place. Orientation is a two-way process in that an employee's questions and concerns are discussed and answered. The goal of orientation is not only to get the new employee paperwork processed and logistics and introductions made, but to help the new employee feel welcome and quickly transition into a productive employee.

Copyright © Mometrix Media. You have been licensed one copy of this document for personal use only. Any other reproduction or redistribution is strictly prohibited. All rights reserved.

# Compensation and Benefits

## Applicable Laws and Regulations Related to Compensation and Benefits

### DAVIS-BACON ACT AND THE WALSH-HEALY ACT

The **Davis-Bacon Act**, passed in 1931, requires contractors and subcontractors working on federally funded projects or federally assisted projects contracted for at least $2,000 to pay wages and fringe benefits at a rate equal to or more than the prevailing wage rates of similar projects in the area. Any employer who performs work applicable to the Davis-Bacon Act must place a WH-1321 poster in a workplace common area detailing the wage protections offered by this act. Additionally, it should be noted that employers operating under the Davis-Bacon Act who fail to comply risk losing both their existing federal contracts and their new contract eligibility for three years.

The **Walsh-Healey Act**, passed in 1936, is almost an extension of the Davis-Bacon Act in that the prevailing wage principle was expanded to include manufacturers and suppliers of goods to employers of federal contractors with contracts that exceed $10,000. Furthermore, time-and-one-half wages for nonexempt workers must be paid for any hours over 40 worked in a week. Work sites that must comply with the Walsh-Healey Act are required to post an "Employee Rights on Government Contracts" notice, including wage amount, in a common work area. Similar to the Davis-Bacon Act, penalties for non-compliance are monetarily severe, with the potential for federal contractors to lose their federal contracts and not be eligible to receive new contracts for three years.

### COPELAND "ANTI-KICKBACK" ACT

The Copeland "Anti-kickback" Act, passed in 1934 and since amended, prevents federal contractors and subcontractors who perform work on covered contracts from persuading an employee to give up any compensation that he or she is rightly entitled to earn based on their contract of employment. All methods of persuasion are prohibited, including force, intimidation, and threat. Prior to the passage of this act, it is estimated that a large number of employees working under a covered federal contract were unfairly intimidated to return wage earnings to the federal contractor as a so-called "kickback" for employment. There are steep criminal and civil penalties for violating the Copeland "Anti-kickback" Act, including prison time, fines, or both.

### FAIR LABOR STANDARDS ACT (FLSA)

The **Fair Labor Standards Act** (FLSA) of 1938, also known as the Wage and Hour Law, sets minimum wage standards, overtime pay standards, and child labor restrictions. The act is administered by the Wage and Hour Division of the Department of Labor. FLSA carefully separates employees as exempt or nonexempt from provisions, requires that employers calculate overtime for covered employees at one-and-one-half times the regular rate of pay for all hours worked in excess of 40 hours during a week, and defines how a workweek should be measured. The purpose of minimum wage standards is to ensure a living wage and to reduce poverty for low-income families, minority workers, and women. The child labor provisions protect minors from positions that may be harmful or detrimental to their health or well-being and regulates the hours minors can legally work. The act also outlines requirements for employers to keep records of hours, wages, and related payroll items. Furthermore, employers subject to FLSA must hang a poster or notice in a common place at the work site whereby employees can easily view the provisions of the FLSA.

Copyright © Mometrix Media. You have been licensed one copy of this document for personal use only. Any other reproduction or redistribution is strictly prohibited. All rights reserved.

## MINIMUM WAGE REGULATIONS

The **Fair Labor Standards Act** (FLSA) established regulations designed to prevent employees from receiving substandard wages and established the minimum wage. The federal minimum wage is the smallest amount an employer can pay for each hour of work and employers are required to pay at least the amount specified by the federal minimum wage to any nonexempt employee. An employee will be considered exempt from this provision if the individual receives a weekly salary of at least $684, if the employee works in a profession not covered by the FLSA or a profession identified as exempt from the minimum wage provision of the FLSA, or if the employer has received special permission to pay less than the minimum wage as part of a Department of Labor program.

## REQUIREMENT TO PAY AN EMPLOYEE MORE THAN THE FEDERAL MINIMUM WAGE

There are two situations in which an organization may need to pay an employee more than the federal minimum wage: (1) if the individual has worked more than 40 hours in a single week and is in a position covered by the Fair Labor Standards Act, and (2) when the minimum wage for the state in which the organization's employees are located is higher than the federal minimum wage. However, most states have their own list of exemptions and requirements so that a particular organization may be part of an industry covered by the Fair Labor Standards Act but not by the regulations set by state law.

## PORTAL-TO-PORTAL ACT

The **Portal-to-Portal Act** was passed in 1947 as an amendment to the Fair Labor Standards Act (FLSA) to clarify when and under what conditions activities are not considered compensable work time. The general compensation rule is that an employee should be compensated for time worked. This act specified what constituted work time and concluded that activities before work, such as getting ready and commuting, are not compensable. Similarly, activities conducted after work are also not compensable work time. Before- and after-work activities are called "preliminary" and "postliminary" activities and are not compensable. The Supreme Court interpreted the act as the employer being responsible for compensating employees for activities that are integral and indispensable for principal job functions performed. If a function is integral to the job duties, then the employer must compensate the employee for that work. The following would be considered exceptions to the Portal-to-Portal Act and therefore must be compensated:

- If an employee must travel to various work sites to perform job duties.
- If an employee must put on and remove protective clothing for their job.
- If a specific type of washing is necessary because an employee is working with toxic or caustic material.

(Note: This is not an exhaustive list.)

## EQUAL PAY ACT (EPA)

The **Equal Pay Act** (EPA), which was passed in 1963, prevents wage discrimination based on gender. It requires an employer to provide equal pay to both men and women performing similar tasks unless the employer can prove that there is an acceptable reason for the difference in pay, such as merit, seniority, quantity or quality of work performed, etc. This act also establishes the criteria that must be considered to determine whether a particular position is similar or not. This includes the following equal work factors:

- **Skills** – The necessary training, education, and experience needed for a particular position
- **Effort** – This includes the physical and mental capabilities required for a given position

Copyright © Mometrix Media. You have been licensed one copy of this document for personal use only. Any other reproduction or redistribution is strictly prohibited. All rights reserved.

- **Responsibility** – This is primarily an issue of accountability and degree to which an employer relies on employees to successfully accomplish their job
- **Working conditions** – The physical working environment, be it hazardous, indoors, outdoors, cold, hot, etc.

## PROVISIONS OF THE EMPLOYEE RETIREMENT INCOME SECURITY ACT

The **Employee Retirement Income Security Act** (ERISA) was passed in 1974 to protect employees who are covered under private pensions and employee welfare benefit plans. It has been amended several times since its enactment. ERISA ensures that employees receive promised benefits and are protected against early termination, mismanaged funds, or fraudulent activities. ERISA mandates that employers adhere to eligibility requirements, vesting requirements, portability practices, funding requirements, fiduciary responsibilities, reporting and disclosure requirements, and compliance testing. Most employees who have at least 1,000 hours of work in 12 months for two consecutive years are eligible to participate in private pension plans. Employees have the right to receive some portion of employer contributions when their employment ends. Employees must be allowed to transfer pension funds from one retirement account to another. Sufficient funds must be available from the employer to cover future payments. Employers must appoint an individual to be responsible for seeking ideal portfolio options and administering pension funds. Employers must adhere to extensive reporting requirements, provide summary plan documents, and notify participants of any changes. Employers are required to complete annual minimum coverage, actual deferral percentage, actual contribution percentage, and top-heavy testing to prevent discrimination in favor of highly compensated employees. Administration of ERISA is handled by the U.S. Department of Labor's Employee Benefits Security Administration, the Treasury Department's Internal Revenue Service, and the Pension Benefit Guaranty Corporation.

## RETIREMENT EQUITY ACT (REA)

The **Retirement Equity Act** (REA), which was passed in 1984, is an amendment to the Employee Retirement Income Security Act (ERISA) designed to establish a number of benefit plan regulations in addition to those originally established by ERISA. These regulations are designed to protect spouses from losing their plan benefits after a plan participant's death or after a divorce, but also include regulations to strengthen the protections offered by ERISA. Protections established by REA include regulations prohibiting benefit plan administrators from considering maternity/paternity leave as a break in service regarding the right to participate in a plan or become vested in a plan, regulations that require pension plans to automatically provide benefits to a spouse in the event of the plan participant's death unless a waiver has been signed by both the spouse and the participant, and regulations that lowered the age an employer had to allow an individual to participate in a pension plan. An employer not complying with this act could face severe criminal and civil penalties.

## CONSOLIDATED OMNIBUS BUDGET RECONCILIATION ACT (COBRA)

The **Consolidated Omnibus Budget Reconciliation Act** (COBRA) of 1986 requires that all employers with 20 or more employees continue the availability of healthcare benefits coverage and protect employees from the potential economic hardship of losing these benefits when they are terminated, working reduced hours, or quit. COBRA also provides coverage to the employee's spouse and dependents as qualified beneficiaries. Events that qualify for this continuation of coverage include the following:

- Voluntary or involuntary termination for any reason other than gross misconduct.
- Reduction in hours that would otherwise result in loss of coverage.
- Divorce or legal separation from the employee.

Copyright © Mometrix Media. You have been licensed one copy of this document for personal use only. Any other reproduction or redistribution is strictly prohibited. All rights reserved.

- Death of the employee.
- The employee becoming disabled and entitled to Medicare.
- The dependent being over 26 and no longer a dependent child under plan rules.

Typically, the employee and qualified beneficiaries are entitled to 18 months of continued coverage. There are some instances that will extend coverage for up to an additional 18 months. Coverage will be lost if the employer terminates group coverage, premium payments are not received, or new coverage becomes available. COBRA is a high-cost plan, typically the cost to the employee is the full cost that the employer pays for health coverage, plus an administrative fee that averages around 2 percent. Alternatives to COBRA are purchasing coverage through marketplace offerings, Medicaid coverage if applicable, or switching coverage through a spouse (again, if applicable) because a qualifying event entitles the spouse to special enrollment.

## FAMILY AND MEDICAL LEAVE ACT (FMLA)

The **Family and Medical Leave Act** (FMLA) of 1993 is a federal regulation that provides employees the right to a maximum limit of 12 weeks of unpaid leave in each 12-month period for the specified care of medical conditions that affect themselves or immediate family members. To be eligible for FMLA leave, an employee must have worked for a covered employer for the preceding 12 months and for a minimum of 1,250 hours during that time. All private employers, public or government agencies, and local schools with 50 or more employees within a 75-mile radius must adhere to the regulations. Qualifying events covered under FMLA include the following:

- The birth or adoption of a new child within one year of birth or placement
- The employee's own serious health condition that involves a period of incapacity
- An ill or injured spouse, child, or parent who requires the employee's care
- Any qualifying exigency due to active-duty foreign deployment by an employee's spouse, child (or children), or parent. Exigencies may include arranging childcare, tending to legal matters, and attending military ceremonies.
- The care of an ill or injured covered service member as long as the employee is a spouse, child, parent, or next of kin. In addition, time to care for military personnel or recent veterans has been expanded to 26 weeks in a 12-month period.

Additionally, employers covered by FMLA must display a poster in a common area workspace that outlines FMLA provisions, including how to file a complaint.

### AMENDMENTS

The **Family Medical Leave Act** (FMLA) has undergone some significant amendments, and human resource practitioners should be aware of the following:

- If an organization fails to denote an employee's leave as FMLA leave, the employee may be eligible to receive compensation for any losses incurred.
- Prior to 2008, all FMLA disputes required Department of Labor or legal intervention. Now, employees and employers are encouraged to work any issues out in-house to avoid the cost of litigation.
- Light duty does not count toward FMLA taken.
- FMLA covers medical issues arising from preexisting conditions.
- Due to their unique scheduling, airline employees are eligible for FMLA after 504 or more hours worked during the preceding 12 months.

Copyright © Mometrix Media. You have been licensed one copy of this document for personal use only. Any other reproduction or redistribution is strictly prohibited. All rights reserved.

## HEALTH INSURANCE PORTABILITY AND ACCOUNTABILITY ACT (HIPAA)

The **Health Insurance Portability and Accountability Act** (HIPAA) was passed in 1996 to provide greater protections and portability in healthcare coverage. Some individuals felt locked into current employer plans and feared that they would not be able to obtain coverage from a new employer plan due to preexisting conditions. As a result, some of the key HIPAA provisions are pre-existing condition exclusions, pregnancy, newborn and adopted children, credible coverage, renewal of coverage, medical savings accounts, tax benefits, and privacy provisions. Employees who have had another policy for the preceding 12 months cannot be excluded from coverage due to a pre-existing condition or pregnancy, and it must be applied to newborn or adopted children who are covered by credible coverage within 30 days of the event. **Credible coverage** involves being covered under typical group health plans, and this coverage must be renewable to most groups and individuals as long as premiums are paid. **Medical savings accounts** were created by Congress for those who are self-employed or otherwise not eligible for credible coverage. Individuals who are self-employed are also allowed to take 80 percent of health-related expenses as a deduction. Finally, HIPAA introduced a series of several regulations that impose **civil and criminal penalties** on employers who disclose personal health information without consent.

## WORK OPPORTUNITY TAX CREDIT (WOTC)

The **Work Opportunity Tax Credit** (WOTC) is a federal tax credit that is provided to employers who hire individuals that are part of targeted groups facing significant challenges or barriers to employment. The tax credit is intended to financially incent employers to hire from these 10 targeted groups:

- Qualified veterans
- Qualified ex-felons
- Designated community residents, meaning individuals living in designated empowerment zones or rural renewal counties
- Vocational rehabilitation referrals
- Summer youth employees living in an empowerment zone
- Supplemental Nutrition Assistance Program (food stamps) recipients
- Supplemental Security Income recipients
- Long-term Temporary Assistance for Needy Families (TANF) recipients
- Qualified long-term unemployment recipients
- Qualified long-term family assistance recipients

It should be noted that there are many stipulations and specific qualifications for all the targeted groups. Generally, the tax credit is based on three factors: the category of the worker, compensation to the employee, and the number of hours they worked. The WOTC is authorized until December 31, 2025 (Section 113 of Division EE of P.L.116-260 – Consolidated Appropriations Act, 2021). The U.S. Department of Labor (DOL), U.S. Department of Treasury, and the Internal Revenue Service (IRS) all play a role in administering the WOTC program with employers.

## UNIFORMED SERVICES EMPLOYMENT AND RE-EMPLOYMENT RIGHTS ACT (USERRA)

The **Uniformed Services Employment and Re-employment Rights Act** (USERRA) of 1994 is applicable to all employers, both public and private. USERRA forbids employers from denying employment, re-employment, retention, promotion, or employment benefits due to service in the Armed Forces; Reserves; National Guard; and other uniformed services, including the National Disaster Medical System and the Commissioned Corps of the Public Health Service. In other words, this statute is designed to prevent those in the uniformed services from being discriminated against or otherwise disadvantaged in the civilian workplace because of their military service or affiliation.

Copyright © Mometrix Media. You have been licensed one copy of this document for personal use only. Any other reproduction or redistribution is strictly prohibited. All rights reserved.

Employees absent in services for less than 31 days must report to the employer within eight hours after arriving safely home. Those who are absent between 31 and 180 days must submit an application for re-employment within 14 days. Those who are absent 181 days or more have 90 days to submit an applicant for re-employment. Employees are entitled to the positions that they would have held if they had remained continuously employed. If they are no longer qualified or able to perform the job requirements because of a service-related disability, they are to be provided with a position of equal seniority, status, and pay. Moreover, the escalator principle further entitles returning employees to all of the seniority-based benefits they had when their service began plus any additional benefits they would have accrued with reasonable certainty if they had remained continuously employed. Likewise, employees cannot be required to use accrued vacation or PTO during absences. USERRA requires all healthcare plans to provide COBRA coverage for up to 18 months of absence and entitles employees to restoration of coverage upon return. Pension plans must remain undisturbed by absences as well. However, those separated from the service for less-than-honorable circumstances are not protected by USERRA.

## MENTAL HEALTH PARITY ACT (MHPA)

The **Mental Health Parity Act** (MHPA), which was passed in 1996, is designed to prevent health plan providers from setting limits on mental health benefits that are stricter than the limits the provider has set for other health benefits. This act prohibits a health plan provider from setting a financial cap on the amount the health plan provider will pay for mental health benefits if that cap is lower than the cap the provider has set for other benefits. For example, if a medical or surgical lifetime cap is $8,000, then the cap on mental health benefits cannot be below $8,000. This act applies to any health plan provider providing coverage for an employer with at least 51 employees, but only if the regulations set by this act will not result in a 1 percent or greater increase in the costs of the provider. It is also important to note that health plan providers are not required to offer mental health benefits, and providers may set other limits related to mental health coverage as long as there is no specific payout limit.

## LILLY LEDBETTER FAIR PAY ACT OF 2009

The **Lilly Ledbetter Fair Pay Act** overturned the 2007 Supreme Court decision in the *Ledbetter v. Goodyear Tire & Rubber Company* case, which ruled that the statute of limitations to make a discriminatory pay claim was 180 days from the first discriminatory paycheck. The Lilly Ledbetter Fair Pay Act of 2009 results in the statute of limitations restarting with each discriminatory paycheck. The act applies to all protected classes and covers both wages and pensions. Due to the scope of the act, employers could face claims years after an employee has left the company. This act was designed to make employers more proactive in resolving pay inequities. Additionally, employers should review their compensation record retention procedures in case they need to produce any related documentation for potential pay disparities.

## PATIENT PROTECTION AND AFFORDABLE CARE ACT (PPACA)

The **Patient Protection and Affordable Care Act** (PPACA) is a comprehensive healthcare law that was passed in 2010 to establish regulations on medical services, insurance coverage, preventative services, whistle-blowing, and similar practices. A few key provisions of PPACA include the following:

- **Individual mandate** – Requires all individuals to maintain health insurance or pay a penalty. It was removed from the statute effective tax year 2019. However, there are a few states that have an individual mandate.
- **State healthcare exchanges** – Provides individuals and families a portal in which they can shop through a variety of plans and purchase healthcare coverage

Copyright © Mometrix Media. You have been licensed one copy of this document for personal use only. Any other reproduction or redistribution is strictly prohibited. All rights reserved.

- **Employer shared responsibility** – Requires that employers with more than 50 full-time employees provide affordable coverage to all employees that work 30 or more hours per week or pay a penalty
- **Affordable coverage** – Does not allow employers to shift the burden of healthcare costs to employees and imposes a penalty for employees who obtain government subsidies for coverage

Additional provisions of the Patient Protection and Affordable Care Act (PPACA):

- **Flexible spending accounts (FSAs)** – Imposes a cap on pretax contributions to flexible spending accounts, health reimbursement arrangements (HRAs), and health savings accounts (HSAs)
- **Wellness incentives** – Allows employers to provide premium discounts for employees who meet wellness requirements
- **Excise tax on "Cadillac" plans** – Will impose excise tax on employers that provide expensive coverage beginning in 2022
- **W-2 reporting requirements** – Requires employers to report the cost of coverage under employer-sponsored group health plans on each employee's W-2 form
- **Summary of benefits coverage** – Requires insurance companies and employers to provide individuals with a summary of benefits coverage (SBC) using a standard form
- **Whistleblower protections** – Amends the FLSA to prohibit employers from retaliating against an employee who applies for health benefit subsidies or tax credits

# Pay Structures and Programs

## IMPORTANCE OF PAY STRUCTURES

**Pay structure** is the way an organization groups jobs and defines the compensation associated with a collection of jobs. Pay structure is critical because every organization needs qualified and talented individuals to build and run a business. One of the best ways to obtain and retain good talent is through a fair and attractive pay structure. Additionally, as in most areas of HR, pay structure needs to demonstrate that an organization has fair and consistent policies surrounding all aspects of pay. This structure will help an organization maintain necessary compliance requirements, as well as clearly demonstrate fair practices as it relates to pay opportunities for all employees. One of the most important considerations in pay structure is the balance between internal and external pay equity. Internal pay equity is how an employee's pay compares to the pay of others in similar positions within the organization. External pay equity is the comparison of pay to similar jobs outside the organization. A balance indicates the pay is fair, which will help attract new employees and also help retain existing employees in the organization.

## CREATING A PAY STRUCTURES

Creating a pay structure can vary greatly, but most organizations begin the process by conducting a job evaluation for each position. A **job evaluation** is the process whereby the value of a job to the organization is determined—it is how a job's worth is established. Once all positions are evaluated and assigned a value, they are categorized based on their importance to the organization. The organization will usually gather information from salary surveys to determine the market median for each category and wages an individual would receive at the midpoint of a similar pay category for another organization. Finally, using all of this information as a guide, a **pay range** is developed for each category. Pay ranges can be a challenge because it is a very fluid process. Occasionally, an employee is paid above the range maximum and sometimes below the range minimum. When an

Copyright © Mometrix Media. You have been licensed one copy of this document for personal use only. Any other reproduction or redistribution is strictly prohibited. All rights reserved.

employee is paid above a range maximum, it is referred to as a **"red circle rate"** and could mean that an employer's ray range is below the market value and should be researched to remain competitive. Alternatively, if the pay rate is below the range minimum, it is called a **"green-circle rate"** and should also be re-examined.

## PAY GRADES AND BANDING

A **pay grade** refers to a compensation job grouping, by level, with similar responsibilities, authority, and experience. This grouping means that within an organization, similar jobs have approximately the same relative value and are therefore paid at similar rates within a pay range. Some compensation structures break out pay grades or ranges into separate **bands** (or levels) so the company can maintain pay equity and stay within budget. This is done by conducting a job analysis and grouping titles into families. For example, those that fall into the first pay grade may have a pay band of $20,000 to $35,000, the second pay grade may have a band of $30,000 to $50,000, and the third pay grade may have a band of $50,000 to $100,000. Jobs may also be evaluated and ranked based upon overall responsibilities and worth to the organization. Although pay bands are broken out based upon job duty and skill level, it is important to recognize whether the company tends to lead, lag, or match current market rates. Matching or leading the market is best for recruitment and retention. The sizes of pay bands tend to grow as you move up the managerial ladder, with executives having the largest pay levels.

## TRADITIONAL SALARY STRUCTURE

A **traditional salary structure** could have multiple pay ranges that correlate to differences in a position. The way it typically works is that a new employee will be offered a salary on the lower end of the pay range and then hopefully advance to a higher pay range depending on their performance evaluation or other means of evaluating the employee. The benefit of an organization using a traditional salary structure is it provides the organization and its employees an easy-to-understand "ladder" or hierarchical system for an employee to advance or be promoted from one pay grade to another. Typically, an organization will first set the minimum and maximum salary range for each grouping. Then, based on the number of groupings, the organization will figure out the logical number of pay grades in their salary structure.

## BROADBAND SALARY STRUCTURE

A **broadband salary structure** takes multiple pay salary grades that only have a modest difference between the minimum and maximum pay scale and combines them into a single band with a much broader difference in the spread. In effect, the organization is collapsing multiple ranges in order to obtain a larger spread between the minimum and maximum point for a salary range. An organization might use a broadband salary structure if they wish to remove hierarchical levels and thereby limit the levels of management, a process sometimes referred to as "flattening" an organization. For example, an organization may have had 10 levels of management with a narrow salary range in each level. They then decide to adopt a broadband salary structure and reduce the levels from 10 to five, thereby also allowing the organization to increase the difference in the salary range. Existing employees are then moved to the most appropriate level within the five options.

Copyright © Mometrix Media. You have been licensed one copy of this document for personal use only. Any other reproduction or redistribution is strictly prohibited. All rights reserved.

Companies may also choose a broadband salary structure in a large organization if managing too many pay grades becomes complex and difficult to equitably administer.

## Traditional Pay Grades Compared to Broadbanding

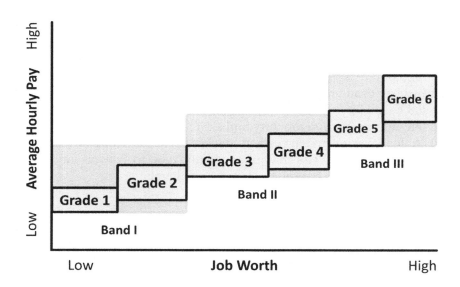

## MARKET-BASED PAY STRUCTURES

A **market-based pay structure** can be thought of as a combination of traditional and broadband structures, except market-based pay is a pay scale based on what similar employers in similar geographic locations pay employees. In other words, appropriate pay is determined by an employer evaluating data from various sources in the job market that summarize pay for similar jobs. Sources include the U.S. Bureau of Labor Statistics and some private companies that offer salary surveys for a fee. Like traditional and broadband, the market-based pay structure also has a pay range for specific jobs. However, what usually happens is the pay range, minimum to maximum, is too slim to be competitive with similar jobs in the external market, while the salary range is usually too high, like the broadband structure. A large majority of businesses utilize a market-based pay structure in their organization.

## VARIABLE PAY

**Variable pay** is employee pay that changes based on predetermined parameters or goals set by an employer. Variable pay is most often used as a monetary incentive to achieve business objectives and reward employees, and is usually a supplement to base salary or wages. An organization that wants to use variable pay to incentivize behavior or performance can accomplish this goal based on criteria such as sales revenue, customer satisfaction scores, percentage increase in clients, and pieces produced. Variable pay is frequently either a dollar amount or percentage based on target

Copyright © Mometrix Media. You have been licensed one copy of this document for personal use only. Any other reproduction or redistribution is strictly prohibited. All rights reserved.

objectives and is included in an employee's overall compensation plan. Following are some examples of how variable pay might work:

- An electrician paid hourly could be paid $30 extra for every referral made.
- An account executive could be paid a salary and, for every quarter that his or her team exceeds their sales objective by 10 percent, could receive an additional $5,000.
- An assembly line worker who exceeds his or her pieces built per hour by 10 percent or more and with no defects could receive an extra $100 per day.

## PAY COMPRESSION

**Pay compression** occurs when a senior employee has a salary that is only slightly more, or in some cases less, than a new hire in the same position. This is a situation whereby beginning salaries for new hires are too close to the salaries for existing employees in the same exact job. In some cases, it is not the same exact job—it could also occur if a new hire makes more money than their manager. Pay compression can be the cause of high turnover and employee disengagement. Causes of pay compression may include the following:

- An organization increases wages to attract new hires and doesn't adjust wages for existing employees according to market changes.
- Internal compensation is not aligned with real-world market salary data.
- Issues with existing organizational pay grades, levels, and bands.

The answer to pay compression is easy, but its implementation and fallout is challenging. The answer is to adjust the inequities and pay employees fair market value wages. This is a costly proposition for most organizations, but if they do not adjust wages accordingly, they risk losing good workers and facing the challenges and costs that come with replacing them.

## DIFFERENTIAL PAY

**Differential pay** is when an organization pays an employee an extra wage for working undesirable shifts or hours. This could mean working through the night or maybe on the weekend or holiday. It is important to note that organizations are not legally obligated to offer differential pay, rather they offer it as a means to incentivize people to work those shifts. However, if a worker works over 40 hours in a week, regardless of shift, then they are entitled to overtime pay according to the Fair Labors Standard Act (FLSA). Most employers offer differential pay as a percentage. For example, suppose XYZ Supermarket offers 20% differential for the overnight shift and the normal day rate of pay is $15 an hour. By multiplying the normal rate of pay with the 20% (15 x 0.20 = 3), the differential would be an additional $3 per hour, meaning the worker doing the overnight shift would earn $18 an hour.

## COST-OF-LIVING ADJUSTMENT (COLA)

A **cost-of-living adjustment** (COLA) is designed to counteract and stabilize inflation by declaring a percentage increase in social security and supplemental income. Usually, a COLA is equal to the percentage rise in the consumer price index for urban wage earners and clerical workers (CPI-W) for a predefined period of time, a calculation that frequently aligns with the calculation for inflation. For example, if a person received $20,000 in social security and the COLA was evaluated at 3.1%, then their benefits would be $20,620 for the year. COLA began in 1975 in response to high inflation and is evaluated every year. The Social Security Administration uses COLAs to protect compensation-based benefits from inflation.

Copyright © Mometrix Media. You have been licensed one copy of this document for personal use only. Any other reproduction or redistribution is strictly prohibited. All rights reserved.

## BONUS PAY

**Bonus pay** is similar to variable pay in that an employee is paid a sum of money based on criteria set by the organization, but not necessarily linked to a clear objective. For example, at the end of the year, an organization might pay employees a bonus, perhaps a percentage of pay or just a lump sum not based on wages. This type of bonus could be offered because the business or the individual achieved certain goals, or the bonus could be made at a manager's discretion to reward the employee(s). Discretion-based bonuses could be given at any interval of time—perhaps by a manager when an employee successfully handled the closing of a deal. Additionally, a bonus could be shared among an entire department, region, team, etc. for a goal achieved or any other valued display of work. There is only a subtle difference between bonus pay and variable pay. Bonuses may be linked to an achievement of predetermined metrics or factors, such as a holiday bonus or manager discretion bonus. Generally, bonuses reward past activities or achievements, whereas variable pay encourages future performance.

## MERIT PAY

**Merit pay** is money awarded to an employee, via a base pay increase, based on predetermined and performance-related goals. It should be noted that the Fair Labor Standards Act (FLSA) does not require or manage merit pay; the management and distribution of merit pay is between the employer and the employee. The overarching goal of merit pay is to motivate employees to meet and hopefully exceed individual predetermined goals. A merit pay program can drive individuals to be more productive and hence an organization more successful. However, the difference between merit pay and other incentive pay programs (variable, commission, etc.) is that it is incorporated into an employee's base salary rather than being a one-time occurrence. Merit increases can vary based on the organization and circumstances, but typically are under 5 percent of base salary. There are many advantages to merit pay, such as monetarily rewarding high performers, assisting with the retention of top talent, and differentiating individual contributions versus team contributions to company goals. On the other hand, there are some issues to be aware of when administering a merit pay program, including making sure there are predefined, clear, measurable performance objectives, as well as managing merit awards in a fair, consistent manner.

## DIRECT MONETARY COMPENSATION

**Monetary compensation** is the money an employee is paid for work performed. Typically, direct monetary compensation falls into four major categories and one quasi-category: hourly wage, salary, commission, bonuses, and tips. **Hourly wages** are based on the number of hours an employee works. Salaried workers are generally compensated a set amount, called a **base salary**, regardless of specific hours worked. Additionally, based on Fair Labor Standards Act regulations and depending on how hourly workers are classified, employees on an hourly wage could be eligible for overtime, while salaried workers are usually ineligible. **Commission** is compensation, usually paid in addition to a salary or hourly wage, for a fixed extra amount or a percentage amount based on achievement of a goal. Commission structures can vary tremendously and must comply with all federal, state, and local laws. However, this type of monetary pay is typically considered **base pay plus commission**. Bonuses, a type of variable pay, do not have to be tied to a specific goal and can be paid at the employer's discretion. **Tips** are the aforementioned quasi-category and are primarily seen in service-oriented industries.

## NON-MONETARY COMPENSATION

Not all compensation is monetary. **Non-monetary compensation** may include a flexible work schedule, free training or education, awards, free coffee and meals, etc. These forms of non-monetary compensation may not be directly included via a dollar amount in an employee's

Copyright © Mometrix Media. You have been licensed one copy of this document for personal use only. Any other reproduction or redistribution is strictly prohibited. All rights reserved.

compensation, but can be immensely valuable to the employee. For example, organizations can promote a type of culture with non-monetary perks such as a relaxed or casual dress code; a game room at work; or initiatives that support a better work-life balance, such as working remotely when needed, time off for personal reasons not counted against paid time off, etc. Often, non-monetary compensation differentiates organizations and contributes to their becoming employers of choice, thereby assisting the attraction of top talent. It should also be noted that non-monetary compensation is sometimes considered an ill-defined gray area, especially when organizations do not reveal the cash equivalent or value of such perks to workers at an individual level.

# Total Rewards Statements

## TOTAL REWARDS

**Total rewards** are all of the compensation and benefits received for performing tasks related to each position. It is important to have an effective total rewards program for two main reasons. First, it encourages employees to join and then stay with the organization. Second, there are legal concerns associated with the minimum amount of compensation an individual can receive for a certain amount of work, making it essential to consider these concerns to avoid unnecessary fines or litigation.

A **total rewards strategy** is a plan used to design a total rewards program. It is based on the organization's total rewards philosophy and is primarily designed to establish the framework for the allocation of program resources. It refers to the ways resources are used to encourage individuals to work for the organization without exceeding limits.

### TYPES OF TOTAL REWARD PHILOSOPHIES

A total rewards philosophy is developed to clearly state reward goals and how those goals will be achieved. Identifying this philosophy is necessary to determine if the rewards are reflecting the values and goals of an organization or if they need to be modified.

The two types of total reward philosophies are entitlement philosophies and performance-based philosophies. An **entitlement philosophy** issues rewards based on the length of time a particular employee has been with the organization. It assumes an individual is entitled to certain rewards because of seniority or length of time in a specific position. Entitlement philosophies encourage individuals to stay with an organization, but do not necessarily encourage effective performance. A **performance-based philosophy**, on the other hand, issues rewards for good performance.

### DESIGNING AN EFFECTIVE TOTAL REWARDS PROGRAM

There are a variety of factors to consider when designing an effective total rewards strategy. The four main factors include the competitive environment, the economic environment, the labor market, and the legal environment. The **competitive environment** is the effect competition has on the ability to allocate resources to the total rewards program. For example, if competitors are offering a specific product at a price that is far lower, the organization may need to reduce the amount of funds allocated to its total rewards program to afford a price reduction. The **economic environment** refers to the effect the economy has on the cost of labor. For example, as the cost of living increases, the cost of labor will usually increase as well. The **labor market** is the availability of skilled employees, and the **legal environment** refers to taxes and regulations.

## TOTAL REWARDS STATEMENT (TRS)

A **total rewards statement** (TRS) is a document that usually has the look and feel of a pay stub and provides detailed information regarding all aspects of an employee's compensation package. The

Copyright © Mometrix Media. You have been licensed one copy of this document for personal use only. Any other reproduction or redistribution is strictly prohibited. All rights reserved.

TRS is an opportunity for employers to communicate and highlight everything they are doing to compensate employees. An employer's TRS is unique and can vary drastically depending on the organization's compensation package. The overarching goal is to clearly communicate not just an employee's direct compensation, but the employer's contribution to the total compensation package. Information contained in a TRS may include base pay; commission or bonuses, if applicable; medical, dental, and any other healthcare benefits; value of paid leave; 401(k) contributions; stock options; premiums for insurance; all perks, including workday flexibility, cell phone reimbursements, lunches, coffee, employee discount programs, tuition reimbursement, childcare, training, wellness programs; and more. A TRS contains all compensation information, both monetary and non-monetary, and its purpose is to communicate all the ways employers reward their employees.

## BENEFITS

Employers benefit from creating and distributing a total rewards statement (TRS) because it helps the employee understand the full value of compensation, both direct and indirect, afforded each employee. Frequently, this type of information can also be used to assist in recruiting and retaining top talent in an organization. A TRS can differentiate the organization, enabling it to possibly achieve a competitive advantage. Typically, employers can realize the following advantages from a TRS:

- **Assists in recruiting** – Clearly communicates full compensation package
- Creates **awareness** about all benefits – Sometimes employees may not know or remember all the benefits that are offered.
- Assists in **employee retention** – Quantifying all compensation allows an employee to see how much an organization values its employees and hopefully fosters a sense of loyalty.
- **Increases productivity** – Awareness of what an organization offers for full compensation and a sense of loyalty with employees because information in a TRS can contribute to a more productive and engaged work force

# Benefit Programs

## NON-DISCRETIONARY VS. DISCRETIONARY BENEFITS

Benefits fit under two basic categories: non-discretionary and discretionary. **Non-discretionary** benefits are benefits that an employer must offer and are mandated under various legal statutes. These non-discretionary benefits can include, but are not limited to, unemployment insurance, Medicare, workers' compensation, social security, unpaid family medical leave, and COBRA. Alternatively, **discretionary benefits** are those benefits that an employer chooses to offer—and thus are not mandated by legal regulations—in order to attract and retain talent. Generally, discretionary benefits comprise three primary areas:

- **Health benefits** – This includes everything under the healthcare umbrella, including medical, dental, vision, prescription, employee assistance programs, disability insurance, and life insurance.
- **Deferred compensation** – This area includes any type of employer-offered retirement plan whereby the benefit is received at a later date than when work is performed.
- **Other** discretionary benefits – This includes perks that do not fit into health benefits or deferred compensation, such as paid time off for holidays, paid vacation time, flexible work schedule, tuition reimbursement, and childcare.

Copyright © Mometrix Media. You have been licensed one copy of this document for personal use only. Any other reproduction or redistribution is strictly prohibited. All rights reserved.

## FLEXIBLE BENEFIT PROGRAMS

**Flexible benefits** are programs offered by an employer that enables an employee to select and create their own customized benefits based on their preferences. In recent years, employees have come to expect benefits that promote work-life balance and support families. To that end, an increasing number of employers offer telecommuting, flex time, and compressed work week options to help workers juggle all of life's different demands. In addition, many workplaces now offer benefits like paid parental leave and designated lactation rooms, making it easier on new parents. Additionally, some employers have started offering paid caregiver leave, which allows workers to care for parents and other relatives without worrying about their paychecks. Small and large businesses alike recognize that flexible benefits are necessary to remain competitive in the marketplace.

## PENSIONS OR RETIREMENT PLANS

Pensions and company retirement plans fund an individual's retirement by providing deferred payments for prior services. These accounts may be funded by the employer through a variety of means. Retirement benefits are accumulated by the total amount contributed plus interest and market earnings. These defined contribution benefit plans are the traditional company-provided plans, such as 401(k)s, 403(b)s, simplified employee pensions (SEPs), SIMPLEs, and IRAs. A defined contribution benefit plan requires separate accounts for each employee participant, and funds are most often contributed by both the employee and the employer. Some employers will implement an auto-enroll policy in which new employees are automatically enrolled and minimum contributions to the plan are withheld from payroll. The contribution rates may even automatically increase on an annual basis. However, the Pension Protection Act of 2006 provides employees with a 90-day window to opt out of these plans and recover any funds contributed on their behalf.

## EMPLOYEE STOCK OWNERSHIP PLANS (ESOP)

An **employee stock ownership plan** (ESOP) is created by establishing a trust into which the business makes contributions of cash or stock that are tax deductible. Employees are then granted the ability to purchase stock or allocate funds into individual employee accounts. The stock is held in an **employee stock ownership trust** (ESOT), and the business can make regular contributions, typically up to 25 percent of its annual payroll. ESOPs became popular because it is believed that employees who have an ownership interest in the business will work more diligently and also have a vested interest in its efficiency and profitability. Although this logic is debatable, many studies have shown that ESOPs actually do motivate employees and support business growth.

## MEDICARE

**Medicare**, established in 1965 as an amendment to the Social Security Act of 1935, is healthcare coverage primarily for people 65 years of age or older. Medicare is not dependent on income levels and is also available to individuals under 65 years of age who are disabled. Employers and employees contribute a percentage of salaries to fund Medicare. There are four types of Medicare coverage:

- Medicare **Part A** – This free coverage is considered mandatory for basic hospital coverage.
- Medicare **Part B** – Optional and additional medical insurance coverage for eligible individuals who pay a monthly fee.

Copyright © Mometrix Media. You have been licensed one copy of this document for personal use only. Any other reproduction or redistribution is strictly prohibited. All rights reserved.

- Medicare **Part C** – Additional healthcare coverage available to those people who qualify for Part A and enrolled in Part B. Typically called Medicare Advantage Plans, Part C provides expanded coverage such as dental, vision, hearing, etc. There is a fee to enroll in these plans.
- Medicare **Part D** – Prescription drug coverage available to those people who qualify for Part A and enrolled in Part B. There is a monthly fee associated with this coverage.

## SOCIAL SECURITY

The Social Security Act was first implemented to force workers into saving a fraction of earnings for retirement and making employers obligated to match those funds. These funds are now withheld as a portion of the **Federal Insurance Contributions Act (FICA) payroll taxes** and regulated by the IRS. The benefits have since been extended to cover four types of insurance benefits:

1. **Old age or disability benefits** – For workers who retire or become unable to work due to disability; based upon eligibility requirements.
2. Benefits for dependents of retired, disabled, or deceased workers – Paid to certain dependents.
3. **Lump-sum death benefits** – Paid to the worker's survivors.
4. **Medicare** – Healthcare protection provided to individuals age 65 and older, consisting of Parts A, B, and D.

## MANAGED CARE HEALTHCARE PLANS

Employers usually provide managed care healthcare plans, which is defined as care that ensures an individual receives appropriate and necessary treatment in the most cost-efficient manner possible. There are many forms of healthcare insurance plans, and the increasing cost of insurance has forced employers to absorb additional costs, pass more costs to employees, or find affordable alternatives. **Fee-for-service plans** allow employees to decide what services they need from any provider; fees are paid by both the employee and the employee's benefits plan through deductibles and co-insurance. **Preferred provider organization (PPO) plans** allow insurers to contract with providers of the employees' choosing with lower fees and better coverage for providers within the organization; fees are paid by deductibles, co-insurance, and co-payments. **Health maintenance organization (HMO) plans** emphasize preventative care through fixed costs regardless of the number of visits, but primary care physicians (PCPs) must refer others, and no other providers are covered; fees are paid by deductibles, co-insurance, and co-payments. **Point of service (POS) plans** are similar to PPO plans with certain elements (PCP referrals) of HMO plans; fees are paid by deductibles, co-insurance, and co-payments. **Exclusive provider organization (EPO)** is a plan whereby no payments or coverage will be made unless the individual uses a provider within the network of coverage. **Consumer-directed health plans** provide tax-favored accounts, such as an FSA or an HSA, to pay for medical expenses and may allow employees to see any provider of their choosing. However, these plans carry high deductibles and may have low or no co-insurance after the deductible is reached.

Copyright © Mometrix Media. You have been licensed one copy of this document for personal use only. Any other reproduction or redistribution is strictly prohibited. All rights reserved.

## HEALTH SAVINGS ACCOUNTS (HSA) AND HEALTH REIMBURSEMENT ARRANGEMENTS (HRA)

Healthcare options offered by employers have shifted in recent years to a more "consumer-directed" initiative in order for employers to reduce costs and allow employees to choose or customize their healthcare spending. As a result of this shift, employer healthcare options tend to be high-deductible plans. For example, an individual employee could have a deductible of $3,000 and a family deductible of $6,000. This means that the employee must pay the deductible out of pocket before medical insurance begins to pay. This is frequently a burden for employees, so many employers have created and administer programs to help offset the employee expense.

- **Health savings account (HSA)** – Employer coordinates the ability for an employee to save monies dedicated for healthcare expenses, pretax, up to an amount determined by the IRS. Employers have the ability to contribute to these accounts, thereby reducing the employee's burden. Additionally, the unused monies saved can roll over to the following year and are portable. Note: IRS-determined expenses are subject to changes on an annual basis.
- **Health reimbursement arrangement (HRA)** – An employer funds a medical plan whereby employees are reimbursed for qualified healthcare expenses. An employee is given these funds from the employer for qualified medical expenses. This arrangement is calculated as a benefit and is not direct compensation. These monies can be rolled over to the following year, but are not portable to a subsequent employer.

## FLEXIBLE SPENDING ACCOUNTS (FSA)

A **flexible spending account** (FSA) is a special account in which an individual can put money in to pay for certain out-of-pocket, non-covered healthcare costs. FSA users do not have to pay taxes on this money. This means the insured can save an amount equal to the taxes he or she would have paid on the money set aside. Money is placed in the account by the enrollee tax free and is taken out tax free or as tax deductible to pay for qualified medical expenses. FSAs are available only with job-based health plans. Employers and the employees themselves can make contributions to the FSA. Individuals cannot use FSA funds on insurance premiums. FSAs are set up by the employer, but funds can be added by either the employer or employee. FSAs can be used to reimburse an enrollee and their dependents' medical, dental, and vision expenses. Funds in FSAs can be used to cover expenses related to prevention diagnosis and treatment of medical illnesses.

### MEDICAL COSTS AND CONTRIBUTION LIMITS

Eligible medical care expenses are defined by the IRS and include costs that relate to disease deterrence, diagnosis, or treatment. Expenses for solely cosmetic reasons are generally not considered expenses for medical care and are not reimbursable. These include procedures and services such as liposuction or Botox treatments and are therefore not eligible under an FSA. Ineligible expenses also include contact lenses and personal trainers, for example. Eligible expenses do, however, include things like service or guide animals and acupuncture. Employees can also open dependent care FSAs, which allow them to use pretax dollars to pay for dependent care, like daycare.

The IRS determines FSA contribution limits annually. The main drawback to the FSA is that it requires careful budgeting because there is a use-it-or-lose-it provision attached to the benefit. If employees do not use the funds within an account during the given plan year, they may lose the money. Exceptions to this are when the employer opts to offer a grace period, granting an additional 2.5 months to use the funds; or a carryover provision, which is limited to $500. Employers are not required to offer either and can offer only one of the two. They may also offer a run-out period, which gives employees an additional 90 days to make claims for reimbursement.

Copyright © Mometrix Media. You have been licensed one copy of this document for personal use only. Any other reproduction or redistribution is strictly prohibited. All rights reserved.

## CAFETERIA PLAN

IRS section 125 defines a **cafeteria plan** as an employer plan providing participants the opportunity to receive certain benefits on a pretax basis. Funds allocated to these benefits are not included as wages for state or federal income tax purposes and are generally exempt from the Federal Insurance Contributions Act (FICA) and Federal Unemployment Tax Act (FUTA). Unused benefit credits can sometimes be re-allocated by the employee to buy more benefits through pretax salary reductions, or the employee may end up losing the unused monies. An employer-sponsored cafeteria plan enables the employee to pick and choose benefits based on their preferences. Qualified benefits under these plans might include the following:

- **Medical healthcare coverage** – Plans may include some or all portions of physician services, office visits and exams, prescription drugs, hospital services, maternity services, mental health, physical therapy, and emergency services.
- **Dental coverage** – Plans may include some or all portions of routine exams, cleanings, X-rays, fluoride treatments, orthodontic services, fillings, crowns, and extractions.
- **Dependent care** – Plans may cover some or all portions of on-site childcare, allowances and flexible spending for childcare, daycare information, or flexible scheduling.
- **Short-term disability** – This provides partial income continuation to employees who are unable to work for a short period of time due to an accident or illness. "Short-term" is usually defined as three to six months.
- **Long-term disability** – This provides partial income continuation to employees who are unable to work for long periods of time due to an accident or illness. "Long-term" is usually defined as over six months.
- **Group-term life insurance and accidental death or dismemberment** – This provides financial assistance to an employee or their beneficiaries if the employee has an accident that results in the loss of limbs, loss of eyesight, or death. The cost of group plans is frequently lower than individual plans, and payments are based upon the employee's age and annual salary.

## EMPLOYEE ASSISTANCE PROGRAM (EAP)

An **employee assistance program** (EAP) is a program sponsored by an employer that provides confidential counseling services to help employees manage all types of stressful life situations or problems. Because it is sponsored by the employer, EAPs are free to employees. It is important to note that the service is confidential, meaning the employer is not aware of the employee's usage. This confidentiality is primarily due to Health Insurance Portability and Accountability Act (HIPAA) regulations, meaning complete confidentiality is maintained with the third-party vendor contracted to provide the counseling. An EAP is designed to help the employee, which in turn allows them to be more productive at work. EAP services can vary, but typically include mental health issues, family problems, financial concerns, legal issues, substance abuse, etc. Usually, the program provides guidance and professional referrals to resources that can help the employee on a short- or long-term basis.

## WELLNESS PROGRAMS

Employer-sponsored **wellness programs** are implemented for three primary purposes: (1) to assist employees in improving their health in an effort to prevent serious health problems, (2) to help employers offset the expense of increasing healthcare costs, and (3) to improve employers' overall benefit offerings to remain competitive for attracting and retaining talent. Wellness programs indicate that employers are investing in their employees' health and well-being. Some companies create awareness about the available programs by encouraging employees to participate

Copyright © Mometrix Media. You have been licensed one copy of this document for personal use only. Any other reproduction or redistribution is strictly prohibited. All rights reserved.

in a voluntary health assessment or screening as an impetus to encourage healthy lifestyle changes. Employers benefit from these changes through decreased absenteeism, decreased healthcare spending, higher employee morale, and improved productivity. Wellness programs can vary tremendously and may include personalized one-on-one health coaching, nutritional counseling, well-being workshops, healthy snacks at work, stress reduction programs, and fitness activities. Some employers will give monetary incentives to encourage participation in wellness programs.

# Payroll Processes

## PAYROLL PROCESSING

**Payroll processing** is a system that an employer utilizes to manage the payment of wages to its employees. It is important to note that payroll processing is more than just issuing a paycheck. There are other components that need to be addressed, such as legal compliance with all federal, state, and local laws and regulations, including reporting requirements; the time period for record retention of information; and all aspects of control and security. Generally, the major steps involved in payroll processing include gathering the time worked per employee for a designated time period, calculating and applying cost of benefits and deductions, distribution of paychecks (direct deposit or paper check), and retention procedures. The employer must then file and remit payroll taxes. An organization can face expensive penalties if payroll taxes are not accurate and/or on time. Most organizations use payroll software or outsource to a third-party payroll processing service.

## PRIMARY DOCUMENTS/ INFORMATION NEEDED TO PROCESS A PAYROLL

There are many documents and information needed to process a payroll. They include, but are not limited to the following:

- Completed **W-4** form (for employees) – This form is completed by employees before or on their first day of work and documents employee withholding information needed so that the employer can deduct the correct amount of federal income tax from their wages.
- Completed **I-9** form – This form is for employment eligibility verification, and must be completed by employees' first day of work. It requires showing the employer a combination of identification documents that prove they can legally work in the U.S.
- **Job application** – This contains consistent, detailed information about an employee such as name, address, education, and dates of employment used to enter information into a payroll system.
- **Bank account information** – This is usually used in order for an employer to directly deposit an employee's pay into their bank account(s).
- **Medical insurance** form – This form details the amount to be deducted from an employee's pay and their permission for the deduction (usually requires a signature).
- **Retirement plan** form – This form details the amount being deducted for various retirement plan options. Similar to medical insurance, an employee signature is required for an employer to deduct from an employee's pay.

## PAYROLL CYCLE

A **payroll cycle** or schedule refers to the frequency that an employer issues pay to an employee. The most common cycle is biweekly, or every other week, for a total of 26 paychecks per year. However, an organization could also offer a weekly cycle, meaning 52 paychecks a year; or possibly a monthly cycle with 12 paychecks a year; etc. An organization can choose their payroll schedule as long as it is in compliance with all federal, state, and local laws and regulations. Many states require employers to pay their employees biweekly, others have more specific requirements, and some

Copyright © Mometrix Media. You have been licensed one copy of this document for personal use only. Any other reproduction or redistribution is strictly prohibited. All rights reserved.

have no specified schedules that must be adhered to. However, an organization must also consider what the employees would prefer. Most employees prefer to get paid more frequently as compared to less frequently, especially those employees earning low wages. Employers must also weigh the cost of processing payroll more frequently because it will cost more. An organization must decide and communicate a consistent payroll schedule.

## PAYROLL POLICY

A payroll policy is a set of guidelines and protocols established to ensure that payroll is accurate, processed on time, and conducted with strict adherence to all payroll laws and regulations.

- To comply with the Fair Labor Standards Act (FLSA), a **standard work week** needs to be defined and usually constitutes seven consecutive 24-hour periods. A work week doesn't have to start on Monday, but rather can begin on any day of the week.
- There should be a system, electronic or paper, in place to **accurately record employee hours** worked, with an approval process to verify the information is correct. State laws and regulations may require employers to give breaks from work for rest, meals, etc., after a given number of hours worked. These breaks need to also be reflected in total hours worked.
- **Overtime hours** must also be outlined, including who is eligible and how much they will be paid for hours worked over 40 in one work week. It should be noted that overtime is usually paid at a rate of one-and-one-half times regular pay rate per hour. However, this can vary from state to state—usually in favor of the employee receiving more wages.
- **How often employees are paid** should be detailed, whether biweekly, weekly, monthly, etc., and what days they will receive their pay.
- A **payroll policy** should also explain deductions: mandatory, such as social security and other taxes; voluntary, like health insurance, and retirement plans, as well as and further explanation of pre- and post-tax information. All the different wage structures should be explained, such as hourly pay, salary, bonuses, commission, and stock options.
- Finally, all time periods for **payroll recordkeeping** should be documented as well as applicable security measures.

## PAID TIME OFF (PTO)

Employees will need to take time off from work to attend to various life circumstances and events. There is no simple formula for an organization to follow when developing guidelines for paid time off (PTO). PTO varies tremendously from organization to organization and much depends on the needs of the business as well as what employees need. Furthermore, PTO must comply with all federal, state, and local laws and regulations. Some organizations like the federal government have rigid guidelines, while others have looser, almost employee-determined PTO days. For instance, some companies might give employees 12 vacation days, six sick days, three bereavement days, 10 holidays, and then let the employee choose and categorize their PTO days. A PTO policy usually states the guidelines and processes for an employee to request PTO and obtain necessary approvals.

### EXAMPLES

There are many categories for paid time off (PTO). Following are some common examples:

- **Personal** time – Time off to attend to various life activities
- **Sick** time – Time off for personal illness, injury, or general medical care. Sick time may also be covered under Family Medical Leave Act, ADA, short- and long-term disability, or workers' compensation.

Copyright © Mometrix Media. You have been licensed one copy of this document for personal use only. Any other reproduction or redistribution is strictly prohibited. All rights reserved.

- **Vacation** time - Time off from work for recreation or fun
- **Holidays** – Time off to celebrate recognized holidays
- **Floating holidays** – Time off to celebrate holidays that might not be recognized by the organization
- **Bereavement** – Time off due to a death in the employee's immediate family. Some organizations even have bereavement PTO days for the death of a pet.
- **Jury duty** – Time off from work for compulsory jury duty
- **Compensatory (comp)** time – Credited time off from work for eligible employees who would prefer time off instead of payment. It should be noted not all employees are eligible for comp time because FLSA mandates that all nonexempt workers must be compensated for time worked, both standard and overtime.
- **Maternity and paternity** leave – Time off following the birth or adoption of a baby.
- **Military** leave – Time off for military service obligations. Includes the U.S. Armed Forces, the National Guard, and state defense forces. USERRA provides certain job protections, and employers also frequently offer a supplement to offset the difference in regular pay and military pay.

## UNPAID LEAVE

**Unpaid leave** is time off from work that is approved by the employer, but not compensated in any way. There are many reasons an employee may need to take unpaid leave. Every employee request and situation must be carefully considered by an employer to make sure they are consistent with organizational policy and legally compliant with all federal, state, and local laws and regulations. If an employee is requesting unpaid leave under the parameters of FMLA, then the employee's unpaid leave is mandatory and the employee is guaranteed to keep their job and benefits upon returning to work. An unpaid leave of absence can also occur when an employee has used up all of their paid time off. Assuming the request does not have to be granted under federal, state, or local laws and regulations, it is up to the employer's discretion and policies. In some instances, the employer can also force an employee to take unpaid leave if the workplace does not have enough work, a practice sometimes referred to as a **furlough**. During a furlough, employees typically have access to benefits. Furloughs are sometimes implemented to avoid a staff reduction such as layoffs. Another example of when employees could be furloughed is when coming to work is temporarily unsafe, like during a national pandemic. Paying or not paying employees during such a furlough is up to the employer's discretion and is dependent on many other factors.

# Uses for Salary Surveys

## SALARY SURVEYS

A **salary survey** is an assessment of the compensation and benefits currently offered by organizations in a particular labor market. It is a collection of information related to how each organization encourages employees to work in the current economic environment. These surveys are usually conducted by individuals or third parties outside the organization and are an essential part of a total rewards planning process because they identify changes in the current labor market that may impact effectiveness.

## TYPES OF SALARY SURVEYS

The three most common types of salary surveys are commissioned surveys, government surveys, and industry surveys. A commissioned survey is prepared from outside the organization. Because these surveys are expensive, they are used to obtain very specific information related to the labor market. A government survey is prepared by a government agency such as the Bureau of Labor

Copyright © Mometrix Media. You have been licensed one copy of this document for personal use only. Any other reproduction or redistribution is strictly prohibited. All rights reserved.

Statistics and usually accomplished without cost to the organization. However, the information is less specific than the information included in other types of surveys. An industry survey is prepared by the members of a particular industry. They are relatively inexpensive and provide more specific information than government surveys.

## REMUNERATION SURVEYS

Competitive compensation structures are not only equitable and motivating, but they should also be legal, cost-effective, and provide security. The most readily available **remuneration surveys** are those conducted by government agencies, such as the Bureau of Labor Statistics (BLS) and wage surveys conducted by private organizations. Government surveys may include local, state, or federal data. The BLS regularly publishes reliable data findings on occupational earnings and benefits of blue- and white-collar jobs. Furthermore, professional organizations, journals, and associations may perform sophisticated surveys to obtain remuneration data of top managers, supervisors, and entry-level workers. Some popular publications are Forbes's CEO compensation report or those compiled by wage survey companies like PayScale or Towers Watson. However, the U.S. Department of Justice has stated that human resource professionals cannot conduct salary surveys on their own. Doing so violates the antitrust safety zone guidelines. Professionals should remember that these surveys frequently consider varying components of compensation, such as base pay, incentives, and benefits.

## ADVANTAGES AND DISADVANTAGES OF USING SALARY SURVEYS

While salary surveys can be very useful to an organization when evaluating their total compensation packages, there can also be drawbacks. Sometimes numbers or data alone do not hold all the answers or may need further explanation in order to strategize effectively. If the positions or benefits and their related data points are not equal, then extrapolating strategies or action plans from a false base can be misleading and ineffective. However, if employees believe they are not being paid fairly or their benefit package is subpar, then possession of industry surveys for comparison is helpful. Salary and benefit surveys are also beneficial when a company compares itself to their competitors in the marketplace. It is important for leaders in an organization to remember that salary and benefit surveys can effectively assist the organization to make decisions, but they are only one tool.

# Claims Processing Requirements

## WORKERS' COMPENSATION

**Workers' compensation** provides employees with coverage of medical expenses and a continuation of income for individuals who sustain work-related injuries. The basic concept makes compensation and expenses the employer's responsibility without liability or fault to the employee, assuming that the employee has adhered to reasonable safety precautions. Each state administers its own workers' compensation per state and federal laws. Each state determines its own workers' compensation rules, including what is covered, eligibility, types of benefits, and how the benefits will be funded. There are **four types of benefits** awarded to employees: medical expenses, wage replacement payments, rehabilitation, and death benefits. The wage replacement payments are often calculated based upon an employee's average weekly wages and become available after a waiting period. Costs are determined by an experience rating based upon an employer's claim history. In other words, organizations and sometimes entire industries with a high occurrence of workers' compensation claims will probably pay more.

Copyright © Mometrix Media. You have been licensed one copy of this document for personal use only. Any other reproduction or redistribution is strictly prohibited. All rights reserved.

## PROCESSING OF A WORKERS' COMPENSATION CLAIM

Most employers carry workers' compensation insurance to cover the expenses related to the treatment of an employee's injury at work. It is important to note the workers' compensation claim process can vary by state. The following is generally how the process works:

1. Medical attention – If employees are injured, the most important thing to do is make sure they get **immediate medical treatment**. Some employer policies require injured employees to get treatment at a specific medical facility or by a specific doctor. If it is not an urgent situation, employees may want to ask their employer if that is necessary. Many policies give injured employees the ability to get a second opinion as well.
2. Employer notification – Employees should **notify their employer immediately** about any injury. Depending on the state, there could be a restricted period of time to notify the employer of a job-related injury.
3. Completion of worker injury form – Usually, an employer will have the injured employee complete a **form detailing specific information** about the injury, including date, time, location, how it happened, parties involved, medical treatment, etc.
4. Employer files claim – The **employer will usually file a claim** with its insurer and the state workers' compensation office. The claim is reviewed and a determination is made if it will be denied or accepted. If accepted, the insurer will detail and communicate the amount of benefits an employee will receive.
5. Employee returns to work – A medical determination is made as to **when the employee can return to work** and if any accommodations need to be made for a defined period of time.

## DISABILITY INSURANCE

Disability insurance is divided into two categories: **short-term disability** (STD) and **long-term disability (LTD)**. These private insurance plans replace a portion of employees' wages if they are out of work due to an injury or illness. Contrary to workers' compensation, the injury or illness does not need to be work-related to qualify for STD or LTD. Many employers offer disability insurance benefits on a fully paid, partially paid, or ancillary basis. Employers should check state regulations to determine if they are required to provide partial wage replacement insurance coverage to eligible employees. STD typically runs for 90 to 180 days, providing employees with 60-75 percent wage replacement following a short waiting period. LTD takes effect after STD is exhausted. Depending on the plan, the LTD coverage may last 24–36 months and run until employees can return to their old job or begin a new one, until they are old enough to collect retirement, or they are able to collect social security disability.

## OBLIGATION IN UNEMPLOYMENT CLAIMS

Unemployment payments are funded by businesses that pay state and federal taxes, and unemployment programs are managed at the state level. Rules governing unemployment and how it is administered can vary from state to state. Generally, when an employer must lay off an employee because of no fault of their own, the employee is eligible for unemployment benefits, although there are some exceptions to this rule. If an employee is laid off, they can file an unemployment claim in their respective state. In turn, the former employer will receive notification of the claim and must verify and provide details. Some of the questions might include working status, be it full-time, part-time, etc.; why the employee was laid off, whether fired, lack of work, etc.; severance pay or other compensation, if applicable; if legally eligible to work in the U.S.; and more. If the former employee's claim is accurate, the employer will accept the claim from the state. If the claim is not accurate, then the employer will have approximately 10 days to contest it. After

Copyright © Mometrix Media. You have been licensed one copy of this document for personal use only. Any other reproduction or redistribution is strictly prohibited. All rights reserved.

the claim is investigated by the state unemployment office, the unemployment program will render a notice of determination detailing if the claim is accepted or denied.

# Work-Life Balance Practices

## WORK-LIFE BALANCE

**Work-life balance** is generally defined as the competing prioritization between one's personal and professional activities. This juggling act has become an increasingly hot topic due to such issues as advances in technology and permitting a physical office location to no longer be the primary place to accomplish work-related tasks. A poor work-life balance can lead to employee stress and burnout, diminished productivity, and lost revenue. As such, it is in the organization's best interest to share some of the responsibility for improving the balance between work and an employee's personal life. Some business leaders maintain that, due to technological advances that everyone should strive for, a "work-life integration" should be the true end goal because complete separation might not be realistic. Achieving a balance then becomes a shared responsibility with the employee and the employer.

## HELPING EMPLOYEES ACHIEVE A GOOD WORK-LIFE BALANCE

An employer can help its employees in a number of different ways, depending on the needs of the business. A **flexible work arrangement** could mean working remotely, scheduling outside typical business hours, part-time arrangements, telecommuting on certain days, job sharing, and shift swapping. Businesses who adopt such measures may experience reduced turnover, increased productivity, and the ability to recruit from an expanded talent pool. In some situations, flexible work arrangements are not possible due to the nature of the business. If that is the case, businesses can also promote campaigns to encourage breaks, regularly review workload balance, taking time off, leading by example, providing resources for working parents, or other perks to ease the burden for their employees. There is not a one-size-fits-all approach for employers to assist workers in finding their individual work-life balance; rather, the program should be customized for the business, as well as recognizing that every employee is different with diverse circumstances. Work-life balance programs can give businesses a competitive advantage, but if poorly designed and implemented or managed incorrectly, the program could unintentionally harm morale and/or be legally detrimental to the company.

## VIRTUAL OR REMOTE WORK ENVIRONMENT

A virtual work environment is possible thanks to technological advancements that have eliminated employers' need for a physical, brick-and-mortar presence or office space. Virtual work environments allow employees to work in remote locations, including home, coffee shops, or basically anywhere that connectivity can be achieved. Work units or teams can collaborate via virtual networks and accomplish work via many formats, such as video conferencing, phone, virtual servers to share and store information, etc. Employers are starting to include virtual or remote policies in their employee handbooks that define expectations when working remotely, with new protocols regarding start time, end time, meal breaks, check-in procedures, etc. Some employers have more informal plans, such as a quick video conference in the morning or at the end of the day, casual conversation to see how everyone on a team is doing, manager office hours, etc. Due to advances in technology and the cost savings achieved from remote work, the trend is that the virtual workplace is growing.

Copyright © Mometrix Media. You have been licensed one copy of this document for personal use only. Any other reproduction or redistribution is strictly prohibited. All rights reserved.

## ADVANTAGES AND DISADVANTAGES

There are many advantages to a virtual or remote work environment:

- Cost effectiveness – Working virtually enables companies to have lower operating costs and be more environmentally friendly. Examples include smaller workspace and less commuting, which respectively cost less to maintain and expend less energy.
- Flexibility – Working remotely or at home is a perk for many employees because it eliminates commuting and promotes better work-life balance.
- Improved productivity – Employees that are able to better balance their work and personal life tend to be happier, and research indicates that happier employees tend to be more productive. Remote work also eliminates many of the distractions that occur in an in-person office environment.
- Bigger talent pool – Virtual work environments mean that recruiting is not restricted by location. This enables an employer to cast a wider net for top talent.

There are also some disadvantages to virtual or remote work environments:

- Preference – Some employees may not like working remotely or do not have a space or environment that is conducive to productively accomplishing work. Remote work can be isolating and many have a hard time separating work and personal life when working from home.
- Difficulties collaborating – Sometimes there is no substitute for face-to-face collaboration. It could take time to figure out ways to make virtual collaboration work well.
- Trust – Employers can monitor technology to see if an employee is active, but there needs to be a level of trust between the employer and employee for this work arrangement to work.

## LEGAL CONSIDERATIONS WHEN DEVISING AND MANAGING WORK-LIFE BALANCE PROGRAMS

Generally, the U.S. Equal Employment Opportunity Commission (EEOC) supports work-life balance programs. However, if the program is not implemented fairly, it could violate Title VII of the Civil Rights Act, requiring equal treatment and preventing discrimination. Some work-life balance programs are left to the discretion of a manager or HR representative. If an employee requests a flexible working arrangement and the manager is not consistent and fair in administrating these requests, the disappointed employee may claim unlawful discrimination. Furthermore, there is the risk of an inconsistent or unfair decision resulting in disparate treatment or disparate impact against a protected class or classes. In addition, an employee could ask for a flexible work arrangement due to a family or medical condition that would otherwise be covered under the Family and Medical Leave Act (FMLA). If the request meets the specific requirements of FMLA, then it should be processed accordingly to avoid legal consequences. Another legal consideration is whether the employee is making the request due to a disability. In this case, the employer may be in violation of the Americans with Disabilities Act (ADA) and the request should have been processed and determined via a reasonable accommodation. Lastly, flexible work arrangements carry the potential for Fair Labor Standards Act (FLSA) wage and hour issues or violations, especially when calculating hours worked. These types of legal considerations, along with monitoring ongoing changes in federal, state, and local laws, should always be considered when a business implements a work-life balance program.

Copyright © Mometrix Media. You have been licensed one copy of this document for personal use only. Any other reproduction or redistribution is strictly prohibited. All rights reserved.

## SABBATICAL LEAVE

A **sabbatical leave** is generally a paid leave from an organization to work on a long-term project. This is typically a four-week to three-month leave to concentrate solely on the project without distraction. Sabbatical leave used to only apply to professors or researchers in academic environments. There has been a slow shift to allow this type of leave in other industries for professional development, authoring articles, etc. Sabbatical leave is usually reserved for more senior, longer-term employees who already have years of experience, but there are no specific legal regulations and little case law precedents for sabbatical implementation. It is wise for organizations to have clearly defined criteria and guidelines when offering sabbatical leave to employees in order to ensure it is implemented in a fair and consistent manner. There are many advantages for an organization to offer sabbaticals: they attract top talent; give employers a competitive edge; demonstrate an employer cares for their employees, thereby promoting loyalty; and promote long-term retention of employees. On the flip side, there are also some disadvantages: cost, decreased productivity due to an employee's absence, administrative challenge to maintain benefits, potential conflict or resentment among employees covering the workload, and the possibility the employee on sabbatical will not return to work.

Copyright © Mometrix Media. You have been licensed one copy of this document for personal use only. Any other reproduction or redistribution is strictly prohibited. All rights reserved.

# Human Resource Development and Retention

## Applicable Laws and Regulations Related to Training and Development Activities

### COPYRIGHT ACT (TITLE 17)

The term **"copyright"** refers to protection from the U.S. government for original works being copied, duplicated, distributed, or otherwise taking credit for someone else's creative expression. **Title 17** of the United States Code includes the **Copyright Act**, first passed in 1976 and amended many times since. The Copyright Act automatically grants protections once the original work is expressed in a medium. In other words, original works are copyright protected once they are printed, created into an object, in a form of technology, etc. However, it is usually recommended that a person or organization register copyrighted material. To be clear, ideas cannot be copyrighted; rather, it is the tangible expression of the idea in some medium that is copyrighted. There are five primary rights or protections afforded to copyright owners: the ability to authorize others to (1) reproduce the work, (2) distribute the work, (3) use the original work as basis for new creations, (4) publicly display copyrighted work, and (5) publicly perform copyrighted work. Ownership of a copyright is important to distinguish—it is either the person who created the work or a work made for hire, whereby the copyright is given to the person or organization that ordered or commissioned the work. In the commissioned work scenario, an employer could be the copyright owner.

### U.S. PATENT ACT

The **U.S. Patent Act** (35 U.S. Code) grants protection for new inventions whereby no one other than the owner of the patent is allowed to do anything that involves using or selling the invention. Article 1, section 8 of the U.S. Constitution states, "to promote the progress of science and useful arts, by securing for limited times to authors and inventors the exclusive right to their respective writings and discoveries." As a result of Article 1, Section 8 of the U.S. Constitution, Congress created the United States Patent and Trademark Office (USPTO) to assess and process applications for two types of patents:

- **Utility** patent – This type of patent is issued for inventions that are new and have a use, such as a new machine, process, or manufacturing system. The USPTO qualifies utility patents in five categories: (1) composition of matter, (2) improvement of an existing idea, (3) machine, (4) manufacture, (5) process. Approximately 90 percent of all patents are utility patents.
- **Design** patent – This type of patent is issued for original designs on an existing product. Sometimes organizations apply for a design patent when the look of a product is changed.

It is important to note that whoever creates the invention is the owner of the patent. However, if the patent was obtained through work, the inventor often contractually agrees to turn over all rights of the patent to the employer.

### TRADEMARK ACT

The **Trademark Act** was passed in 1946 and amended several times. A trademark is any "marking," meaning a logo, slogan, phrase, company name, or combination of attributes that distinguishes a

Copyright © Mometrix Media. You have been licensed one copy of this document for personal use only. Any other reproduction or redistribution is strictly prohibited. All rights reserved.

product or service from others. This distinction enables the product or service to have a competitive advantage in market recognition. In some ways, a trademark makes a product or service unique or authentic. The Trademark Act gives certain rights to the owner of the so-called "marking" to prevent other individuals or organizations from using it without authorization. Trademarks, both registered and unregistered with the USPTO, are protected from infringements. In other words, if an organization uses a trademark that is similar or likely to be confused with a widely recognized trademark, it is considered infringement and grounds for legal actions.

## TITLE VII OF THE CIVIL RIGHTS ACT OF 1964

**Title VII of the Civil Rights Act of 1964** prohibits discrimination or segregation in all aspects of employment based on five factors: race, color, national origin, religion, and gender. Included in the act is also the stipulation that all employees have equal opportunity for advancement. Training is usually necessary for job advancement, and as such all employees must have equal opportunity to attend trainings when offered. Frequently it is not possible to have everyone attend every training program, so employers often must select employees for specific trainings. Employers should be fair and consistent in the training selection process to ensure their selection procedures do not have an adverse impact on minorities or women. Employers should also be careful their selection processes for training do not discriminate against or favor only certain employees.

## AMERICANS WITH DISABILITIES ACT AND THE AGE DISCRIMINATION IN EMPLOYMENT ACT

The Americans with Disabilities Act prohibits any type of discrimination against a qualified person with a disability. Furthermore, an employer cannot discriminate against someone who is perceived as having a disability or associates with someone who is disabled. Additionally, accommodations or modifications must be made by the employer so long as it does not impose a financial hardship on that employer. Such accommodations might be necessary so the disabled individual has the ability to attend trainings or other opportunities for professional development or career advancement. Accommodations might include access to a training facility or classroom, interpreter (if applicable), note taker, extended break time, preferential seating, etc.

The Age Discrimination in Employment Act prohibits discrimination in all aspects of employment for individuals 40 years of age and older. Employers should be careful to give all employees an equal opportunity to attend training and career advancement and make sure training opportunities do not have an adverse impact on older workers.

# Training Delivery Format

## ADDIE MODEL

The **ADDIE model** is a set of instructional design guidelines commonly used by organizations to develop human resource development (HRD) programs. This model consists of five separate steps and each step is identified by one of the letters in the term "ADDIE." "A" represents the **analysis** step, the first "D" represents the **design** step, the second "D" represents **development**, the "I" represents **implementation**, and the "E" represents **evaluation**. Each step of the model establishes a basic set of guidelines and procedures an individual or organization can follow to develop a training or instructional program piece by piece. This procedure is commonly used in human resource development because it is a simple but effective way of creating a training program. The ADDIE model can also be applied to a variety of fields and is not limited to training programs.

## DECIDING TRAINING DELIVERY METHODS

A **training delivery method** is simply a tactic or approach deployed for teaching the desired material or content. A training delivery method could be thought of as a means for an individual to

Copyright © Mometrix Media. You have been licensed one copy of this document for personal use only. Any other reproduction or redistribution is strictly prohibited. All rights reserved.

learn material in the manner that will optimally keep the participant engaged and interested. There is not one superior training delivery method because it depends on many factors: the goal of the training, budgetary constraints, time frame for the training, equipment needed, and a clear understanding of the audience. Typically, a delivery method for training is decided after an understanding of the expected learning outcomes for the intended audience with the goal of the best return on the training investment. A training method must also take into consideration the workplace culture, be it slow-paced, fast-paced, casual, or formal, and be careful to recognize that different generations have different learning preferences which might also impact the method(s) chosen for an effective training program.

## TRADITIONAL CLASSROOM TRAINING

A **traditional classroom training** is conducted in a teaching space and allows for face-to-face instruction. This mode of training can take place internally at an employer's work site, externally at a training facility, or possibly at an industry conference. Classroom training offers many options to deploy multiple learning modalities. To begin, a classroom can be conducive to teaching new information to a small or large number of students. A classroom presentation can be made lecture style, with or without visual aids; or can include demonstrations of material, allowing for multiple formats to teach information. If the group is small enough, classroom training can be an environment for interactive discussion, whereby the instructor gauges students understanding and immediately changes course if needed. Depending on the training, classroom training can permit employees to interact with one another, thereby enhancing the learning experience. Lastly, a classroom environment provides a human element that is challenging to capture in other training delivery formats.

## ON-THE-JOB TRAINING (OTJ)

**On-the-job training** (OTJ) is usually provided by mangers or supervisors utilizing real time demonstration of the material or equipment the employee will be using to complete job tasks. This hands-on approach is sometimes more effective than lecturing or a more theoretical approach. Seeing and being allowed to perform the desired function is a simple and cost-effective method for learning. This method also allows for immediate feedback and helps to ensure the employee is immediately productive. However, there can be disadvantages to OTJ trainings. First, the person teaching may not be a certified trainer, but rather someone who knows how the work needs to be accomplished. Teaching requires clear communication and patience, and not everyone possesses necessary teaching skills. Second, another reason for OTJ training is to get the new employee up to speed quickly and, by doing so, there could be safety issues and potential accidents. This is especially true of high-risk jobs. Lastly, OTJ training could be distracting to coworkers, creating work disturbances and causing lack of concentration, especially in a space-constrained environment.

## E-LEARNING OR VIRTUAL LEARNING

**E-learning**, also known as virtual learning, is a training delivery format that permits students to learn via a form that utilizes technology. E-learning can take a number of different formats, including web-based, mobile computer applications, and virtual classrooms. E-learning can be **synchronous**, whereby the instructor and students are interacting in real-time. Alternatively, e-learning can also be **asynchronous**, enabling students to access the same training and related materials on demand at different days and times. There are many benefits to using e-learning, such as delivering a large volume of information quickly, assisting globalization efforts through virtual learning, scheduling flexibility, cost effectiveness, etc. However, there are considerations that should be examined when utilizing e-learning, including technology constraints and user access,

Copyright © Mometrix Media. You have been licensed one copy of this document for personal use only. Any other reproduction or redistribution is strictly prohibited. All rights reserved.

concerns about intellectual property, lack of face-to-face interaction possibly causing uneasiness with students, and the potentially significant costs involved in training development.

## BLENDED LEARNING OR HYBRID FORMAT

A **blended learning** or hybrid format combines multiple methods of delivering training material. Research suggests that a mix of learning strategies and formats might be more effective than one single method. Typically, blended or hybrid learning involves face-to-face, traditional classroom instruction combined with an online, technological component that might also give the student control over their pace of learning. Following are two examples of blended or hybrid learning:

- A course with synchronous learning in a virtual setting using video and independent, web-based, self-paced learning modules that compliment classroom instruction.
- A training program that involves a web-based book with case studies and traditional face-to-face classroom instruction coupled with a mobile application for simulation exercises.

Blended learning or hybrid instruction has many advantages: it works well with different student learning styles, enables both independent and collective learning, supports learning in a global work force, provides scheduling flexibility, etc. On the other hand, there are some concerns that must be addressed, such as more advanced planning being necessary, students needing to be organized in how they will attend, students potentially needing more motivation with this format, a feeling of not being connected and needing more encouragement, development costs, etc. This integrated, blended learning environment is constantly evolving as technology affords the organization more options.

# Techniques to Evaluate Training Programs

## PERFORMING A NEEDS ANALYSIS BEFORE DESIGNING A TRAINING PROGRAM

It is important for an organization to perform a needs analysis before designing a training program for several different reasons. First, an organization can accurately identify problems. Second, even if a particular problem is known prior to the analysis, it can be difficult to identify the cause of that problem. Third, and most importantly, it is impossible to design an effective training program without first identifying the specific knowledge, skills, and abilities required to achieve goals or correct a problem. A needs analysis can be an essential part of the training development process because it helps to identify and inform about problems so that possible solutions can be found.

## KIRKPATRICK'S FOUR-LEVEL EVALUATION MODEL

It is important to analyze the effectiveness of training programs so as not to waste resources. Donald Kirkpatrick introduced a **four-level training evaluation model** for planning, evaluating, and preserving. The four levels of the Kirkpatrick evaluation model are as follows:

- **Reaction** – Measures how people react to the training, often a survey upon completion that asks for feedback or satisfaction levels on the subject, the material, the instructor, and so on.
- **Learning** – Measures what objectives people have learned from the training program. Could be in the form of a questionnaire, assessment, etc.
- **Behavior** – Measures how far the performance or behavior of people that received the training has changed and observes how they apply what has been learned to their environment.
- **Results** – Analyzes noticeable effects of training, such as changes in production, efficiency, and quality.

Copyright © Mometrix Media. You have been licensed one copy of this document for personal use only. Any other reproduction or redistribution is strictly prohibited. All rights reserved.

## PRE- AND POST-TRAINING EVALUATION

The end goal of any training is to have the participants learn and apply the new knowledge or material in the most effective manner possible. Information obtained in a **pre-training survey** can help ensure the training meets expected learning outcomes, gauge student expectations, and provide information about the students' abilities and their learning preferences. The data gathered from the pre-training evaluation will help the instructor customize the training to improve learning. Pre-training survey questions need to be tailored for the intended audience—the right questions need to be asked in the right format. This can vary tremendously depending on the training and the participants. The objective is to have a clear assessment of the participant's skill-based knowledge before the training. Meanwhile, the questions asked in a **post-training survey** should measure if the content taught was learned and understood. Frequently, skills-based questions in the post-training survey will be similar to those asked in the pre-training survey. This is intentionally done to measure if the information taught was truly learned, meaning there should be improved scores in the post-training evaluation. Organizations typically will do another survey anywhere from 30 days to six months after the training to gauge training effectiveness.

## CONDUCTING PARTICIPANT TRAINING SURVEYS

Training is an essential function for almost any organization. Sometimes, in cases of sexual harassment, corporate policy, discriminatory practice and legislation, etc., it can even be mandatory. In other cases, it is a necessity because information and technology are constantly advancing. Additionally, companies spend a considerable amount of money on training and should see a return on their investment. Therefore, organizations should always evaluate and assess training effectiveness. One of the ways to assess training is through a training participant survey. This type of survey involves asking employees questions to better gauge how they view the effectiveness of the training. Individuals have different learning styles and learn in many different ways. Their input can help an organization improve future training programs. The survey is usually done electronically and can vary enormously depending on the training needs and makeup of the organization. Generally, questions will either be quantitative, meaning they are evaluated on a numeric scale; or qualitative, meaning they require verbiage and/or accurate responses. Possible questions might be:

- What was your overall impression of the training program?
- What particular part of the training did you feel was the most useful?
- On a scale of 1 to 5, with 1 being the worst and 5 the best, answer the following questions:
    o How would you rate this training program?
    o How would you rate the instructor?
    o How would you rate the technology used?
    o How would you rate your ability to immediately use the information learned?

## AFTER-ACTION REVIEW

The term **"after-action review"** was originally used by the military after field operations as a structured approach to identify the group's strengths, weaknesses, and areas for improvement based on real-life events. Many companies, including GE, BP, and Motorola, use an after-action review to improve their operations. This approach is focused on three primary questions:

- What was supposed to happen and what actually happened?
- What went well and why?
- What can be improved and how?

Copyright © Mometrix Media. You have been licensed one copy of this document for personal use only. Any other reproduction or redistribution is strictly prohibited. All rights reserved.

An after-action review is a structured debriefing that allows an organization to gain insights and knowledge that will enable it to learn from past missteps or mistakes so they are not repeated. Moreover, this reflective, knowledge-is-power method can correct situations that were not ideal and/or help replicate situations that were handled well. Following are the typical processes and objectives when conducting an after-action review:

- Conduct the after-action review as soon as possible after the event so it is fresh in everyone's memory.
- Include everyone involved and set ground rules so that honest opinions are offered with respect to all present.
- Ask all structured questions (listed above) and document responses for lessons learned.
- Document a report detailing all learned strengths, weaknesses, and areas for improvement or areas to be replicated.
- Implement needed changes immediately.

# Career Development Practices

### CAREER PLANNING VS. CAREER MANAGEMENT

Career development is comprised of two separate-but-related processes: career planning and career management. Simply put, **career planning** is all about individuals and their career path preferences and goals. Career planning involves assessing individual interests and abilities in order to develop a career plan. **Career management** is more about the organization's involvement in helping to guide, match, and implement an employee's career preferences and goals to align with the organization's goals. Additionally, an employer will also use this information to assess staffing and training programs. In turn, an organization is then well-positioned to strategically assist the individual reach both their goals and the organization's objectives. Hence, in this respect, career planning and career management are mutually beneficial processes.

### DUAL CAREER LADDER PROGRAM

A "ladder" is a metaphor for moving up a singular or linear path to the top, like climbing rungs on a ladder. In other words, someone's progression up the career ladder means they are progressing in a logical manner in their given field. A dual career ladder program provides a career path for both management progression and also a more technical career progression, thereby allowing the employee to move easily between the two ladders. For example, maybe a technical engineer has progressed along a logical, linear career path from entry-level engineer to senior engineer, but doesn't want to advance up the engineering ladder any further. Instead, suppose this engineer would like to be able to shift from a technical role to management, with a group of senior engineers under him. Or, suppose this person loves being a senior engineer and wants to continue on the technical career path and become a lead senior engineer. An organization with a dual career ladder would make either of these scenarios possible and thereby give the employee more options to move up vertically, horizontally, or any combination thereof. A dual career ladder gives employees more career opportunities, helps to attract and retain top talent, and ideally improves productivity for

Copyright © Mometrix Media. You have been licensed one copy of this document for personal use only. Any other reproduction or redistribution is strictly prohibited. All rights reserved.

the organization. Dual career ladders are more prevalent in the medical, scientific, and engineering industries.

## Dual Career Path

## CAREER DEVELOPMENT ACTIVITIES

There are many activities an organization or employee can utilize to assist in their career development:

- **Coaching** – There are two different types of career development coaching: internal and external. **Internal coaching is** ongoing discussion between employees and their managers, spontaneous or planned, where advice or guidance is shared. **External coaching** is conducted with a certified professional who can assist employees in obtaining specific career outcomes and could also offer assessments.
- **Mentoring** – This is a relationship with an experienced member of an organization helping a less experienced employee. Mentoring can involve, but is not limited to, advising, being a role model, teaching how to build a network, and sharing connections. A mentor is usually not an employee's supervisor.
- **Self-assessment tools** – There are numerous self-assessment tools that can assist employees in their career journeys to learn more about their interests and how that corresponds to their careers (Myers Briggs, Self-Directed Search, etc.).

Copyright © Mometrix Media. You have been licensed one copy of this document for personal use only. Any other reproduction or redistribution is strictly prohibited. All rights reserved.

## EMPLOYEE DEVELOPMENT PROGRAM

**Employee development programs** provide opportunities for employees to learn new ideas and have different career experiences that enable them to grow and prepare for future roles.

- **Continuing education** – Many organizations will fund educational experiences benefitting the employee and organization alike. This could mean obtaining an industry certification, a college course, trade course, etc.
- **Company committees** – Some organizations form committees to address specific issues on a project, in a particular business unit, or for the community. These opportunities could enable an employee to gain some leadership experience, enrich their knowledge in a certain area, network with other colleagues, help their community, etc.
- **Apprenticeship** – The U.S. Department of Labor – Bureau of Apprenticeship and Training regulates apprenticeships because most of them need to comply with Fair Labor Standards Act (FLSA) regulations. Apprenticeship programs are designed and organized by both union and non-union employers and provide training and on-the-job opportunities.
- **Job adjustments** – Job movement can be a **job rotation**, moving between jobs to learn about new positions; **job enlargement**, when an employer would add more tasks requiring the same skill level; and **job enrichment**, adding more depth to already-known skills.

## JOB SHADOWING

**Job shadowing** is a beneficial way to follow a professional in a particular area of interest and observe what he or she does at work. It is an opportunity for an individual to learn firsthand what is involved with a certain position or career and the skills needed to meet the demands of the position. The time period to job shadow can vary from one day to possibly several weeks, and depends on the agreed-upon arrangement with the employer. Additionally, job shadowing programs can be formal; coordinated with a high school or university, including alumni; or could be a casual, informal arrangement. Whether an individual is switching careers or just exploring career options, job shadowing can be beneficial. It exposes a person to a particular career on a short-term basis and helps someone decide if a given career piques their interest. If the career or position is of interest, the job shadowing experience is an excellent start to building a network in the field.

## SUCCESSION PLANNING

**Succession planning** is a method of planning how management and executive vacancies will be filled so a company has highly trained replacements should the need arise. First, determine what the requirements are for key positions and create profiles that outline responsibilities. The experience, education, career progress, and future career interests of managerial candidates should also be reviewed. Then the performance of prospective managers should be assessed to determine whether they are promotable and identify developmental objectives to prepare for advancement opportunities. Performance should be evaluated based upon traditional goals and standards. Developmental objectives might include seminars, training programs, special projects, or temporary assignments.

# Performance Appraisal Methods

## PERFORMANCE APPRAISAL METHODS

There are many different performance appraisal methods. Some involve feedback from the immediate supervisor and some involve the feedback of peers, clients, or subordinates. Many organizations begin the process with self-appraisals. **Self-appraisals** are most beneficial when used for personal development and identifying training needs, but less beneficial when they are used as a

Copyright © Mometrix Media. You have been licensed one copy of this document for personal use only. Any other reproduction or redistribution is strictly prohibited. All rights reserved.

basis for the formal evaluation process. Good supervisors are able to evaluate performance and give meaningful feedback. Hence, it should not be surprising that **supervisor appraisals** are typically required as at least one major component of the overall performance appraisal process. One type of appraisal that considers feedback from multiple sources is a **360-degree appraisal**. These appraisals have rapidly grown in popularity and are expected to share a broader perspective of performance because they include feedback from everyone the employee interacts with— managers, peers, clients, and subordinates.

## FORMS OF RANKING

Ranking procedures put employees in order from highest to lowest based upon evaluation characteristics such as performance. There are three main forms of ranking: straight ranking, alternate ranking, and paired comparison. **Straight ranking** involves listing all employees in order, with number one being the best, number two being second best, number three being third, and so on. **Alternate ranking** entails choosing the best and the worst from a list of all employees, removing these names from the list, and repeating until there are no names left. **Paired comparison** consists of evaluating only two employees at a time, deciding which is better, and continuing until each employee has been paired against every other employee. Ranking procedures assist with distributing budgeted pay increases that are more clearly tied to performance and eliminate some of the biases found in traditional review criteria. The forced-distribution method, also known as **forced ranking**, uses a bell curve in which the majority of employees will receive an average score and a small group will receive extremely high or extremely low performance scores.

## RATING APPRAISAL METHODS

There are a variety of rating appraisal methods, but the two most common are the checklist method and the rating scale method. The **checklist method** is a series of statements describing a certain level of performance. The performance evaluator can then check a box next to the statement that best describes the individual's performance in each performance area. The **rating scale method** rates an individual's performance on a point scale, usually a 1–3, 1–4, 1–5, or 1–10 scale, with lower numbers representing poor performance and higher numbers representing superior performance.

## BEHAVIORALLY BASED APPRAISAL METHODS

Greater focus on accountability and results has led to new approaches for appraising performance. The three main **behaviorally based appraisal methods** include management by objectives, behavioral anchored rating scale, and behavioral observation scale. **Management by objectives** is proactive rather than reactive. It focuses on predicting and shaping the future of the company, accomplishing results rather than simply following directions, improving competence and effectiveness, and increasing the participation and engagement of employees. **Behaviorally anchored rating scales** (BARS) assign numerical values to performance based upon a given range, such as a five-star system or a scale from 1 to 10. The BARS method analyzes the job description for a particular position and identifies the tasks that must be performed for the organization to function effectively. Once the tasks are identified, a determination is made about the specific way the individual should behave to perform each task. For example, if communication is identified as a necessary skill for a management position, then an individual in that position must be able to keep others informed. A series of ranked statements are then designed to describe how effectively the individual performed. Performance appraisers can then choose the statement that best describes the employee's behavior. The key benefits of behaviorally anchored rating systems are that they create agreement by being less subjective and more based upon observations, whereas characteristics are more carefully considered. **Behavior observation scales** are similar to behaviorally anchored rating scales, but with greater focus on frequency of behavior than on quality of performance, such as a sliding scale of "always," "sometimes," and "never."

Copyright © Mometrix Media. You have been licensed one copy of this document for personal use only. Any other reproduction or redistribution is strictly prohibited. All rights reserved.

## NARRATIVE APPRAISAL METHODS

The three most common narrative appraisal techniques are the critical incident method, the essay method, and the field review method. The **critical incident method** documents each performance problem related to an employee occurring during a set period so that the evaluator can discuss problems with the employee at the end. The **essay method** requires performance evaluators to write a short essay about each employee describing their performance during the period in question. The **field review method** is a method in which an individual other than the employee's direct supervisor or manager performs the appraisal and writes down a series of assessments and observations about that particular employee's performance.

## ERRORS OCCURRING IN THE PERFORMANCE APPRAISAL PROCESS

Errors can occur when assessing employee performance. It is important to be aware of and hopefully avoid some of the following common errors:

- **Recency and primacy error** – A **recency** error is when the appraiser evaluates an employee on their more recent activities and not earlier performance. Alternatively, a **primacy** error is when an appraiser values an employee's earlier performance with greater emphasis than their more recent performance.
- **Halo and horn effect** – A **halo** effect is exemplary in one area and rated outstanding because of the one area of expertise, thereby negating the other categories. A **horn** effect is just the opposite, where one area of weakness overshadows all the other areas.
- **Strictness and leniency** – Some appraisers may believe the agreed-upon standards for performance are too low and therefore do not rate performance in a fair manner. In other words, they are reluctant to give the highest rating because, from their perspective, no one is ever that good. **Strictness** gives no room for fallacy. Conversely, **leniency** is when an appraiser gives an undeserving employee an overinflated appraisal.
- **Bias** – This occurs when an appraiser's prejudices and values cloud their judgment, causing them to evaluate someone's performance through their own belief system and not necessarily the organization's.

## LEGAL CONSIDERATIONS IN THE PERFORMANCE APPRAISAL PROCESS

The EEOC clearly explains that performance appraisals, in accordance with Uniform Guidelines, must be job-related. Additionally, in a performance appraisal, careful attention is necessary to avoid any form of discrimination covered under Title VII of the Civil Rights Act of 1964 and related anti-discrimination laws. Evaluation criteria should be formally assessed in a structured format that limits subjective responses and increases validity of data about performance. The goal is for performance to be rated against objective, predefined standards. Information and documentation must be based on genuine interaction with the employee being appraised. Furthermore, the actual appraisal meeting should have some mechanism or protocol in place to prevent one manager from dominating the discussion and unfairly influencing employee rating. Overall, the performance appraisal process should be equitable and fair for all employees.

# Performance Management Practices

## COMPONENTS AND BEST PRACTICES OF PERFORMANCE MANAGEMENT SYSTEMS

**Performance management** is the human resource function concerned with setting performance standards, evaluating employee effectiveness against those standards, identifying any problem areas, and implementing interventions to correct said problems. Performance management is vital

Copyright © Mometrix Media. You have been licensed one copy of this document for personal use only. Any other reproduction or redistribution is strictly prohibited. All rights reserved.

because an organization cannot thrive if individuals, teams, and departments aren't effective in their roles.

The performance management process can vary from organization to organization, but most firms follow three basic steps:

- Through activities like goal setting, needs analysis, and the creation of a corporate value statement and code of conduct, company leaders and human resource professionals establish organizational goals. They then identify the knowledge, skills, behaviors, and tasks required to achieve those goals and inform employees how to best work to meet those company objectives.
- The firm's management then needs to monitor employee performance, document any problems, and help employees correct those problems if possible.
- At predetermined intervals, typically once a year, managers will conduct in-depth performance appraisals for each employee. These appraisals measure performance during the preceding period. Often, the manager and employee will set goals for the employee to work toward in the new appraisal period.

## SETTING PERFORMANCE GOALS

A performance goal is a written declaration of an anticipated end result in a specified period of time. These goals are usually discussed between an employee and their manager. Performance goals are then chosen and agreed upon based on company objectives and/or the employee's personal aspirations. Goals are desired outcomes that specify defined measures such as time frame, quantity, quality, or a percentage. Employee performance goals should link into and support the overall strategic plan of the company or unit, and at the same time should assist in keeping the employee engaged and motivated. It is an opportunity for an employee to formulate a plan with their manager to focus on those job duties, responsibilities, and tasks that will best enable individual achievement of goals that carefully integrate with company goals. To be effective, performance goals should be evaluated and perhaps re-evaluated in a timely fashion, perhaps every quarter, six months, or annually. Performance goals are not written in stone and can be updated or revised as needed to maintain motivation over time.

## SMART PERFORMANCE GOALS

**SMART** is an acronym that stands for "specific, measurable, achievable, relevant and timebound." The idea is that every goal an employee sets should be "SMART." Performance goals should be as follows:

- **Specific** – The goal should clearly define what is to be achieved as specifically as possible. For example, a goal to "improve diversity in company" is not specific at all, but a goal to "begin an electronic diversity awareness monthly communication about a different aspect of diversity" is very specific.
- **Measurable** – Performance goals should be quantifiable in some unit of measurement. For example, "reduce return processing" isn't measurable, but "reduce return processing time by 10 percent before December 31" has a clear and unmistakable deadline.
- **Achievable** – A goal should be a challenge for the employee and require a high level of effort, but also should be reasonable and realistic.
- **Relevant** – All performance goals should link to organizational goals.
- **Timebound** – There needs to be a due date or period of time in which the goal will be achieved. Time is usually reflected as a specific date or numeric period, like December 31 or the end of the third fiscal quarter, respectively.

Copyright © Mometrix Media. You have been licensed one copy of this document for personal use only. Any other reproduction or redistribution is strictly prohibited. All rights reserved.

## 360-DEGREE FEEDBACK

The **360-degree feedback performance assessment** is a multi-source performance feedback tool that derives its data from evaluations obtained by an employee's supervisor(s), peers, subordinates, and sometimes others outside the organization such as vendors, partners, etc. The idea is that 360 degrees form a perfect circle, hence feedback from all directions can give comprehensive feedback based on their interactions with the employee. These directions include supervisors from above, subordinates from below, and peers along the sides. Peers may also be joined by employees from other organizations. This process captures information from a variety of viewpoints and perspectives. The majority of organizations utilize 360-degree feedback for developmental reasons. However, there are some organizations that use it as part of a performance evaluation, in which case it might be called a 360-degree review. There are advantages to using 360-degree feedback, such as providing a comprehensive perspective from multiple people who have interacted with the employee; or asking if someone's opinion makes them feel valued, thereby possibly boosting morale and, if executed correctly, giving a complete or holistic picture of the employee. Conversely, 360-degree feedback can render results that are misleading because people may have different ulterior motives or their own agenda when completing the form and many people are untrained to give this type of feedback. Additionally, it can be a time-consuming process as the form typically takes 45 minutes to one hour to complete. That means time away from work, which also comes at a certain price to an organization.

## IMPORTANCE OF DOCUMENTING EMPLOYEE PERFORMANCE

Up-to-date performance documentation is important to maintain in an employee's personnel file as it frequently demonstrates the reasoning why decisions, both positive and negative, were made. This documentation is especially useful in an employee's performance appraisal because it demonstrates performance with examples. Some managers find it useful to keep a performance diary, documenting a record of key activities or tasks executed by the employee. Employee performance documentation is essential in the event of a lawsuit. Furthermore, the documentation must be accurate, objective, and specific. The following are some guidelines to maintain when documenting employee performance: document right away to avoid anything being forgotten, keep notes on all employees, separate fact from opinion, make sure notes are objective, remove emotion from documentation, and be respectful when writing. Performance documentation is not exclusively useful to avoid possible legal issues, but it can be leveraged to improve an employee's performance and to create a professional development plan or possibly reward outstanding performance.

## BENCHMARKING

**Benchmarking** is a process or system by which an organization measures its performance against other similar business groupings considered to have best practices, sometimes called "best in class." In order to grow, companies must compare given functions and practices to best in class in order to improve efficiencies and productivity. In HR, benchmarking is frequently used to compare an organization in the areas of recruitment, employee retention, salary, performance, employee engagement, HR strategies, etc. An organization can choose to conduct **internal benchmarking**, whereby they closely exam and compare the efficiencies realized in their own organization; or **external benchmarking**, which involves an organization comparing its functional information against other industries. The objective is to discover what areas of the business could benefit from improvement to hopefully maintain a competitive advantage and cultivate a culture of continuous improvement. Some specific benefits of benchmarking may include lowered labor cost, increase in sales and profits, operational efficiencies, increased productivity, quality improvements, etc.

Copyright © Mometrix Media. You have been licensed one copy of this document for personal use only. Any other reproduction or redistribution is strictly prohibited. All rights reserved.

Benchmarking may be the impetus that drives change, so organizations must prepare accordingly with change management education in the organization.

## BALANCED SCORECARD

A **balanced scorecard** is a strategic performance management tool that was developed by Robert Kaplan and David Norton in 1996. The tool is designed to identify, report, and improve an organization through four perspectives in time:

1. **Financial** - View of the organization by various stakeholders.
2. **Customer** – How customers view the organization.
3. **Business process** – What the organization excels at.
4. **Learning and growth** – How the organization continuously improves.

This tool and subsequent reports can be used by leadership and management to better monitor the actions or activities within their span of control and keep track of the results.

## PERFORMANCE FEEDBACK TECHNIQUES

How performance feedback is delivered plays a vital role in how it is received and subsequent outcome(s). First, whenever possible, feedback should be given in private and always in a respectful manner. It is important to remember that feedback is not negative. Rather, performance feedback is an opportunity for a supervisor to discuss information that should help make the employee more productive and provide clear direction and priorities moving forward. This should be a two-way discussion and not a supervisor speaking at length to a silent employee. It is important for a manager not to come across as overbearing or cruel, but rather approach feedback in a manner that is sincerely helpful. The manager giving feedback should actively listen to the employee and recap or clarify what the employee is saying if needed, as well as empathize with the employee's point of view. A manager should be cognizant that the words being used to describe an undesired behavior are factual, not judgmental. For example, "Ann, could you just stop making so many errors on the same XYZ activity? Try harder!" is judgmental. However, "Ann, it seems there are some issues doing XYZ. What are your thoughts?" is better. A manager should be specific when providing feedback, both positive and negative. For example, "Derrick, you are doing a good job!" isn't specific; instead, a manager should say something like, "Derrick, your closing numbers are great, 35 percent above the department average and 98 percent customer satisfaction ratings. That's awesome!"

## PERFORMANCE MANAGEMENT SOFTWARE

The performance management process needs to be effective to be productive. If the process is too cumbersome, then there is the risk it becomes a "check-the-box" routine and not as productive as it could be. The end goal is to improve the performance of employees. Many companies utilize various forms and formats of performance management software, both web-based and mobile, to augment the process for efficiency. Software can vary, but most enable the manager to easily keep a record of all performance-related discussions, track progress against goals, and illustrate how progress against goals is linked to the company's strategic objectives. Most also provide a way of capturing skills for each employee, which in turn can assist with succession planning in case an employee leaves the organization. Many even have the capability to facilitate 360-degree feedback between managers, employees, and peers. Additionally, the majority of software packages are capable of producing helpful dashboards, illustrating progress and standard and customized reports to assist management when evaluating performance. Performance management software can be a stand-alone product or part of a more integrated and robust HR system.

Copyright © Mometrix Media. You have been licensed one copy of this document for personal use only. Any other reproduction or redistribution is strictly prohibited. All rights reserved.

# Employee Relations

## Applicable Laws Affecting Employment in Union and Nonunion Environments

### LABOR UNION

A **labor union** is a group of workers who organize together as a collective to negotiate with an employer to advance their rights and interests. This negotiation process with an employer is called "collective bargaining." The concept is that a group of individuals banding together is more powerful than a single person fighting for more rights. The formation of unions began in the 1790s and reached its prime in the 1940s and 1950s. Union contracts typically specify safe working conditions, health benefits and compensation in the event of an injury, and retirement stipulations. Additionally, labor unions were extremely influential in ending the practice of child labor. Organized labor unions have diminished since the 1950s, but have meaningfully impacted the economic, political, and workplace environment since its inception. Unions have been partially responsible for a significant amount of federal legislation protecting worker interests and rights, as well as the creation of the U.S. Department of Labor.

### NORRIS-LAGUARDIA ACT

The **Norris-LaGuardia Act**, which was passed in 1932, protects the right to unionize. This act grants employees the right to form unions and initiate strikes. In addition to granting the right to unionize, this act also prohibits the court system from using injunctions to interfere with any nonviolent union activity and prohibits employers from forcing employees to sign "yellow-dog" contracts. A **yellow-dog contract** refers to any contract that prohibits an employee from joining a union or any contract that requires an employee to agree to be terminated if it is discovered that they are a member of a union or intend to become a member of a union. The act stated that members belonging to a union have "full freedom of association," meaning they are free without legal penalty to strike, picket, or initiate boycotts.

### NATIONAL LABOR RELATIONS ACT (NLRA)

The **National Labor Relations Act** (NLRA) was passed by Congress in 1935 after a long period of conflict in labor relations. Also known as the Wagner Act, after the New York Senator Robert Wagner, it was intended to be an economic stabilizer and establish collective bargaining in industrial relations. Section 7 of the NLRA provides employees with the right to form, join, or assist **labor organizations** as well as the right to engage in **concerted activities** such as collective bargaining through representatives or other mutual aid. Section 8 of the NLRA also identifies five **unfair labor practices**:

- Employers shall not interfere with or coerce employees from the rights outlined in Section 7.
- Employers shall not dominate or disrupt the formation of a labor union.
- Employers shall not allow union membership or activity to influence hiring, firing, promotion, or related employment decisions.
- Employers shall not discriminate against or discharge an employee who has given testimony or filed a charge with the NLRA.
- Employers cannot refuse bargaining in good faith with employee representatives.

116

Copyright © Mometrix Media. You have been licensed one copy of this document for personal use only. Any other reproduction or redistribution is strictly prohibited. All rights reserved.

## TAFT-HARTLEY ACT

Because many employers felt that the NLRA gave too much power to unions, Congress passed the Labor Management Relations Act in 1947. More commonly known as the **Taft-Hartley Act**, it sought to avoid unnecessary strikes and impose certain restrictions over union activities. The act addresses **four basic issues**: unfair labor practices by unions, the rights of employees, the rights of employers, and national emergency strikes. Moreover, the act prohibits unions from the following:

- Restraining or coercing employees from their right to not engage in union activities.
- Forcing an employer to discriminate in any way against an employee to encourage or discourage union membership.
- Forcing an employer to pay for work or services that are not needed or not performed.
- Conducting certain types of strikes or boycotts.
- Charging excessive initiation fees or membership dues when employees are required to join a union shop.

## LANDRUM-GRIFFIN ACT

The government exercised further control over union activities in 1959 by the passage of the Labor Management Reporting and Disclosure Act. More commonly known as the **Landrum-Griffin Act**, this law regulates the **internal conduct of labor unions** to reduce the likelihood of fraud and improper actions. The act imposes controls on five major areas: reports to the secretary of labor, a bill of rights for union members, union trusteeships, conduct of union elections, and financial safeguards. Some key provisions include the following:

- Granting equal rights to every union member with regard to nominations, attending meetings, and voting.
- Requiring unions to submit and make available to the public a copy of its constitution, bylaws, and annual financial reports.
- Requiring unions to hold regular elections every five years for national organizations and every three years for local organizations.
- Monitoring the management and investment of union funds, making embezzlement a federal crime.

> **Review Video: US Employment Law: Employee and Labor Relations (NLRA)**
> Visit mometrix.com/academy and enter code: 972790

## NATIONAL LABOR RELATIONS BOARD (NLRB)

The National Labor Relations Board (NLRB) is a federal agency that protects the right of employees to choose whether they want to be represented by a union or not. It is designed to handle activities related to investigating and preventing employers and unions from taking part in unfair labor practices. The National Labor Relations Board can take a number of actions related to employer unfair labor practices, including requiring employers to rehire or return positions to employees that were affected by an unfair labor practice, requiring employers to resume negotiations with a union, and disbanding unions that are controlled by an employer. The National Labor Relations Board may also take a number of actions related to unfair union labor practices, including requiring unions to refund membership fees with or without interest to union members that have been charged unreasonable fees, requiring unions to resume negotiations with an employer, and requiring unions to accept the reinstatement of any employee if the union specifically discriminated against that employee.

Copyright © Mometrix Media. You have been licensed one copy of this document for personal use only. Any other reproduction or redistribution is strictly prohibited. All rights reserved.

## WORKER ADJUSTMENT AND RETRAINING NOTIFICATION ACT (WARN)

The **Worker Adjustment and Retraining Notification Act** (WARN), passed in 1988, states companies must give 60 days' notice in advance of closings and mass layoffs. WARN applies to union and non-union environments, employers with 100 or more full time employees, or total employees working a cumulative of 4,000 hours per week at all locations. WARN specifically states that notification must be given to the following: local government, state dislocated worker units, and the workers or their representatives. There is a difference between a closing and a mass layoff. A closing is a temporary or permanent shutdown of one or more sites or business units at one location in a 30-day period, impacting 50 or more full time employees. A mass layoff, sometimes called a reduction in force (RIF), is also defined as a 30-day period, but it is always an employment loss for 50 or more full-time employees, if the layoffs comprise 33 percent of the workforce at the site, or impacts 500 or more full-time employees. It is important to note this is an involuntary employment termination for six months or a 50-percent-or-more reduction of hours worked each month for six months. There are a few exceptions to the WARN Act, such as natural disasters and "other unforeseeable business circumstances."

## SEXUAL HARASSMENT

**Sexual harassment** was formally recognized by the Supreme Court in the 1980s when they interpreted Title VII of the Civil Rights Act of 1964 to include discrimination based on "sex." As a result, sex discrimination was expanded to include sexual harassment and thereby applies to employers with 15 or more employees. The U.S. Equal Employment Opportunity Commission (EEOC) maintains that sexual harassment can occur in many ways:

- The victim or the harasser can be either male or female.
- The harasser can be anyone that the victim interacts with in the work environment: direct supervisor, colleague, vendor, etc.
- A victim of harassment doesn't necessarily have to be the person harassed; it can also include anyone affected by the offensive conduct.
- Sexual harassment can happen without economic injury or discharge of the victim.
- All harassment must be unwelcome.

While federal legislation (Title VII) covers sexual harassment, states also may have specific laws that strengthen "sex" protections and the prohibition of sexual harassment in the workplace. Many states also require employers to offer some form of sexual harassment training at work.

### TYPES OF SEXUAL HARASSMENT

Title VII of the Civil Rights Act of 1964 prohibits sexual harassment. There are two different types of sexual harassment in the workplace: quid pro quo and hostile work environment.

**Quid pro quo** literally means "this for that." This type of harassment occurs when a supervisor, manager, or someone with authority demands some form of sexual interaction in exchange for an employment-related benefit, be it more compensation, a promotion, maintenance of job, etc. In other words, the person with authority basically states, "If you do some sexual favor for me, then I will do some work benefit for you." A worker is then coerced or forced into unwelcome sexual demands to avoid negatively impacting their job.

A **hostile work environment** occurs when an employee is confronted with unwelcome, sexually offensive conduct that is severe and in a clear, pervasive pattern, thereby creating an abusive

118

Copyright © Mometrix Media. You have been licensed one copy of this document for personal use only. Any other reproduction or redistribution is strictly prohibited. All rights reserved.

environment. Some of the circumstances that should be examined in a possible hostile environment are as follows:

- How often the offensive, discriminatory action occurs
- How severe the actions are
- Whether the conduct can or has caused physical harm, is intimidating, or is more subtle
- Whether it unreasonably prevents the employee from performing his or her job

The goal for organizations is to try and prevent sexual harassment. This can be done by clearly communicating the organization's policy that sexual harassment will not be tolerated and providing training. However, if sexual harassment occurs, there needs a to be a formal complaint process whereby it is immediately investigated, and swift and fair action is taken to stop the harassment.

## DISPARATE IMPACT

**Disparate impact** is a type of discrimination in which an employer institutes a policy that appears to be reasonable, but prevents individuals of a certain color, with certain disabilities, with a certain military status, of a certain national origin, of a certain race, of a certain religion, or individuals of a particular gender from receiving employment or any of the benefits associated with employment such as promotions or pay. It refers to a policy that makes sense, but is actually unfair because it makes things more difficult for individuals of a certain group to receive the job or benefit. For example, a policy stating individuals applying for an office job must be at least 5'10" and weigh at least 185 pounds may create a disparate impact if it makes it more difficult for individuals belonging to one of the protected groups, such as women, to get the job. However, a physical attribute directly linked to the work that must be performed is not discriminatory so long as it correlates with the essential job requirements. For example, a firefighter has to fulfill certain physical requirements to perform the essential functions of the job. Disparate impact discrimination was first identified by the Supreme Court in *Griggs v. Duke Power Co.*

## DISPARATE TREATMENT

**Disparate treatment** is a type of discrimination in which an employer deliberately treats an individual differently because of that individual's age, color, disability, military status, national origin, race, religion, and/or gender. It refers to any instance in which an employer uses a different set of procedures, expectations, or policies than they would normally use simply because the individual belongs to a particular group. For example, a business that requires female employees to follow a strict dress code while the male employees of the business can wear whatever they like would be guilty of disparate treatment because of treating employees differently based on gender. In general, an individual claiming disparate treatment must prove that they are a member of a protected class. They must then prove they were qualified but were not hired. If the employer then continues the application process after rejecting a qualified candidate because of a protected class criterion, then this might be considered unlawful discrimination and thus disparate treatment. This type of discrimination was first identified by Title VII of the Civil Rights Act.

# Employee and Employer Rights and Responsibilities

## EMPLOYMENT AT WILL

The **employment at-will doctrine** states that an employer can terminate an employee without reason or warning, and also that an employee can choose to resign or leave an organization without reason or warning. An employer's employment at-will policy should appear in the employee handbook and be clearly communicated to all employees. Additionally, the policy is usually in the contract for employment, if applicable. This type of employer-employee relationship offers ultimate

Copyright © Mometrix Media. You have been licensed one copy of this document for personal use only. Any other reproduction or redistribution is strictly prohibited. All rights reserved.

flexibility. However, it is very important to note that just because an employer or employee can do something—like abruptly terminate an employee or unexpectedly quit a job without notice—does not mean that they should. Wrongful termination in at-will employment situations is protected by federal and state laws, and state laws can vary tremendously. Some of the areas protected in a case of wrongful termination can include age, gender, sexual orientation, race, religion, disability, whistleblowing, retaliation for a legally protected act, and many others. All states have some type of at-will employment, but many states place stipulations and limits on how it is interpreted.

## EXCEPTIONS TO THE EMPLOYMENT-AT-WILL DOCTRINE

There are a few exceptions to employment at will and they too can vary in execution from state to state:

- **Employment contracts** – If an employee is working under a collective bargaining agreement or other type of specified employment contract, then the employee may have more rights than typical at-will employees.
- **Public policy exception** – Some states prevent an employer from firing an employee in violation of state public policy. For example, in some states with this exception, an employer cannot terminate an employee that was injured on the job and is filing a worker's compensation claim.
- **Implied contracts** – Some states prevent an employer from firing an employee if an implied contract for employment is established between the employer and employee. This is challenging to prove in cases of implied contracts, where nothing is directly stated or written, and the burden rests with the employee. The employee can reference the employer handbook or historical proof that termination is for cause.
- **Good faith and fair dealing exception** – Some states specify this exception to prevent an employer from terminating employees to circumvent an employer obligation such as paying workers for earned commissions, retirement agreements, healthcare, etc.

## EMPLOYER AND EMPLOYEE RIGHTS WITH SUBSTANCE ABUSE

There are federal and state laws outlining polices an employer can develop to combat drug and alcohol abuse in the workplace. Generally, employers implement three policies that address this type of abuse: (1) unequivocally prohibit alcohol and drug use on the job, (2) provide permission to test for drug use (within guidelines), and (3) fire employees who have been proven to use illegal drugs. Employers should document their drug and alcohol polices, including what could happen if someone fails a drug test. Employees also have some protections afforded to them from both federal and state laws, whereby the employer may have to provide some accommodations to address the substance abuse problem. It is important to keep in mind that the Americans with Disabilities Act (ADA) and the Rehabilitation Act of 1973 include drug and alcohol polices, and some states have their own policies. Following are some examples to keep in mind:

- The ADA does not prohibit an employer from testing for illegal drug use, although it must follow any applicable state protocols.
- Some states restrict pre-employment drug testing until the candidate has accepted the job. It is usually a good practice to test all candidates instead of singling out any one individual.
- Some states can randomly test workers for drugs, especially where safety is an issue. However, there are also some states where an employer must have a reasonable suspicion before requiring an employee to be drug tested.

Copyright © Mometrix Media. You have been licensed one copy of this document for personal use only. Any other reproduction or redistribution is strictly prohibited. All rights reserved.

- An employer, if applicable and possible, must offer reasonable accommodations for employees with substance abuse problems, in their past or currently, to attend to medical care.
- Under the ADA, a person considered an alcoholic might be considered an "individual with a disability" and treated accordingly.

## EMPLOYERS AND AN EMPLOYEE RIGHTS TO PRIVACY

There is no specific federal law that compels employers to inform employees about any type of monitoring in the workplace. Therefore, U.S. employers have the right to monitor employees with such things as surveillance cameras, internet tracking, email or phone tracking applications, etc. The ability to do this is a double-edged sword for employers. Technology affords employers many ways to monitor, which is helpful for reducing liability and perhaps increasing productivity. However, at the same time, employees almost have no choice other than to surrender most of their privacy while at work. There is much debate among employers as to the ethical, moral, and legal decisions to reduce employee privacy rights. There is also the question of where it ends, such as should an employer use a candidate's social media presence when making a decision to hire or not? The debate continues about how a company can strike a balance between employer rights and employee privacy. Every company is different and needs to evaluate if the monitoring is worth the effort and what the monitoring is doing to drive better business results. Additionally, a company may want to consider how the monitoring will impact its culture: will employees want to work for a company that aggressively monitors its employees? There are no right or wrong answers, but it is helpful for companies to be clear and transparent about employee privacy and monitoring activities.

## DEFAMATION

**Defamation** is when a person intentionally makes a false and malicious statement causing harm to a person's reputation in a given community. If doing harm by speaking, it is called **slander**. If it is in written form, it is called **libel**. For example, if someone makes a negative statement during a reference check regarding a former employee, or over-the-top positive comments, then the person giving the reference could be liable for making distorted false claims. Another example of this type of misrepresentation could be when an employee is upset because he or she was passed over for a promotion and decides to spread a rumor that the person who received the promotion lied about their qualifications. It is important to note that the First Amendment, which protects free speech, does not protect someone guilty of defamation, and as a result, the person can face legal consequences. Many companies have implemented policies to try and reduce the likelihood of harmful gossip and rumors that cause needless stress and negatively impact productivity.

## FRAUDULENT MISREPRESENTATION

**Fraudulent misrepresentation** is an intentionally false statement that deceptively causes someone to enter into a contract. Basically, someone can be accused of fraudulent misrepresentation if a statement of fact is a blatant lie, and this lie creates a false pretense under which another person enters into a contract. For example, suppose an employer says to a prospective applicant that the company is doing great financially and job security is strong. Hearing this, the applicant turns down other jobs for the one with the most job security. He accepts the position and learns three months later that the company has not been profitable in many months and the employer knew the job would only be temporary without any job security whatsoever. This is a case of fraudulent misrepresentation whereby the job applicant entered into a contract of employment with an expectation of job security when the employer knew that was not true. Fraudulent misrepresentation can occur in any form that results in the other party being deceived with false information, a half-truth, or silence when there was an opportunity to speak up. Also,

Copyright © Mometrix Media. You have been licensed one copy of this document for personal use only. Any other reproduction or redistribution is strictly prohibited. All rights reserved.

fraudulent misrepresentation requires the deceived party to enter into a contract; this is different from defamation, which is when an intentionally false statement is made about a person without the involvement of contracts.

# Methods and Processes for Collecting Employee Feedback

## CONDUCTING AN EMPLOYEE ATTITUDE SURVEY

An employer would conduct an employee attitude survey to better understand what employees think about the company and its work environment. Employee attitude surveys can either measure employee satisfaction or opinions on specific issues. Some of the information that might be collected and evaluated include workplace culture, communication effectiveness, management effectiveness, safety at work, and specialized initiatives in the organization. There are many advantages for an organization to conduct an employee attitude survey:

- Employees like to feel valued, so asking them their perspective on a number of key topics helps them feel their voices count while also helping employers adjust course if necessary. Also, it demonstrates the organization cares about their employees.
- Employee attitude surveys are anonymous, which encourages honesty. Employers gain the honest opinions of employees because of this format. It provides a better understanding of the organization's strengths and weaknesses as viewed from employees.
- New ideas resulting from the survey could lead to better development and training programs.
- These surveys boost employee engagement and two-way communications.

There are also some disadvantages an organization should consider before implementing an employee attitude survey:

- Surveys set the expectation that an employer will act upon its employees' responses. If the employer just wants to know employee thoughts and does not plan to implement changes or communicate rationales, then employee morale could drop.
- It could be time consuming to design, implement, evaluate, and execute changes based on the survey.
- Completing a survey could be thought of as an annoyance and employees may choose not to participate, resulting in a low response rate that may not be worth the effort.
- Employees may not give undivided attention to the survey and perhaps concentrate only on areas they view negatively, which could be misleading for employers.

## PULSE SURVEY

A **pulse survey** is different from an employee attitude survey in that it is shorter in format, can measure anything, and can be administered more frequently. Hence, it gives an organization the ability to assess any specific topic on a more frequent basis. Pulse surveys can vary greatly and frequently track the same topic or item over time. These short, usually easier-to-administer surveys also enable an organization to evaluate and act upon the information quickly. Therefore, there is sentiment among employees that the organization is listening to them more and genuinely trying to implement changes that mutually benefit the employees and the organization. As a result, employees feel valued. Some of the topics or items a pulse survey might measure include effectiveness of business metrics, effectiveness of specific employer initiatives, and training effectiveness. A pulse survey is nimble and its flexibility allows an organization to measure the effectiveness of a specific issue over time, allowing the organization to shift course if needed. Pulse survey results are sometimes viewed as a monitoring tool.

Copyright © Mometrix Media. You have been licensed one copy of this document for personal use only. Any other reproduction or redistribution is strictly prohibited. All rights reserved.

## FOCUS GROUPS

Focus groups can be used to glean employee views and concerns. They may be used to assess a new benefit plan or organizational change. Most focus groups contain five to 12 voluntary participants, with three to 10 groups in total. Participants should be informed about the subject of the focus group, about who will benefit, and that the information will be kept confidential. Participants may be selected at random or through the use of certain applicable filters. Focus group organizers should ensure that power differentials within the group are avoided. It is also important to involve participants from various levels of staff so they can fully represent the affected population. A neutral facilitator should be chosen to lead the discussion and ask open-ended, guided questions. Following the meeting, collected data should be analyzed and reported.

## EMPLOYEE FOCUS GROUPS

Focus groups can be used to investigate ideas, opinions, and concerns. Focus groups can be beneficial for clarifying supplemental research because they are relatively timely and inexpensive. The topic and objectives of the group should be clearly defined before potential participants are identified. Participants should be notified that their identities will be anonymous and that all information will be confidential. Once a pool of participants has been selected and separated into groups, a trained facilitator should be chosen and a guide of discussion questions should be constructed. Most studies will contain three to 10 focus groups, each with five to 12 voluntary participants. A private location is ideal, and many discussions will last approximately 90 minutes. Finally, all collected information will be analyzed and reported.

## SUGGESTION BOXES

A suggestion box is a place, either physical or virtual, where employees can give their anonymous opinions about anything in the work environment, working conditions, or ways to improve efficiencies or profitability. A suggestion box is a tool to help employees feel more engaged and involved, as well as to assist the organization become a better place to work. A suggestion box improves communication, increases innovative thinking to help solve organizational problems, and could improve employee morale. If the organization is using a physical box, then the box should be placed in a location where all employees have access. A physical box should also be locked shut, with access limited only to those with keys. If a virtual box is being used, then IT needs to ensure suggestions are truly anonymous. Before implementing a suggestion box, an employer should be prepared to take it seriously by being welcoming of suggestions and eager to read and act upon them. A program, including guidelines, should be developed to administer and promote the suggestion box. Additionally, incentives could be offered for participating. Employers should read suggestions on a regular basis and be sure to thank employees for their input.

## STAY INTERVIEWS

A **stay interview** is a discussion between a manager and an employee with the goal of the employer ascertaining why a valued employee continues to work for the organization and if there is anything the employer can do to make improvements. The goal is to retain top talent and have a better understanding of what the organization is doing poorly, as well as learn what the organization is doing well. While employee satisfaction and engagement can be measured in an attitude survey, a stay interview allows for an immediate two-way conversation, enabling the employer to ask follow-up questions. Generally, stay interviews are conducted by employers once or twice during the onboarding process, typically over a six-month period; and then annually, usually six months apart

Copyright © Mometrix Media. You have been licensed one copy of this document for personal use only. Any other reproduction or redistribution is strictly prohibited. All rights reserved.

from an employee's annual performance appraisal. Following are some questions an employer might ask during the approximately 30-minute stay interview:

- What do you enjoy about working here?
- What are a few things you look forward to every day?
- What can we do to make your job more satisfying?
- Do you feel valued and utilized in your current position?

## EXIT INTERVIEWS

Exit interviews are opportunities for organizations to gather honest feedback as to why an employee is choosing to leave the organization. Exit interviews are almost always encouraged because they yield information that may help the organization improve and retain employees in the future. In most organizations, a member of the human resources team, acting as an impartial and neutral party (and not as the employee's direct supervisor), conducts the exit interview to put the employee at ease. Following are ways to make an exit interview as productive as possible:

- Try to make the employee feel comfortable. Remind them their input is extremely valuable and thank them for their time and expertise.
- Ask open-ended questions and repeat responses to ensure understanding. Yes-or-no questions should be avoided, and notes should be taken about what the employee said and did not say.
- The most important question to ask is why the employee started to look for another job.

Typically, HR analyzes and summarizes the information obtained from an exit interview and shares the information with the organization's leadership team to examine areas for improvement.

# Workplace Behavior Issues

## ETHICAL AGENTS

**Ethics** are the moral principles, values, and accepted standards of behavior that determine whether an action is right or wrong. The Society for Human Resource Management (SHRM) Competency Model defines ethical practice as "the knowledge, skills, abilities, and other characteristics needed to maintain high levels of personal and professional integrity and to act as an ethical agent who promotes core values, integrity, and accountability throughout the organization."

Ethics and compliance officers ensure that business is conducted in accordance with rules, legal regulations, and industry standards of practice. Additionally, an ethical agent makes moral judgments based on fundamental ethical principles that are rooted in their personal character, not based on a situation's potential gains. Ethical dilemmas occur when a corporation or individual is faced with a conflict of interest or actions that are blatantly wrong, deceptive, or may have uncertain consequences. Many ethical conflicts value profit over moral principles. Over the past few decades, ethics and business conduct have received increasing attention that has led to more stringent compliance regulations, like the Sarbanes-Oxley Act.

## CODE OF CONDUCT

A **code of conduct** is a set of behavioral rules rooted in moral standards, laws, and best practices that a company develops, adopts, and communicates to employees. It outlines expected behavior and defines what behavior will not be tolerated. The document should also state what disciplinary actions employees could face if they violate the code.

Copyright © Mometrix Media. You have been licensed one copy of this document for personal use only. Any other reproduction or redistribution is strictly prohibited. All rights reserved.

Employee involvement in the development of a code of conduct will lead to greater employee buy-in and adherence. The code should be written in ambiguous language that can be applied to specific situations as they arise. Upon finalization, the code should be shared with all employees. Employees should then be required to sign a document acknowledging receipt and understanding of the new code.

> **Review Video: Ethical and Professional Standards**
> Visit mometrix.com/academy and enter code: 391843

## ABSENTEEISM

**Absenteeism** is when employees do not arrive at work when scheduled. **Tardiness**, a form of absenteeism, occurs when an employee arrives late for work. Absenteeism and tardiness both negatively impact an organization's productivity, financial performance, and administrative cost to operate. Taking pre-approved time off for personal reasons or vacation is a benefit, and time for an employee to "recharge" away from work is beneficial. Additionally, the organization's management team knew in advance and could plan accordingly. Time off for illness cannot usually be predicted and is generally encouraged in order to not make an entire office sick. Plus, there are many legal protections afforded an employee for illness-related absences. Absenteeism is usually regarded as habitual time off for either legitimate or illegitimate reasons. Employers can develop policies for absenteeism that might involve improving communications about their excusable and inexcusable absences, one-on-one discussions with the employee, and recognition programs to reward good attendance. However, an employer should be careful when disciplining an employee for excessive absenteeism to ensure the discipline is not in violation with federal, state, or local laws and regulations, such as USERRA for military leave, occurrences covered under the Family Medical Leave Act (FMLA) and other protected activities depending on state laws (voting, children's activities, medical).

## AGGRESSIVE BEHAVIOR IN THE WORKPLACE

Aggressive behavior in the workplace is typically a response to stress that should be recognized and handled immediately before it causes more harm. Aggression and violence could be displayed in any number of ways, such as physical assault, intimidation, threats, stalking, property damage, verbal and written abuse, and much more. It can also occur between employees, employee to customer, employee and a family member, an outsider with ideological differences than the business, etc. The U.S. Department of Labor maintains that some people work in and around circumstances that present a greater danger of violence than others: people who handle cash, work in high-crime areas, or deliver services or goods. There are many triggers for aggression to occur—money issues, job loss, demotion, personal loss, holidays, etc. Sometimes, there is nothing an employer can do to prevent aggression or violence, like a terrorist incident. Other times, there are warning signs that an employee might become aggressive at work: unexplained drastic changes in behavior, absenteeism, performance decline, chatter about unfair treatment, overly emotional reaction to situations, expressions of paranoia, etc. The goal is to recognize the signs and address them, usually with a zero-tolerance policy for aggressive or violent behavior. Following are some options for organizations addressing aggressive behavior:

- Educate employees about safety and zero tolerance for violence, including resources such as an HR contact, company security group, and key phone numbers or websites for help. Tell employees not to do anything or go anywhere they feel unsafe.
- Maintain vigilant security at the work site—surveillance cameras, identification tags, electronic entry, etc.
- Conduct training programs or resources to de-stress.

Copyright © Mometrix Media. You have been licensed one copy of this document for personal use only. Any other reproduction or redistribution is strictly prohibited. All rights reserved.

There is not a specific remedy if aggressive behavior is observed because it is dependent on a number of factors. Nevertheless, when encountering aggressive behavior, try to stay calm and de-escalate if possible, and never hesitate to call the police for assistance.

## DEALING WITH EMPLOYEE CONFLICT

Employee conflict, or disagreement among employees, will occur. Not all conflict is unproductive. Many times, employee disagreement or conflict that occurs in a constructive, respectful manner leads to innovation, increased creativity, and ultimately improvements. However, there are times when just the opposite occurs and employee conflict is a negative experience for all involved. Following are some strategies for an organization to address negative employee conflict:

- Ask questions and gain a complete understanding of the problem. First, evaluate if the conflict involves any EEOC violations such as discrimination or harassment. Assuming no EEOC violations, gain an understanding as to the root cause of the problem, not the fallout. Depending on the situation, encourage employees to work it out on their own, if possible. This is a judgment call.
- If intervention becomes necessary to prevent escalation, do so immediately. Listen to both sides, ask questions, and restate issues for clarification. Make sure both parties understand they must let each other speak uninterrupted and address each other with respect. Encourage both parties to devise a way to manage going forward, and assist in devising a written plan that both agree to follow. Reference the employee handbook for behavioral expectations.
- Offer training or personality assessments to help conflicted employees improve their communication style and encourage managers to lead by example.

## INSUBORDINATION

**Insubordination** is when an employee overtly refuses to do or comply with a reasonable work request from their manager. The manager's request must meet two basic criteria: (1) the employee must thoroughly understand the request, and (2) the request cannot be dangerous or unethical. Claims of insubordination must be thoroughly investigated by human resources from a position of neutrality, and a conclusion must be drawn as to why the employee is refusing to complete the assignment. The incident should be documented. If this is a one-time occurrence that is unlikely to happen again, then a discussion of ways to behave going forward is appropriate. However, if insubordination becomes a pattern, then disciplinary action should be followed—possibly a verbal warning, written warning, suspension, or a combination of other similar alternatives. Termination is even possible if no other remediation helps to rectify the situation. Insubordination should always be thoroughly investigated, documented, and addressed immediately and appropriately before it leads to a decline in productivity, possible employee turnover, or a hostile work environment.

## ILLEGAL HARASSMENT

**Illegal harassment** usually involves unwelcome verbal exchanges, unwelcome physical contact, or unwelcome actions that are based on a person's race, religion, gender, sexual orientation, national origin, age, disability, genetic information, military membership, or veteran status. The action(s) taken must meet the threshold of a "severe and pervasive" work environment, characterized as hostile, abusive, or intimidating for "a reasonable person." If this type of harassment is present, it could be a violation of the following federal regulations: Title VII of the Civil Rights Act of 1964, the Americans with Disabilities Act (ADA), the Age Discrimination in Employment Act (ADEA), the Genetic Information Nondiscrimination Act (GINA), or the Uniformed Services Employment and Re-employment Rights Act (USERRA). Additionally, many states and local laws provide even more

Copyright © Mometrix Media. You have been licensed one copy of this document for personal use only. Any other reproduction or redistribution is strictly prohibited. All rights reserved.

enhanced legal protections against harassment. Harassment interferes with an employee's ability to accomplish their work. All allegations of harassment should be reported, investigated immediately, and acted upon appropriately by the employer.

## CONDUCTING HARASSMENT TRAINING

Companies should complete regular harassment training because employers must exercise reasonable care to avoid and prevent harassment. It should be noted that several states have mandatory harassment training for certain types of employees. Otherwise, employers may be found liable for the harassing behaviors of vendors, clients, coworkers, and supervisors. **Harassment** is defined as any demeaning or degrading comments, jokes, name-calling, actions, graffiti, or other belittling conduct that may be found offensive. Any form of derogatory speech can be considered harassment, including neutral words that may be perceived in a vulgar or intimidating way. Furthermore, the Civil Rights Act of 1964 protects individuals from harassment on the basis of race, color, religion, gender, or national origin. More importantly, damages awarded under Title VII can total anywhere from $50,000 to $300,000, depending upon the size of the employer.

## BULLYING IN THE WORKPLACE

**Bullying** is a form of aggressive behavior in the workplace that includes numerous forms of mistreatment in order for the bully to assert control and attack another person's self-confidence and/or self-esteem. Bullying can be overt, such as yelling, obscene language, and public humiliation. However, bullying can also be much more subtle, such as failing to invite a targeted employee to an essential meeting, withholding needed resources, sabotage, micromanagement, and inequitable treatment. In either case, while bullying is obviously detrimental to the victim, it may also damage the business by harming productivity and/or incurring legal costs. Many organizations have modified their harassment policies to specifically address bullying. Changing the policy needs to be combined with an awareness campaign so that employees understand what bullying is, what its consequences are, and how to report it. There should be a process for reporting claims of bullying so that the victim feels comfortable—such as a contact in human resources. All reported bullying incidents should be investigated immediately and, if necessary, met with action. Also, Title VII of the Civil Rights Act of 1964 and EEOC could offer protections against harassment in the form of bullying, depending on the circumstances and investigative findings.

# Methods for Investigating Complaints or Grievances

## INVESTIGATING EMPLOYEE MISCONDUCT

The investigation process usually begins when a complaint is received or if it is determined there is reasonable cause to investigate an employee's conduct. The organization should identify exactly what is being investigated, what sort of evidence is needed to prove or disprove the misconduct, who should be interviewed during the investigation, and which questions need to be asked to gather the necessary evidence. Next, the organization needs to interview the person making the complaint, the individual the complaint is against, and any other employees who have relevant information. Finally, the organization should come to a decision and take appropriate action.

## WEINGARTEN RIGHTS

In *National Labor Relations Board v. Weingarten*, the Supreme Court established the right of employees to have union representation at investigatory interviews in which the employee must defend conduct or behavior. If an employee believes that discipline or other consequences might follow, he or she has the right to request union representation. However, management does not need to inform an employee of their Weingarten rights. It is the employee's own responsibility to

Copyright © Mometrix Media. You have been licensed one copy of this document for personal use only. Any other reproduction or redistribution is strictly prohibited. All rights reserved.

know and request representation. When requested, management can (1) stop questioning until a representative arrives, (2) terminate the interview, or (3) ask the employee to voluntarily relinquish their rights to representation. The company does need to inform the representative of the interview subject, and the representative does have the right to counsel the employee in private and advise them what to say.

## GRIEVANCES

A **grievance** is a work-related complaint or formal dispute that is brought to the attention of management. However, in nonunion environments, grievances may encompass any discontent or sense of injustice. Grievance procedures provide an orderly and methodical process for hearing and evaluating employee complaints and tend to be more developed in unionized companies than in nonunionized companies as a result of labor agreement specifications. These procedures protect employee rights and eliminate the need for strikes or slowdowns every time there is a disagreement.

Disagreements may be unavoidable in situations where the labor contract is open to interpretation because negotiators cannot anticipate all potential conflicts. Formal grievance procedures increase upward communication in organizations and make top management decisions more sensitive to employee emotions. The first step to resolving grievances is for a complaint to be submitted to the supervisor or written and submitted to the union steward.

If these parties cannot find a resolution from there, the complaint may be heard by the superintendent or plant manager and the industrial relations manager. If the union is still unsatisfied, the grievance can be appealed to the next step, which may be arbitration if the company is small. Large corporations may have grievance committees, corporate officers, and/or international union representatives who will meet and hear grievances. However, the final step of an unresolved dispute will be binding arbitration by an outside third party, where both parties come to an acceptable agreement.

## RESOLVING DISCRIMINATION COMPLAINTS

Resolving discrimination complaints requires an employer to decide between two different paths:

1. An employer can follow the process defined by the Equal Employment Opportunity Commission (EEOC) and thus be subject to further investigation by the state or local Fair Employment Practice Agency (FEPA). An employee has 180 days from the date of the incident to file a discrimination complaint with the EEOC. After an investigation, probable cause will or will not be found and the process can go one of two ways:
   a. Probable cause found – The EEOC will try conciliation and the employer can agree to settle, or litigation could be pursued with the EEOC or private court.
   b. Probable cause not found – After the 180-day period is over, the employee can ask for a right-to-sue letter and then has 90 days to file in court. At this point, the EEOC's involvement with the matter ends.
2. An employer can make the decision to settle the alleged charges instead of facing an investigation by FEPA.

An employer must contemplate a number of issues before deciding which path is best. Typically, employers will weigh the costs involved in a one-time settlement versus a possibly extended period of legal disruption that could cost both time and money. An open investigation could harm a company's reputation whether the allegations are true or not. Also, if a company believes the claim

Copyright © Mometrix Media. You have been licensed one copy of this document for personal use only. Any other reproduction or redistribution is strictly prohibited. All rights reserved.

of discrimination might be truthful, the one-time settlement might make sense in order to quickly pivot, address, and rectify any possible systemic discriminatory practices within the company.

## FRONT PAY

When an employer is found guilty of discrimination, the employee who brought forth the complaint is usually permitted to return to their position in the organization. However, the court will sometimes instead rule for front pay. **Front pay** is money awarded to the employee from the employer in a discrimination situation. Generally, the amount awarded is equal to lost wages. There are three situations whereby front pay is required for the employer:

1. The position left vacant by the employee discriminated against is no longer available.
2. The employer has taken no action to rectify the discriminatory practice(s) occurring within the organization.
3. The returning employee could be facing an unreasonable, possibly hostile work environment if he or she were to return to the prior position.

## MEDIATION PROCESS

The goal of the **mediation process** is to solve a dispute without having to take more aggressive legal steps. A mediator is specially trained to work with two or more disagreeing parties to reach an agreeable resolution. It should be noted that there is a difference between mediation and arbitration. Arbitration can be the final judgment for a dispute, meaning that if mediation doesn't work, the parties involved can move to arbitration or litigation. Mediation is considered non-binding.

Typically, both parties must mutually agree on a mediator to start the process. A mediator speaks with both parties and there are agreed-upon ground rules, such as logistics, when the negotiation will occur, what specifically will be discussed, who should be involved, and protocol or procedures for discussion. During the agreed-upon negotiations, the mediator will work with both parties to problem solve and create a reasonable solution to move forward. Frequently, this requires compromise on both sides. If a resolution or compromise is agreed upon, both parties must sign documentation stating they will abide by the agreed-upon plan. If a resolution is not reached during the mediation process, then the parties can either pursue arbitration or litigation to resolve the dispute.

## TYPES OF ARBITRATION

**Arbitration** is a formal way to settle disputes outside of court. Frequently, parties in a dispute try arbitration if mediation does not work. Parties must agree on a neutral, third-party arbitrator, who listens and makes decisions based on the information and facts presented during the questioning and subsequent discussions. There are many types of arbitration:

- **Binding** arbitration – During this type of arbitration, both parties are required to abide by the final judgment. In other words, the party that "loses" the arbitration must carry out the final judgment. Also, it is important to note that, in binding arbitration, this is the end of the legal process: both parties have no other legal recourse with regard to the dispute after a decision is rendered in binding arbitration.
- **Non-binding** arbitration – This type follows the same process as binding arbitration, except the decision rendered does not have to be followed and cannot legally be enforced. Additionally, if either party chooses, they can pursue further legal action.

Copyright © Mometrix Media. You have been licensed one copy of this document for personal use only. Any other reproduction or redistribution is strictly prohibited. All rights reserved.

- **Compulsory** arbitration – In this situation, both parties are required by law to enter into the arbitration process. Generally, this occurs due to one of two reasons: (1) a court order dictated that compulsory arbitration is mandatory, or (2) an agreed-upon contract could state that disputes require compulsory arbitration to be resolved.
- **Voluntary** arbitration – The parties in dispute mutually agree to willingly participate in the arbitration process in the hopes of avoiding potentially expensive and time-consuming legal alternatives.

## TYPES OF ARBITRATORS

There are three different types of arbitrators that could lead the resolution of a dispute. Which type of arbitrator an organization chooses is dependent on the circumstances and previously agreed-upon contracts, if applicable.

- **Permanent** arbitrator – This type of arbitrator usually judges cases for a particular organization or during the life of a contract. In either case, the arbitrator has intimate knowledge of the organization and material being discussed. This knowledge makes arbitration highly efficient, but it is important that both parties continue to believe the arbitrator is unbiased.
- **Ad-hoc** arbitrator – In this situation, an arbitrator is mutually agreed upon by both parties, but the arbitrator does not have a previously established relationship with either party. Usually, an ad-hoc arbitrator is chosen in random, one-time situations.
- Arbitrator **panel** – This group of arbitrators, usually three, are similar to ad-hoc arbitrators in that they do not have a previously established relationship with the parties involved. This type of panel is sometimes referred to as an arbitral tribunal or a tripartite panel. In the case of a tripartite arbitration panel, the representation is as follows: one arbitrator represents the management, one arbitrator represents the union, and one is neutral. In most cases, the neutral arbitrator is the one who makes the deciding vote.

# Progressive Discipline

## POLICIES, PROCEDURES, AND WORK RULES

The goal of an organization's policies, procedures, and work rules is to help an organization achieve its goals in an equitable and efficient manner. However, there is a difference between the three terms:

- **Policy** – An overarching or broad statement describing the company's basic philosophy and standards for all related management and employee activities. For example, a company might have a policy stating the company will "reimburse for educational tuition if the course is related to work the employee performs. All coursework must be pre-approved by the management team." This is a broad statement that explains the policy for tuition reimbursement, but doesn't give specifics—it only states that there is an educational reimbursement policy.
- **Procedure** – This specifies very specific steps or methods to process or handle employee activities. For example, if an employee wants reimbursement for taking a course, they might have to follow these steps: (1) Meet with immediate supervisor to discuss, (2) obtain form XYZ and have it signed by the supervisor with several supporting attachments, (3) supervisor must obtain approvals from certain department heads, etc.

Copyright © Mometrix Media. You have been licensed one copy of this document for personal use only. Any other reproduction or redistribution is strictly prohibited. All rights reserved.

- **Work rule** – These rules stand as a guide for clear action to be taken or not taken in a specific situation. These rules are usually black and white, designed to leave no room for ambiguity or interpretation. For example, "Educational reimbursement will be granted only if an employee takes a class at a college accredited by the following institutions ..."

## DELIVERING DISCIPLINARY ACTION

Disciplinary actions, whether part of a union contract or not, should always be fair to all. Therefore, employees should have a process or the ability to defend their actions against any accusation of wrongdoing. In other words, employees should be given the opportunity to present their side of the story in their words. An employer should be consistent in delivering discipline, meaning similar treatment to what others have received for equivalent offenses. A manager should always be able to produce strong, preferably documented evidence of an employee's wrongdoing. Keep in mind that disciplinary actions are rarely straightforward, and usually are complicated with other factors that must be taken into consideration. HR usually reviews disciplinary actions before they are implemented, trying to mitigate risk for the company. Following are some considerations HR should examine: any EEO violations; consistency in treatment; potential tort or other legal liabilities; compliance with union contracts (if applicable); and always complying with federal, state, and local laws and regulations.

## WARNING IN A PROGRESSIVE DISCIPLINE PROCESS

A **warning** is usually a clear indication that a supervisor or the management team is dissatisfied with an employee's work or attitude. A warning is typically the first step in a progressive discipline process, with the goal being to correct the undesired action(s). A warning can be either verbal or in writing. Following are the differences:

- **Verbal** – A verbal warning could be informal and more of a discussion with the employee about their undesired actions and what should be done to improve. It is important the employee leave the conversation with a clear understanding of the corrective action that must be taken, and what could happen next if the action is not corrected.
- **Written** – A written warning is similar in tone to a verbal warning, except the manager delivers a document or letter detailing the issue with an employee's actions and/or attitude, and clear expectations about what specifically needs to be corrected. A written warning will also document possible consequences if the issue in question is not corrected.

## ESCALATING CORRECTIVE ACTIONS

**Escalating corrective actions** are measures taken by an employer, usually a manager, to fix a problem or wrongdoing that an employee is continually repeating even after initial interventions are taken, such as a verbal and/or written warning. It should be noted that an employee issue can be behavioral or any other aspect of their work that impacts performance. When initial interventions with the employee do not produce the desired results, then escalating corrective actions need to be taken. Employers may document these specific measures in their employee handbook, or they can be unique and consequences may need to be altered slightly. Also, in the case of a union environment, there may be very specific disciplinary actions that contractually must be adhered to because they are specified in the collective bargaining agreement. Escalating corrective actions is a logical sequence of discipline that could include required training, suspensions with or without pay, demotions, and sometimes termination. Following is an example of escalating corrective actions:

1. Verbal warning
2. Written warning

Copyright © Mometrix Media. You have been licensed one copy of this document for personal use only. Any other reproduction or redistribution is strictly prohibited. All rights reserved.

3. Mandatory training (if applicable)
4. One-day suspension
5. One-week suspension
6. Two-week suspension
7. Termination

Every step needs to be documented: what was incorrect or unacceptable, the expected behavior or performance measure going forward, the discipline being dispensed, and consequences if the corrective actions are not taken.

## TERMINATION IN THE PROGRESSIVE DISCIPLINE PROCESS

**Termination** is when an employee is removed from their job. It is oftentimes described as a separation from employment. Involuntary terminations can result from the employee's failure to abide by the progressive discipline plan due to poor performance and/or behavior, or could be a policy violation. Usually, it is preferable for an employee to know well in advance that continued actions which remain uncorrected could result in termination. Managers should ensure employees understand the gravity and consequences of failure to correct wrongdoing. If a decision is made to terminate an employee, it should be done swiftly and employers should take necessary measures to make sure managers understand departing employees must be treated with dignity and respect during the termination process. Typically, a private meeting is held between the manager, an HR representative, and the employee. The manager delivering the termination should get right to the point and be clear, yet remain sympathetic and patient. Additionally, at the termination meeting, the manager or HR representative should be prepared to discuss the employee's last paycheck and any other financial matters that need to be settled. Final pay and other financial matters are sometimes dictated by state law and regulations. As always, employers should adhere to all federal, state, and local laws and regulations when terminating an employee.

# Offboarding or Termination Activities

## CONSIDERATIONS OF TERMINATIONS

**Voluntary terminations** may be caused by a variety of reasons, such as new job opportunity, relocation, or personal obligations. **Involuntary terminations** most often occur as a result of employment problems, such as poor performance, excessive absenteeism, insubordination, or theft. Employers should have controls that require all terminations to be reviewed in advance to avoid the risk of legal or contract violations. The review should determine whether there are valid, job-related reasons for the termination. If the termination is due to a particular incident, the review should conclude that a proper investigation has been documented. Additional documentation should show that the employee was made aware of performance problems and had an opportunity to correct behaviors. Terminations should also be consistent with prior treatment of other employees. Finally, it is imperative to ensure that the employee is not a victim of retaliation of any civil rights violations.

## OFFBOARDING

The terms "onboarding" and "offboarding" are analogous to getting on and off a vessel for an ocean voyage. Employment is being compared to a journey on the ocean. The complexity of the voyage dictates the steps needed for the onboarding and offboarding processes. The same holds true for employment. Every organization wants the beginning and ending of employment to be a good experience. **Offboarding** is a process that includes all decisions and steps that need to be completed when an employee separates from an organization. Offboarding is also an opportunity to talk with an exiting employee about ways to improve the organization. It is important to remember

132

Copyright © Mometrix Media. You have been licensed one copy of this document for personal use only. Any other reproduction or redistribution is strictly prohibited. All rights reserved.

that, when an employee leaves an organization, he or she could be a loyal supporter of the organization, or they may speak negatively about the employer. Offboarding gives an employer one final opportunity to influence how the employee feels when they leave. A good offboarding process can help minimize the chance that potential ill feelings might linger. Offboarding leaves a lasting impression in the minds of employees separating from an employer.

### STEPS INCLUDED IN OFFBOARDING PROCESS

Employers' offboarding processes can differ depending on the organization and functions of a job. Following are some of the items that might be included in the offboarding process:

- Planning for the transfer of knowledge from the departing employee to their replacement (if appropriate)
- Reviewing final pay, benefits, and financial information including retirement options, unused vacation, health coverage, and COBRA (if applicable)
- Collecting all computer equipment, phone, and other technology-related items
- Collecting other employer-issued items, such as uniforms, credit card, and automobile
- Collecting physical keys and/or security badges
- Deactivating access to company intranet and other systems (email, databases, etc.), as well as related rights and passwords
- Verifying accurate contact information – mailing address, phone number, and email address
- Conducting an exit interview – Usually done by a human resources representative to understand the employee's viewpoint on their overall work experience and other concerns that will enable the organization to improve going forward

## WRONGFUL TERMINATION

**Wrongful termination** occurs when an employee is illegally terminated from employment or fired in such a way as to violate an agreed-upon contract or public policy. Laws can vary enormously from state to state on criteria for wrongful termination. Following are some more specific reasons for a wrongful termination: discrimination, the employer asked the employee to pursue an illegal act, breach of contract, whistleblowing violation of company policy, etc. There is not a specific law or regulation that specifically shields or protects an employee against wrongful termination; rather, it is usually other laws such as discrimination, whistleblower protections, public policy, or collective bargaining agreement laws. The majority of states recognize some form of at-will employment, meaning the employer does not need a reason to fire an employee, and an employee is permitted to leave employment without reason or notice. Just because an employer can fire an employee without reason does not mean that they should do so. However, the employer cannot terminate an employee in such a manner that breaks an existing law or violates the company's own policies.

# Employee Relations Programs

## RECOGNITION PROGRAMS

**Recognition programs** are an important part of the employee experience that enhance employee engagement and positively help shape company culture. Recognition should be tailored to the organization and its employees—there is not a one-size-fits-all plan. However, the goal of most recognition programs is to help make employees feel valued or appreciated and frequently serve as an incentive to strive towards. Recognition programs can reward any number of desirable attributes or events, such as going above and beyond, team effort, wellness objectives, innovation,

Copyright © Mometrix Media. You have been licensed one copy of this document for personal use only. Any other reproduction or redistribution is strictly prohibited. All rights reserved.

quality improvements, and career celebrations. Recognition rewards can vary, but may include the following:

- A heartfelt, verbal (or written) thank you
- A meal celebration
- A point-based system for employees to choose a reward
- Treats or candy
- Gift cards
- Unique experiences such as concerts, sporting events, shows, etc.

A recognition program provides an employer with the ability to create a workplace of choice where employees thrive. Recruitment and employee retention is positively influenced by an effective recognition program. Successful recognition has the following characteristics: recognition is genuine, all employees have an opportunity to give and receive recognition, the reward is done in a timely manner, it is specific, it is connected to the company's purpose, is presented in a public forum, etc. There are software programs and vendors that also can help an organization design and administer recognition programs.

## SPECIAL EVENTS

Company-sponsored special events can vary, but all serve as a way to leverage and promote employee engagement and build a positive company culture. Some special events can be recurring, such as holiday dinners, summer picnics, Friday social nights, or Tuesday tacos in the office. These events may be social outings with or without employee family members. However, they serve to build camaraderie among employee team members and give them opportunities to socialize with one another outside of the work environment. This may help build a stronger, more productive work team, as well as improve employee satisfaction. Events can also incorporate an element of community service, including serving food at a local food kitchen, volunteering at an animal shelter, or building homes for those in need. Some special events might also include wellness-related campaigns, company walking or running teams, weight loss or healthy eating initiatives, or yoga classes at lunch. Special events demonstrate that the employer cares about the employees' health and well-being.

## APPROACHES TO AN INCLUSIVE WORKPLACE

The first step toward establishing an inclusive workplace is to identify any areas of concern. An internal workforce should reflect the available labor market. Examine the corporate culture and communications to ensure that they advocate for a diverse and inclusive workplace. Review or amend policies and practices to support an inclusive culture. Focus on the behavioral aspects of how people communicate and work together. Are all perspectives respected and input from all positions valued? Address any areas that might not welcome protected classes or disabilities. Then brainstorm approaches and ideas for an inclusive workplace. Once a diverse culture is established, target recruiting efforts to reach a broad audience. Some ideas may include college recruiting, training centers, career fairs, veteran's offices, and state unemployment offices or career centers. Set business objectives for areas that can be improved upon, document what changes will be implemented, and review progress.

## DIVERSITY AND INCLUSION TRAINING

Although people most often think of diversity as the inclusiveness of minorities, diversity may also embrace a robust variety of traits such as generation, gender, sexual orientation, race, ethnicity, language, religious background, education, or life experiences. Diversity is the ability to consider and value the perspectives of all people. It is important for human resource practitioners to

Copyright © Mometrix Media. You have been licensed one copy of this document for personal use only. Any other reproduction or redistribution is strictly prohibited. All rights reserved.

recognize that everyone has both conscious and unconscious biases. **Diversity and inclusion training** supports establishing a nonjudgmental and collaborative workforce that is respectful and sensitive to differences among peers. Additionally, it can teach humility and self-awareness. Training program methods may be extensive or address specific gaps. Moreover, diversity and inclusion training may introduce new perspectives to the workforce, promoting creativity and innovation.

## ADVOCATING FOR A DIVERSE AND INCLUSIVE WORKPLACE

Diversity fosters the potential for more perspectives, creative ideas, and innovation. **Inclusion** involves realizing and accepting the benefits and competitive advantage to be had when everyone feels welcome and respected. This environment can be developed with openness, cultural sensitivity, and equal support. Human resource practitioners can advocate for a diverse and inclusive workplace by reflecting how it can align with business objectives. Building diverse teams can improve problem-solving and productivity and may increase customer satisfaction by providing better representation of an employer's stakeholders. Once buy-in has been gained from upper management, a diversity committee can collaborate to design and communicate initiatives.

## OPERATING IN A DIVERSE WORKPLACE

HR practitioners should identify if there are any areas of concern or need in the organization. Do current employees fairly represent the available talent pool? Human resources should work to address any unconscious biases or prevailing attitudes in policies or practices that do not support diversity initiatives. They can further support diversity by drawing attention to and eliminating discriminatory perspectives or prejudices. They should train managers on how to fairly and consistently conduct interviews and to supervise employees from various backgrounds. Moreover, providing appropriate accommodations to employees in need can increase safety, efficiency, and team morale.

# Workforce Reduction and Restructuring Terminology

## DOWNSIZING

**Downsizing**, sometimes referred to as "workforce reduction," is a strategically planned and necessary elimination of jobs in order to make an organization potentially more competitive and ideally more profitable. This process is intended to reduce operating costs for the purpose of maximizing production, which is intended to drive profitability in a positive direction. Downsizing can occur for any number of reasons, including possibly decreasing profits over a period of time, closure in parts or entire lines of the business, and acquisitions that might involve duplication of functions. Downsizing is not linked to employee performance and is usually regarded as a complex process due to all the factors that must be taken into consideration. Organizations need to identify exactly what downsizing will achieve, create reliable and legally defensible selection criteria, develop a plan for work redistribution (if applicable), and gauge how downsizing will impact the business in the short- and long-term. Typically, the process of downsizing negatively impacts both productivity and morale. Hence, the employer should communicate with employees throughout the process and keep the lines of two-way communication open in order to minimize disruption to the business.

## OPTIONS BEFORE IMPLEMENTING A DOWNSIZING PLAN

The decision to downsize is rarely an easy one. However, it is oftentimes a necessity for a business to stay viable. The negative effect of downsizing on a business culture and its brand in the

Copyright © Mometrix Media. You have been licensed one copy of this document for personal use only. Any other reproduction or redistribution is strictly prohibited. All rights reserved.

marketplace is challenging. Therefore, many businesses look for alternatives to downsizing before implementing a reduction in force. Some of these alternatives include the following:

- Implement an immediate **hiring freeze** and work with employees on work redistribution if needed.
- Reduce employees' hours.
- Create an **early retirement program**, whereby the company can offer eligible employees financial incentives to leave. Eligibility can be tied to years of service and/or age to incentivize the most senior employees to take early retirement.
- **Reduce pay** in order to avoid layoffs, although the employer must pay careful attention to legal regulations and consistency in implementation.
- Place employees on **furloughs** if the financial distress is temporary.
- Encourage employees to **voluntarily leave with incentives** that could include a generous severance package and/or outplacement services.

## REDUCTION IN FORCE (RIF)

Following are the steps for conducting a layoff or reduction in force (RIF):

1. Select employees for layoff using seniority, performance, job classification, location, or skill.
2. Ensure selected employees do not affect a protected class to avoid adverse or disparate impact.
3. Review compliance with federal and state WARN Act regulations, which require employers to provide 60 days' notice to affected employees while specifying whether the reduction in force is permanent or for a specified amount of time.
4. Review compliance with the Older Workers Benefit Protection Act that provides workers over the age of 40 the opportunity to review any severance agreements that require their waiver of discrimination claims. The act allows a consideration period of 21 days if only one older worker is being separated and 45 days when two or more older workers are being separated. They also must receive a revocation period of seven days after signing the agreement. Additionally, they must be informed of the positions and ages of the other employees affected by the layoffs so that they can assess whether or not they feel age discrimination has taken place.
5. Determine if severance packages, including salary continuation, vacation pay, employer-paid COBRA premiums, outplacement services, or counseling might be available to affected employees. Typically, employees laid off in a RIF will sign a document called a separation and general release, whereby the employee signing the document accepts a severance package and agrees to not sue or make any claims against a company. It is important to note that a company is never required to offer a severance package.
6. Be empathetic, have tissues, ensure that all required documentation is available to the employee, and review all information in detail when conducting meetings with employees.
7. Inform the current workforce by communicating sustainability concerns, methods used to determine who would be selected for the reduction in force, and commitment to meeting company goals and objectives to maintain morale and productivity.

## OUTPLACEMENT FIRMS

An **outplacement firm** is an external vendor that is contracted by an organization in the event the organization needs to reduce its workforce and lay off a large number of employees—sometimes referred to as a "reduction in force" (RIF). Outplacement firms, sometimes called career transition services, offer services to outgoing employees to cope with the loss of a job and assist in finding a new job. Usually, outplacement firms are contracted and paid for by the organization that is laying

Copyright © Mometrix Media. You have been licensed one copy of this document for personal use only. Any other reproduction or redistribution is strictly prohibited. All rights reserved.

off its employees. This service is typically part of an employee severance benefit and therefore offered at no cost to the exiting employee. Services provided by an outplacement firm can vary, but some of the most common offerings are career assessments, career coaching, job search programs, and resume and networking workshops. Depending on the options selected by the organization, services can be in-person, one-on-one, group and/or video appointments. The reason an organization may choose to utilize the services of an outplacement firm include it being the moral or conscientious and responsible thing to do, it may reduce the risk of litigation, and it protects the employer's reputation by assisting their displaced employees.

## MERGERS VS. ACQUISITIONS

Mergers and acquisitions are similar in many ways, as both terms refer to a type of structural change in which two organizations join together to form a single organization. However, it is important to realize that the two terms are not exactly the same, as each term actually refers to a different way in which an organization's structure changes. A **merger** refers to a situation in which two or more organizations agree to combine into a single organization because both organizations will benefit from the merger. An **acquisition**, on the other hand, refers to a situation in which an organization purchases enough of another organization's stock to take control of the organization's operations. This can actually be an important difference to keep in mind because all of the organizations involved in a merger must agree to the merger in order for the merger to take place, while the organizations involved in an acquisition do not necessarily need to agree to the acquisition in order for the acquisition to take place.

## DIVESTITURE

A **divestiture** is the opposite of an acquisition, whereby a company separates a portion of itself, usually a division or subsidiary, in a form of restructuring.

Companies that initiate a divestiture typically seek to remove a business line that is unrelated to its core operations or is simply a poor fit that requires inordinate management attention. A subsidiary that operates in an aging business with modest growth prospects may be sold or spun off in order to focus on more promising opportunities.

Alternatively, the divestment may be required by a regulatory authority, such as in compliance with an antitrust adjudication.

Copyright © Mometrix Media. You have been licensed one copy of this document for personal use only. Any other reproduction or redistribution is strictly prohibited. All rights reserved.

# Health, Safety, and Security

## Applicable Laws and Regulations Related to Workplace Health, Safety, Security, and Privacy

### OCCUPATIONAL SAFETY AND HEALTH ACT (OSHA)

The **Occupational Safety and Health Act** (OSHA), passed in 1970, created a national policy for health and safety in the workplace. In addition, an agency called the **Occupational Safety and Health Administration** was formed under the U.S. Department of Labor and is charged with administering and enforcing OSHA. This act basically requires employers to provide a safe work environment free of health hazards, and remain in compliance with OSHA safety standards. If an employer is in violation of any safety standard, they are required to fix it or face severe financial penalties as well as the possibility of being shut down. OSHA requires employers to provide relevant safety training to employees and display OSHA posters in common areas that explain employee safety rights. Accurate and specific records must be maintained and reported to the Occupational Safety and Health Administration if a workplace injury or illness occurs. OSHA also grants employees the right to a safe work environment and requires employers to be transparent in their communication about potential workplace hazards. If an employee reports a safety concern or possible violation to the Occupational Safety and Health Administration, the employer is not permitted to retaliate against the employee. In fact, employees can request an inspection and can meet privately with the OSHA inspector without fear of retaliation from the employer. If employees believe they are working in dangerous or life-threatening conditions, they have the right under this act to refuse to work. Following are a few of the most referenced OSHA standards and amendments: emergency exit procedures, occupational noise exposure, machine guarding, hazard communication, bloodborne pathogens, confined space entry, and personal protective equipment.

### DRUG-FREE WORKPLACE ACT

The Drug-Free Workplace Act of 1988 requires that government contractors make a good faith effort to ensure a drug-free workplace. Employers must prohibit illegal substances in the workplace and must create drug awareness trainings for employees. Any federal contractor with contracts of $100,000 or more, and all organizations that are federal grantees, must adhere to a set of mandates to show they maintain a drug-free work environment:

- Employers must develop a written policy prohibiting the production, distribution, use, or possession of any controlled substance by an employee while in the workplace.
- Employers are required to develop standards of enforcement, and all employees must receive a copy of the policy and understand the consequences of a violation.
- Employers need to implement drug awareness trainings to help employees understand the hazards and health risks of drug use.
- Although drug testing is not required, it is intended that employers have some type of screening in place.

### AMERICANS WITH DISABILITIES ACT (ADA)

The Americans with Disabilities Act (ADA) is a federal law that protects people with disabilities. One of the stipulations of the Act is to provide reasonable accommodations to individuals with physical or mental disabilities. Employers are encouraged to provide accommodations as long as they do not impose a financial burden or undue hardship on the organization. For example, ramps may be needed for an employee to safely enter and exit the building and move freely within the

Copyright © Mometrix Media. You have been licensed one copy of this document for personal use only. Any other reproduction or redistribution is strictly prohibited. All rights reserved.

building. The ADA requires that all public buildings be accessible for disabled persons. Employers should keep in mind the ADA provides protections for mental and physical medical conditions, and could include an employee who is temporarily disabled. In the case of a temporary disability, the employer must still consider if the employee can safely perform their job with accommodations or consider if it would be safer to temporarily reassign the employee to a different job. Also, the courts have recently recognized certain infectious diseases as a disability under the ADA.

## INTERSECTION OF HIPAA WITH WORKPLACE SAFETY AND PRIVACY

The **Health Insurance Portability and Accountability Act** (HIPAA), passed in 1996, specifies regulations an employer must comply with to protect the health and medical records of employees registered in an employer-sponsored healthcare plan. These regulations dictate how protected healthcare information (PHI), maintained by a designated employee-sponsored healthcare plan, can be shared with employers. Safety and HIPAA regulations intersect if OSHA must collect health information that is otherwise protected healthcare information under HIPAA. The **HIPAA Privacy Rule** states that covered entities such as healthcare providers and plans must protect health and medical records and may not disclose health information unless the individual provides written authorization for the release of those records. Most employers are not covered healthcare providers, and as such do not have to comply with the HIPAA Privacy Rule for health disclosures. Therefore, an employer that must comply with OSHA recordkeeping can disclose private healthcare information for public health activities. These activities under OSHA reporting could include government-required recording and reporting of workplace injuries or illnesses.

## SARBANES-OXLEY ACT (SOX)

The **Sarbanes-Oxley Act** (SOX) was passed in 2002 to provide accountability, standards, and oversight to prevent corporate fraud. The act was largely in response to major corporate accounting scandals in the early 21st century like WorldCom and Enron. In turn, the passage of SOX created the **Public Company Accounting Oversight Board** (PCAOB) as an oversight agency for the accounting industry. However, the Securities and Exchange Commission (SEC) enforces compliance with SOX. SOX holds senior executives responsible for any accounting misconduct or manipulation. Additionally, the law protects shareholders from any activity that might mislead or influence investors about the company's financial health and outlook. Under SOX, a public corporation is required to accurately report financial information both to investors and the SEC. If the information reported to the SEC is later found inaccurate or altered in any form, there are large financial penalties and stringent white-collar crime consequences. Additionally, SOX offers protection to whistleblowers who report fraud and could potentially testify against their employer.

# Risk Mitigation in the Workplace

## RISK MANAGEMENT

**Risk management** is a methodical approach an organization engages in to identify, target, and initiate steps to minimize threats that could negatively impact an organization's health, safety, security, and privacy. While employers must abide by all federal, state, and local laws and regulations, they also have an obligation to protect employees from risks that could seriously harm the company, negatively impact morale, or create a financial burden. A **cost-benefit analysis**, or observing the potential cost of an endeavor against the benefit it will bring, is one of the methods an organization can utilize to evaluate risk. This type of evaluation relies on predicting the future based on available current information. Hence, there is an element of uncertainty with cost-benefit analysis that forces an organization to carefully examine all options and possible outcomes. Additionally, there are always unknowns in a situation, such as new obstacles or threats.

Copyright © Mometrix Media. You have been licensed one copy of this document for personal use only. Any other reproduction or redistribution is strictly prohibited. All rights reserved.

Accordingly, there is a method to evaluate these risks called **enterprise risk management**. This methodology forces an organization to factor in those risks that have the likelihood of occurring, or whose impact is the most drastic. This allows organizations to strategically plan for worst case scenarios and the possibility of perceived risks becoming realities.

## EMERGENCY ACTION PLANS

All emergency action plans should explain the alarm system that will be used to inform employees and other individuals at the worksite that they need to evacuate. They should also include in-depth exit route plans that describe which routes employees should take to escape the building, as well as in-depth plans that describe what actions employees should take before evacuating, such as shutting down equipment, closing doors, etc. All emergency action plans should also include detailed systems for handling different types of emergencies and a system that can be used to verify that all employees have escaped the worksite.

## PREPARING FOR EMERGENCIES AND NATURAL DISASTERS

Because it is an employer's obligation to provide a safe and healthy work environment, many companies have begun to create **emergency and disaster plans** for handling situations such as fires, explosions, earthquakes, chemical spills, communicable disease outbreaks, and acts of terrorism. These plans should include the following steps:

1. Clarify the **chain of command**, and inform staff who to contact and who has authority.
2. Someone should be responsible for **accounting** for all employees when an emergency occurs.
3. A **command center** should be set up to coordinate communications.
4. Employees should be **trained annually** on what to do if an emergency occurs.
5. Businesses should have **first-aid kits and basic medical supplies** available. This includes water fountains and eye wash stations in areas where spills may occur.
6. An **emergency team of employees** should be named and trained for the following:
   a. Organizing evacuation procedures
   b. Initiating shutdown procedures
   c. Using fire extinguishers
   d. Using oxygen and respirators
   e. Searching for disabled or missing employees
   f. Assessing when it is safe to re-enter the building

## CHARACTERISTICS OF EFFECTIVE SAFETY AND HEALTH MANAGEMENT PLANS

According to the Occupational Safety and Health Administration (OSHA), there are four characteristics a safety and health management plan should have to be considered effective. First, an effective plan should establish a **specific system** that an organization can use to identify hazards in the workplace. Second, the plan should establish a **training program** that teaches employees to avoid hazards and perform tasks in the safest way possible. Third, an effective safety and health management plan should include **specific procedures and programs** designed to eliminate hazards that the organization identifies or, at least, minimize the risk that a hazard will injure or kill an employee or cause an employee to become ill. Finally, it should allow employees at all levels of the organization to be **involved in the identification, prevention, and elimination** of hazards in the workplace.

## WORKPLACE VIOLENCE

Workplace violence can be a physical act against someone or it can be verbal abuse, threats, and intimidation. No matter what type, workplace violence is disturbing and dangerous, regardless of

Copyright © Mometrix Media. You have been licensed one copy of this document for personal use only. Any other reproduction or redistribution is strictly prohibited. All rights reserved.

whether it is physical or psychological. There are numerous reasons why an employee may exhibit violent behavior and could include a history of family abuse, drug or substance abuse, mental illness, etc. Workplace violence not only causes harm to the victim, but could also cause financial harm to a business, with damage to reputation possibly resulting in loss of clients, suppliers, or advertisers. Sometimes workplace violence is random and difficult to predict and prevent. However, there are steps an employer can take to reduce the chances of workplace violence:

- Establish a zero-tolerance policy against workplace violence that is documented and communicated to employees.
- Provide access to an employee assistance program (EAP) whereby employees can speak to a mental health counselor for referrals and appropriate treatment.
- Have only alcohol-free company events, possibly reducing the chances of workplace violence.
- Incorporate a violence prevention program into onboarding safety training.

# Security Risks in the Workplace

## BASIC SECURITY CONCERNS

Employers have an obligation and a responsibility to keep employees and the work environment safe, and should have a security plan in place to help achieve that goal. This includes every contingency from a bad crisis to an uninvited visitor. A well-conceived security plan can reduce panic and enable employees to calmly respond to different types of crises. A security plan can include any or all of the following: photo badges, keycard access systems, locks on rooms and closets, alarm system with back up, concealed alarms, visible and hidden cameras, exterior fencing and gates, exterior lighting, security guards, etc. Typically, security plans are designed with key management team members, including human resources, to ensure the plan is comprehensive. Additionally, the security plan should highlight specific roles and backups in the event of a security breach. Having a security plan also helps to prevent panic in the event of a workplace emergency. Organizations should periodically review and practice planned drills to reinforce preparedness.

## DISASTER RECOVERY PLAN

Certain information should be included in every organization's disaster recovery plan. Equipment and locations that can be utilized temporarily in the event of an emergency should be identified. Also, agencies and personnel that may be able to help the organization continue functioning immediately after an emergency should be identified. It is also wise to establish a set of procedures the organization can use to bring the personnel and equipment together after an emergency. Disaster recovery plans should also identify alternative sources the organization can use to receive supplies or products if the emergency disables the organization's normal supply chain.

## INFORMATION TECHNOLOGY (IT) SECURITY

IT security is becoming a more serious topic and rapidly gaining more attention. It is important for human resource practitioners to be conscientious of controls to mitigate organizational exposure and risk. Some companies may have IT security policies and acknowledgements in place to identify and document compliance and security controls and to reduce liability. Multiple layers of corporate IT security might include the encryption of data files, firewalls, access controls or logins, systems monitoring, detection processes, antivirus software, cyber insurance, and so on. Implementing stronger IT security can provide companies with benefits such as mitigating lost revenue, protecting brand reputation, and supporting mobilization.

Copyright © Mometrix Media. You have been licensed one copy of this document for personal use only. Any other reproduction or redistribution is strictly prohibited. All rights reserved.

## CYBERCRIMES

**Cybercrime** is when a computer or element of technology is used to commit an illegal act such as violating privacy or stealing data, money, intellectual property, and identities. Cybercrime is a criminal activity even if the activity is not specifically monetary, such as spreading viruses or causing other forms of technological harm. In fact, companies could be held liable if they do not impose actions or precautions to prevent cybercrimes from occurring. Furthermore, the financial cost of cybercrime can be astronomical to a business. The reality is that a large majority of work is completed with data and the transfer of data by employees. Therefore, it is extremely important for organizations to conduct background checks that include a criminal history of potential hacktivism. Employers should take steps to allow and promote open communication and report any suspected cybercrime the moment there is an indication that something might be wrong. Employers should communicate the importance of not opening anything via email or any other form of technology or software that could be linked to scams, hacking, phishing, etc. Companies should make every effort possible to protect their data, including not transferring data on unsecured or unencrypted servers, not posting company information on public social media sites, updating antivirus protection software, requiring mandatory frequent password changes, etc. An organization's best defense against cybercrime is vigilance in monitoring and taking every possible systemic precaution to protect its data.

## THEFT AND FRAUD

Theft and fraud in the workplace are extremely costly to an organization and every effort should be made to prevent them from happening. **Theft** is when property or information is taken without consent. **Fraud** is when some form of deception is utilized to take something for personal gain. Fraud is a form of theft. Employees may steal for any number of reasons: a sense of entitlement, the belief they are underpaid, because it was easy, and more. Furthermore, theft could include almost anything that belongs to the company. Common types of theft include cash, products, equipment, services, ideas, and data. Fraud is a variation of theft and could include inflation of expense accounts, falsified payrolls, fabricated receipts, unrecorded vacation or personal time, forgeries, entertainment expenses without a legitimate link to a business purpose, fictitious purchase orders, etc.

Regardless of why or what is stolen, theft and fraud are illegal, and should be investigated by the company if suspected. To help prevent theft and fraud, organizations should consider the following:

- Conduct background checks on employees before hiring.
- Maintain an inventory control system (if applicable).
- Establish and communicate an employee theft policy, including consequences if found guilty after an investigation.
- Install security cameras (if appropriate).

## EQUIPMENT DAMAGE OR DESTRUCTION

Company equipment is typically provided to and/or utilized by employees to efficiently perform the function of their job. Equipment provided can include laptops, printers, cell phones, cars, etc. Over time, and for various reasons, equipment can be damaged or destroyed. As a result, this hurts a company both monetarily and timewise via work disruption. There are policies and steps an organization can take to mitigate equipment damage or destruction. To begin, companies should have an equipment property policy. This policy should reinforce that all equipment provisioned to or used by employees is the property of the company and is to be used only for company purposes. There should be a procedure in place of who to notify and when in the event equipment is damaged, lost, stolen, or destroyed. The policy should also state disciplinary actions that could occur if the

Copyright © Mometrix Media. You have been licensed one copy of this document for personal use only. Any other reproduction or redistribution is strictly prohibited. All rights reserved.

damage was due to negligence. Employers should consult all federal, state, and local laws and regulations, as they vary from state to state, with regards to recovering lost expenses for equipment. Additionally, if equipment is damaged or destroyed due to unforeseen conditions such as fire, water, or disaster, companies should consult their insurance policy and/or other federal, state, and local resources.

## MINIMIZING PASSWORD BREACH RISKS

Passwords are needed for almost every program that is opened on a computer, and are critical to develop and maintain in such a way to minimize risk to the company. Many companies have developed password polices to help manage the process and ensure it is being monitored and enforced with regularity. Most password policies are developed with the whole lifecycle of the password in mind. For example, the creation of passwords, the interval of time they are changed, and guidelines for the prevention of password theft. Research indicates data breaches involving passwords are more likely to occur with a phishing attack or someone inside the company getting knowledge about passwords, such as being left out on a drawer or written on a piece of paper, than by outside hacking. Following are some guidelines that could be adopted while drafting a password policy:

- Passwords should be strong, complex, and challenging for someone to guess—typically they should be combinations of uppercase letters, lowercase letters, numbers, punctuation marks, special characters, and preferably over eight characters long. Passwords should not be obvious or easy to determine. For instance, Password123! would be a poor password.
- Passwords should be changed at regular intervals of time and not repeated. The recommended interval for changing passwords is 30 days. Default passwords, those given by IT for various reasons, should be changed immediately after logging in.
- Passwords should not be shared with anyone. If this occurs, then the employee should change the password immediately.
- Employers should educate employees on ways to avoid phishing scams that might be used to steal passwords.
- To prevent discovery, passwords should be neither written down nor stored in an employee's workspace.

## CORPORATE ESPIONAGE

**Corporate espionage** is a type of spying between companies that involves taking some type of information that would provide one with an unfair advantage over the other. This type of secret could be (but is not limited to) trade secrets, competitor's plans for future products, services or endeavors, and strategic plans. Corporate espionage can range from a disgruntled employee leaving a company for a competitor and sharing some type of secret, to hacking into or launching malware on a competitor's system. Obtaining information about competitors is not always a crime. For example, a retail company could send secret shoppers to a competitor's retail company to evaluate how they do specific functions. In this case, they are obtaining information in a legally acceptable manner. However, intentionally and often deceptively obtaining a trade secret without the owner's consent is not legal. Evaluating legality in corporate espionage is extremely complex. The federal Economic Espionage Act of 1996 essentially makes it illegal to steal commercial secrets. If found guilty, financial penalties could be severe, possibly including prison time. Additionally, violators could be subject to civil ligation. It is important to note that some states have even more stringent laws and regulations to combat corporate espionage.

Copyright © Mometrix Media. You have been licensed one copy of this document for personal use only. Any other reproduction or redistribution is strictly prohibited. All rights reserved.

# aPHR Practice Test

**1. The Drug-Free Workplace Act is applicable to which of the following groups?**

    a. Most federal contractors and grant recipients
    b. Most workplaces with 100 or more employees
    c. Most federal and state employees
    d. Most employees within a blue-collar industry

**2. Which of the following recruiting methods is the MOST cost-efficient?**

    a. Referral programs
    b. Internships
    c. Alumni networks
    d. Online job boards

**3. Weak passwords can pose a threat to Internet security and sensitive organizational data. Which of the following security measures can HR consider to eliminate the use of passwords in the workplace?**

    a. Multifactor authentication
    b. Biometric technology
    c. Virtual private network
    d. Random password generator

**4. If a Human Resources professional makes decisions and regards other business functions as dynamic, interactive teams rather than silos or independent entities, which of the following skills are they utilizing?**

    a. SWOT analysis (environmental analysis)
    b. Systems thinking
    c. Strategic thinking
    d. Growth-share matrix analysis

**5. Which of the following types of organizational culture is at the HIGHEST risk of innovation stagnation?**

    a. High-Performance
    b. Mechanistic
    c. Learning
    d. Authoritarian

**6. Which of the following HR functions is LEAST likely to utilize an external provider?**

    a. Workforce planning
    b. Workers compensation administration
    c. Workforce recruiting
    d. Payroll processing

Copyright © Mometrix Media. You have been licensed one copy of this document for personal use only. Any other reproduction or redistribution is strictly prohibited. All rights reserved.

**7. When designing a recruiting strategy for a reception desk attendant, which workforce team or individuals will be the most critical to collaborate with to determine the information needed for the number of positions to fill?**

a. Executive leadership
b. Finance and administration
c. Line managers
d. Incumbent reception desk attendants

**8. In a company that is expanding in size and geography, which of the following areas of expertise will be MOST critical to consider when selecting a benefits broker?**

a. Insurance coverage
b. Direct connection with employees
c. Insurance compliance
d. Existing benefit analysis

**9. Which of the following technologies or technological services facilitates an organization's integration of IT needs across multiple business functions such as HR information systems, front line operations, sales and marketing, and customer history?**

a. Software as a service
b. Best of breed systems
c. Enterprise resource planning system
d. Employee self-service technologies

**10. Which of the following would be an example of disparate impact during the recruiting process?**

a. Selecting only male applicants to interview for a position that requires strength and stamina
b. Requiring a college degree for an entry-level position at a department store
c. Rejecting job applicants who report to an interview with a religious headdress
d. Offering higher compensation rates to applicants who look similar to the interviewer

**11. Which of the following mitigation methods would be the most appropriate to give employees the power to hold one another accountable to stopping theft in the workplace?**

a. Strong whistleblower policy and practices
b. Transparent surveillance practices
c. Frequent team meetings to review theft prevention
d. Trainings that simulate how to confront theft in the workplace

**12. The MOST proactive and effective way to improve an organization's response to workplace emergencies is:**

a. Facility signage directing appropriate emergency response
b. After-action debriefs
c. Clearly communicated policies and procedures
d. Practical exercises and drills

Copyright © Mometrix Media. You have been licensed one copy of this document for personal use only. Any other reproduction or redistribution is strictly prohibited. All rights reserved.

**13. Pay for performance style compensation structures improve performance as a result of a(n) _____ and a(n) _____**

    a.  Incentive effect; spillover effect
    b.  Competitive position; sorting effect
    c.  Incentive effect; sorting effect
    d.  Competitive position; spillover effect

**14. Which of the following conditions must be met to require a medical exam as a post-offer employment opportunity?**

    a.  The prospective employee must display clear signs of illness or impairment
    b.  A company physician must perform all exams
    c.  There is a bona fide business necessity to require an exam for the position
    d.  All data related to exam results must be safely and securely stored with the prospective employee's personnel file

**15. Which of the following recruitment sources has the potential to reach the greatest number of possible candidates?**

    a.  Company intranet posting
    b.  Job fair at local educational institution
    c.  Open house hiring event
    d.  Social media job posting

**16. Which performance appraisal method involves categorizing employees according to the mean (or average) performance and labeling approximately 20% of employees as exceeding expectations, 70% as meeting expectations, and 10% as not meeting expectations?**

    a.  Relative Percentile Method
    b.  Paired Comparisons
    c.  Alternation Rank Order
    d.  Forced Distribution

**17. While labor strikes are generally protected by the National Labor Relations Act (NLRA), there are limitations. Which of the following limitations to labor striking refers to the potential of a strike's impact affecting national health or safety?**

    a.  Duty to bargain
    b.  Secondary strikes
    c.  Taft-Hartley injunctions
    d.  Healthcare institutions

**18. When determining an organization's pay practices for its national headquarters in a US city where the national minimum wage is $7.25, the state minimum wage is $12.50, and the city minimum wage is $15.00, which of the following levels of law supersedes the others?**

    a.  Municipal
    b.  State
    c.  Federal
    d.  International

Copyright © Mometrix Media. You have been licensed one copy of this document for personal use only. Any other reproduction or redistribution is strictly prohibited. All rights reserved.

**19. Which of the following exceptions to at-will employment is applicable in all states?**

a. Good faith and fair dealing exception
b. Implied contracts
c. Public policy exception
d. Employment contracts

**20. When an HR practitioner is informing an organization's employees of their rights as workers, which of the following is required by federal law to be displayed as a detailed poster?**

a. Health Insurance Portability and Accountability Act (HIPAA)
b. Genetic Information Nondiscrimination Act (GINA)
c. Equal Pay Act (EPA)
d. Fair Labor Standards Act (FLSA)

**21. Which of the following law sources MOST closely impacts how an organization will design and enact its workforce policies and practices?**

a. Statutes
b. Agency guidelines
c. Regulations
d. Executive orders

**22. When selecting employees for developmental opportunities, which of the following is the LEAST appropriate factor to consider?**

a. Amount of time that has passed since the employee was last offered a developmental opportunity
b. Consistently positive performance evaluations
c. Family or personal circumstance that may prevent the employee from benefiting from the opportunity
d. Amount of time employee has been part of the team being considered for the opportunity

**23. Which flexible staffing practice would be the MOST appropriate to accommodate difficult-to-predict spikes in staffing needs?**

a. Job sharing
b. Temporary employees
c. On-call workers
d. Contract workers

**24. When considering different styles of learning, which of the following approaches of training would be MOST effective when teaching employees to use a new piece of equipment?**

a. Sending all employees a training video detailing the functions of the equipment and how to operate it
b. Issuing a printed copy of the equipment manual to all departments to read and review as a team
c. Bringing in an equipment technician to demonstrate the equipment functions to each team of employees
d. Issuing employees a how-to guide to read on their own and then following up with hands-on training sessions conducted in teams

Copyright © Mometrix Media. You have been licensed one copy of this document for personal use only. Any other reproduction or redistribution is strictly prohibited. All rights reserved.

**25. For how long must an organization retain pre-employment records such as the original job posting, resumes, and interview notes?**

    a.  6 months
    b.  12 months
    c.  24 months
    d.  36 months

**26. In addition to performing a job analysis, which of the following organizational tools is MOST valuable to utilize when updating job descriptions?**

    a.  Environmental scans
    b.  Employee timesheets
    c.  Performance appraisals
    d.  Customer feedback

**27. When performing a job analysis, which of the following data sources can provide the most strategic view of job tasks and conditions?**

    a.  Accounts from job incumbents
    b.  Accounts from direct supervisor
    c.  Observations from HR professionals
    d.  Vision description from senior management

**28. Which is the MOST effective way to gain employee buy-in when defining and introducing organizational values?**

    a.  Manager compliance and leadership during the introduction phase
    b.  CEO town hall with interactive question and answer segment during the introduction phase
    c.  Executive guidance and expertise during the design phase
    d.  Employee input during the design phase

**29. Which of the following is TRUE about an employee's Weingarten rights during an investigation?**

    a.  An employee does not have to be part of the union to exercise his or her Weingarten rights
    b.  A union representative is permitted to object to intimidation or confusion tactics taken by the employer during an investigatory interview
    c.  An employer is required to approach collective bargaining meetings with a genuine intent to reach an agreeable resolution
    d.  An employee may elect to have an attorney present in lieu of a union representative during investigatory interviews

**30. When having a difficult conversation with an employee regarding company policy, the employee appears highly agitated when stating his or her viewpoint. What is the FIRST communication technique that a Human Resources professional can utilize to improve the potential outcomes of the interaction?**

    a.  Respond by explaining the benefits of the policy that the employee does not understand
    b.  Listen intently without preconceived opinions or responses
    c.  Ask open-ended questions to improve his or her understanding of the employee's viewpoint
    d.  Tell the employee to calm down if he or she wishes to continue the conversation

Copyright © Mometrix Media. You have been licensed one copy of this document for personal use only. Any other reproduction or redistribution is strictly prohibited. All rights reserved.

**31. Which of the following is an advantage of a matrix-style reporting structure?**

    a. Increased partnership between functional and product processes
    b. Consistent expectations for employee outcomes
    c. Clear reporting lines and responsibilities
    d. Reduced time spent in meetings

**32. When measuring the impact of a new wellness initiative, which of the following metrics could suggest a successful initiative when negatively correlated?**

    a. Employee grievance rate
    b. Employee satisfaction ratings
    c. Employee retention
    d. Employee absence rate

**33. Which of the following tools found in performance management practices can BEST inform an appraisal or evaluation design that aligns with a team or organization's financial and non-financial objectives?**

    a. Competency Clusters
    b. Organizational Vision
    c. Balanced Scorecard
    d. Work Analysis

**34. Which of the following workplace practices is the MOST effective at preventing defamation lawsuits against the employer?**

    a. Instituting a strict no-referral policy
    b. Closely monitoring all written workplace interactions
    c. Training managers on fact-based communication methods
    d. Avoiding all types of opinions when writing performance reviews

**35. A 'no vacation policy' vacation policy can also be referred to as an unlimited vacation time policy and describes a work-life balance practice that does not limit time spent away from work based on a pre-determined bank of vacation days. In addition to high quality communication practices and fully committing to the policy, which of the following is an important building block for a successful 'no vacation policy' vacation policy?**

    a. Compensation
    b. Progressive Discipline
    c. Performance Management
    d. Data Analysis

**36. Which of the following career development practices is MOST closely aligned with an organization's strategic plan?**

    a. International assignments
    b. Succession planning
    c. Employee mentoring
    d. Tuition reimbursement programs

Copyright © Mometrix Media. You have been licensed one copy of this document for personal use only. Any other reproduction or redistribution is strictly prohibited. All rights reserved.

**37. When recruiting for an open nursing position, the HR manager receives 64 applications. After reviewing the following application breakdown information, what is the yield ratio of highly qualified candidates?**

| Application Sources | | Application Quality | | Application Progression | |
|---|---|---|---|---|---|
| Internet Job Board (IJB) | 42 | Not Qualified | 14 | Invited to Interview | 12 |
| | | Qualified | 24 | | |
| | | Highly Qualified | 4 | Accepted Invitation to Interview | 8 |
| Local Nursing College Job Fair (JB) | 22 | Not Qualified | 7 | | |
| | | Qualified | 7 | Job Offers Extended | 3 |
| | | Highly Qualified | 8 | | |
| *Total* | 64 | *Total* | 64 | Job Offers Accepted | 2 |

    a.   0.125
    b.   0.188
    c.   0.286
    d.   0.484

**38. If an organization's compensation philosophy states that the base pay structure for jobs deemed critical to the organization's overall mission will be set at the 50th percentile of the market and that their total possible performance incentives will be set at the 75th percentile of the market, what does this mean?**

    a.   A job deemed critical will be compensated a higher rate than 50% of the other positions within the company.
    b.   An employee in a critical position can earn 25% more through incentives in addition to their base pay.
    c.   The organization's compensation philosophy suggests a market match strategy for jobs deemed critical to the organization's overall mission.
    d.   A job deemed critical will likely share similar base pay practices with external jobs of a similar nature.

**39. Which of the following conditions may suggest that a contracted worker should be reclassified as an employee?**

    a.   When the contracted worker changes their working hours to match company employees
    b.   When the contracted worker performs similar tasks alongside regular employees
    c.   When the contracted worker loses money on a project
    d.   When the contracted worker takes on another project with the same company

Copyright © Mometrix Media. You have been licensed one copy of this document for personal use only. Any other reproduction or redistribution is strictly prohibited. All rights reserved.

**40. Total rewards statements can communicate a variety of compensation details. Which of the following is LEAST likely to be found on a total rewards statement?**

a. Employee stock options
b. Health benefits
c. Social Security deductions
d. Work-life balance policies

**41. Creativity in benefits plans can create appeal for both current and prospective employees while also increasing the costs of total compensation. Which of the following practices would be MOST effective at balancing employee appreciation and rising costs?**

a. Passing part of the benefits costs onto employees
b. Tying benefit availability to employee tenure
c. Only offering benefits for full-time staff
d. Personalizing benefits options

**42. Unemployment insurance programs are intended to support all of the following EXCEPT:**

a. Engagement of unemployed workers during short-term layoffs
b. Stabilization of the working environment by employers
c. Income for unemployed workers to maintain quality of life
d. Finding and securing of a new job by unemployed workers

**43. If a company is planning to introduce new remote work opportunities for its workforce, which internal business partner would be the LEAST critical to collaborate with when designing the new policy?**

a. Line Managers and Employees
b. Information Technology (IT)
c. Legal
d. Marketing and Sales

**44. Which of the following is FALSE about the potential effects of a dual career ladder program for career development?**

a. A dual career ladder gives high-performing employees the ability to advance without becoming supervisors
b. A dual career ladder may increase the turnover of senior staff who have nowhere left to advance
c. A dual career ladder program is more common in technical fields like medicine, science, and engineering
d. A dual career ladder may foster resentment from other organizational leadership who feel the compensation practice does not fit the responsibilities

**45. Which form of data collection would be the MOST effective to collect qualitative and multi-perspective information regarding employee opinions?**

a. Online survey
b. One-on-one interview
c. Focus group
d. Workplace observation

Copyright © Mometrix Media. You have been licensed one copy of this document for personal use only. Any other reproduction or redistribution is strictly prohibited. All rights reserved.

**46. Which of the following interview questions is an example of a question that could be used in a behavioral interview?**

    a. What do you value in a workplace environment?
    b. In the event that you encounter conflict with a coworker, how would you respond?
    c. Can you tell me about a time when you made a mistake in the workplace?
    d. Tell me why you are the best fit for this position?

**47. In a company with a competitive culture and a strategy that emphasizes growth and desired outcomes as a result of increased production rates, which of the following appraisal methods would be MOST effective for line workers?**

    a. Behavior observation scale
    b. Behaviorally anchored rating scale
    c. Field review
    d. Straight ranking

**48. Which of the following career development practices would be MOST appropriate for a supervisor to consider when guiding an employee who has expressed interest in advancing into a leadership position one day?**

    a. Job enlargement
    b. Job rotation
    c. Job enrichment
    d. Job transfer

**49. Which of the following classifications of workers are NOT covered under the Fair Labor Standards Act (FLSA)?**

    a. A part-time store clerk at a large grocery chain
    b. An independent contractor completing a project for a local hospital
    c. A full-time teacher's aide who is paid an hourly wage
    d. A full-time exempt director who oversees a local childcare facility

**50. Which of the following retirement plan options incurs the highest financial burden for employers?**

    a. Employee pension
    b. Employee stock ownership plan
    c. 401(k)
    d. Profit-sharing plan

**51. Which of the following organizational structures most closely aligns with an authoritarian style organizational culture?**

    a. Virtual
    b. Modular
    c. Matrix
    d. Vertical

Copyright © Mometrix Media. You have been licensed one copy of this document for personal use only. Any other reproduction or redistribution is strictly prohibited. All rights reserved.

**M⊘metrix**

**52. Which of the following HR metrics would be the MOST useful for measuring the financial effectiveness of a team's structure and size?**

a. Cost per hire
b. Revenue per employee
c. Time to hire
d. Retention rate

**53. When measuring the effectiveness of a training program, which of the following measures best indicates the level of training optimization?**

a. Usage or training participation
b. Knowledge retention of training material
c. Return on investment
d. Measurable change in behaviors based on training material

**54. What is one DISADVANTAGE to utilizing a group interview style?**

a. Group interviews take additional time and resources to execute
b. Group interviews are less effective when assessing multiple candidates
c. Group interviews are ineffective at determining how well candidates work together
d. Group interviews can be intimidating for candidates

**55. What is the primary benefit to utilizing an enterprise risk management method when working to mitigate risks in the workplace?**

a. It accounts for the potential financial implications of risk occurring or not occurring
b. It is a strategic approach to assessing the likelihood and impact of potential risks
c. It eliminates the potential for certain risks to occur
d. It spans across an organization's functions and locations

**56. Unless otherwise stated by the Equal Employment Opportunity Commission (EEOC), an EEO-1 Component 1 report must be filed annually by private employers with over 100 employees. The primary data collected in this report includes all of the following information EXCEPT:**

a. Job category
b. Sex
c. Religion
d. Race

**57. Which regularly updated tool can Human Resources utilize to clearly and concisely communicate organizational policies and procedures?**

a. Company Mission Statement
b. Employee Handbook
c. Job Descriptions
d. Organizational Chart

Copyright © Mometrix Media. You have been licensed one copy of this document for personal use only. Any other reproduction or redistribution is strictly prohibited. All rights reserved.

**58. Which of the following is FALSE when referencing an employee's rights to participate in concerted activities?**

    a. Concerted activities and an employer's rights to activities on their private property must be balanced

    b. Protected concerted activities are only applicable to union members

    c. Employees discussing and sharing wage and compensation information is considered a concerted activity

    d. Employers prohibiting discussion of a pending sexual harassment investigation is considered an unfair labor practice

**59. Which of the following learning activities would be most effective to teach one-on-one communication techniques for customer service representatives?**

    a. Concept mapping

    b. Case studies

    c. Role-play

    d. Video example

**60. Which of the following post-offer activities helps to protect the employer from future negligent hiring claims?**

    a. Drug testing

    b. Background check

    c. Medical exam

    d. Aptitude assessment

**61. The primary goal of progressive discipline is to:**

    a. Punish an employee for poor decisions

    b. Reshape employee behavior to align with business expectations

    c. Remove the employee from the workforce

    d. Set an example for the employee's team of the consequence of poor performance

**62. Payouts from workers' compensation insurance assist an employee who is injured or has fallen ill as a result of his or her job in all of the following ways EXCEPT:**

    a. Medical expenses

    b. Dependent benefits

    c. Wage replacement payments

    d. Death benefits

**63. Prior to downsizing or restructuring, an organization can take steps to curb the potential fallout to employees and to the company. Which of the following workforce actions would be MOST appropriate for a situation in which a company is planning a major restructure?**

    a. Furloughs

    b. Hiring freeze

    c. Pay reduction

    d. Early retirement options

Copyright © Mometrix Media. You have been licensed one copy of this document for personal use only. Any other reproduction or redistribution is strictly prohibited. All rights reserved.

**64. When transforming an in-person training into a virtual training, which of the following is the biggest strategic difference to consider in the training design?**

a. Learning tools and materials
b. Facilitator consistency
c. Content visualization
d. Student attention span

**65. When designing a compensation system or practice, during which step of the design process would a salary and benefits survey be most useful?**

a. Job Analysis
b. Job Documentation
c. Job Evaluation
d. Pay Structure

**66. While similar in purpose and function, orientation and onboarding are two distinct processes for new employees. Which of the following is NOT one of the differences between the two processes?**

a. Orientation typically covers administrative processes and introductions whereas onboarding covers more strategic topics and introductions
b. Orientation typically spans from a few hours to a few days whereas onboarding can last as long as several months to a year or more
c. Orientation typically covers the specific duties and role of the new employee's position whereas onboarding can provide a wider view of the organization's culture
d. Orientation typically is a formal process where onboarding is a strictly informal process

**67. During a workforce reduction, expansion, or restructure, which of the following is the MOST critical responsibility for the HR team?**

a. Completing any associated hiring or layoff paperwork
b. Honest and timely communication with the workforce
c. Designing the new workforce hierarchy
d. Salary negotiations with incoming employees

**68. Which of the following workplace incidents would NOT require an organization to record the details on the OSHA Form 300?**

a. A remote worker falling down the stairs in his or her home while on the clock and breaking a limb
b. A change in hearing test results for a worker in one or both ears
c. An employee calling in sick from work due to exposure to chemicals while on the job
d. A temporary change in job duties as a result of an injury experienced in the workplace

**69. An "Employee Records Confidentiality Policy" may include all of the following EXCEPT:**

a. Standard procedures for protecting employee data
b. A guarantee that employee data will not be compromised
c. Contact information or reporting procedures that employees can utilize if they have questions or concerns regarding their personal data
d. The type of information collected by the organization

Copyright © Mometrix Media. You have been licensed one copy of this document for personal use only. Any other reproduction or redistribution is strictly prohibited. All rights reserved.

**70. The Consolidated Omnibus Budget Reconciliation Act (COBRA) set what benefits standards for employers?**

a. Employer rules when providing a pension
b. Required leave rules for companies with 50 or more employees
c. Continuing health care coverage for employees who are laid off or resign from their positions
d. Prohibition of discrimination on the basis of a protected class in the administration of benefits

**71. Which of the following is TRUE of an employer's responsibilities when regarding employees and substance abuse?**

a. Alcoholism can be considered a disability and may require reasonable accommodations
b. Employers are not permitted to randomly test employees for drugs
c. While employers do not need to tolerate poor or unsafe performance, illicit drug use is protected under the ADA
d. It is best practice to only test candidates suspected of drug use during pre-employment drug screening

**72. Which of the following pay structure designs can be MOST helpful for an organization that is transitioning from a vertical organizational hierarchy to a more horizontal organizational design?**

a. Broadband salary structure
b. Market-based salary structure
c. Pay grade salary structure
d. Outcome-based salary structure

**73. When designing the onboarding experience for a new employee, which training tool would be MOST impactful for a new professional entering their desired field?**

a. Mentor system
b. Role-specific training
c. Teambuilding event
d. Job rotation

**74. When determining the match accuracy of data from an external compensation survey, which characteristic best indicates the data's comparability to existing internal pay practices?**

a. Job Coverage (Job Comparability)
b. Geographical Origin
c. Effective Data Age
d. Labor Market Coverage

**75. Which U.S. federal regulation sets the legal standards and expectations for child labor standards, minimum wage, overtime pay, and recordkeeping?**

a. Sarbanes-Oxley Act
b. Fair Labor Standards Act
c. Lilly Ledbetter Fair Pay Act
d. The Patient Protection and Affordable Care Act

Copyright © Mometrix Media. You have been licensed one copy of this document for personal use only. Any other reproduction or redistribution is strictly prohibited. All rights reserved.

**76. Which of the following employee relations programs would be most effective at connecting employees across the company who share a diversity dimension (such as race, ethnicity, religion, etc.)?**
   a. Employee assistance program
   b. Diversity council
   c. Company wellness program
   d. Employee resource group

**77. What holistic business statement reflects the desired future state of the organization?**
   a. Mission Statement
   b. Vision Statement
   c. Organizational Values
   d. Business Goals and Objectives

**78. Which of the following communication media would be most effective for a Human Resources Representative to assist a supervisor struggling to get along with a new employee on their team?**
   a. Peer review
   b. Mediation
   c. Arbitration
   d. Grievance hearing

**79. An employee has been working with a company for four months. In that time, he or she has reported five to ten minutes late to work on five separate occasions. The employee's manager did not address the specific instances of tardiness with this employee but has included the organization's late policy in monthly team-wide emails. When the employee shows up late for a sixth time, what is the most appropriate step along the progressive discipline process for the manager to take with this employee?**
   a. Verbal Counseling
   b. Formal Warning
   c. Final Warning
   d. Termination

**80. Which of the following is FALSE as it pertains to retaliation in the workplace?**
   a. Retaliation does not need to affect the terms and conditions of the job
   b. Retaliation charges must be connected to a corresponding discrimination charge
   c. Retaliation is the leading charge filed with the Equal Employment Opportunity Commission (EEOC)
   d. Treatment does not need to be discriminatory in nature to be considered retaliation

**81. Which of the following is the MOST appropriate goal to set as a result of diversity and inclusion training in the workplace?**
   a. To demonstrate to shareholders the organization's commitment to an inclusive workplace
   b. To eliminate discrimination and harassment in the workplace
   c. To change what employees believe about other ways of life
   d. To increase employee awareness of diversity issues and improve collaboration skills

Copyright © Mometrix Media. You have been licensed one copy of this document for personal use only. Any other reproduction or redistribution is strictly prohibited. All rights reserved.

**82. An employer has scheduled and arranged a special training opportunity for the sales team members as a reward for increased revenue in the previous quarter. One member of the team is unable to attend the training as scheduled due to a physical handicap that prevents him or her from entering the facility. Which of the following responses would be the MOST appropriate for the employer seeking to provide reasonable accommodations for the employee?**

    a. Securing an alternate location for the training with handicap accessibility.
    b. Providing the employee with a self-guided virtual training option that teaches the same material.
    c. Sending the employee to a different training that takes place in an accessible facility.
    d. Building the required accessibility features at the training facility.

**83. Which of the following internal recruiting sources would be the MOST appropriate when gauging the interest in a future position opening?**

    a. Job bidding
    b. Employee referral
    c. Social media
    d. Succession planning

**84. According to the Worker Adjustment and Retraining Notification (WARN) Act, how many days in advance must an organization with 100 or more employees notify the affected individuals prior to a mass reduction in force?**

    a. 14
    b. 45
    c. 60
    d. 90

**85. When designing the benefits package, which of the following benefits is the MOST likely to improve employee turnover rate?**

    a. Paid time off
    b. Pension plan
    c. Tuition reimbursement
    d. Profit-sharing

**86. A large corporation with a wide array of services and products is seeking to define its strategic position by 'changing the way customers experience' those services and products. Which of Michael Porter's competitive business strategies does this approach reference?**

    a. Low-Cost Leadership
    b. Differentiation
    c. Focused Cost Leadership
    d. Focused Differentiation

**87. Which of the following is NOT a benefit of outsourcing staffing needs?**

    a. Increased access to certain skills or expertise
    b. Improvement in data security
    c. Reduction in staffing costs
    d. Increased free time to focus on core business functions

Copyright © Mometrix Media. You have been licensed one copy of this document for personal use only. Any other reproduction or redistribution is strictly prohibited. All rights reserved.

**88. Which of the following is NOT an advantage when an organization shifts from the traditional annual process of performance appraisals to a more frequent and ongoing schedule of performance reviews?**

    a. Increased individual and organizational agility
    b. Time and money savings
    c. Development of a feedback culture
    d. Enhanced employee engagement

**89. There are a variety of practices for flexible working arrangements within work-life balance practices. Which of the following refers to an employee's ability to determine his or her start and end times for each workday?**

    a. Telecommuting
    b. Variable workweek
    c. Job sharing
    d. Flexible work hours

**90. While recruiting for a manager position, the HR team states that it is looking for "highly qualified candidates who are available on weekends and who will bring new energy and a fresh face to the team." Which of the following laws is the most likely to be cited if a candidate feels these search criteria are discriminatory?**

    a. Americans with Disabilities Act
    b. Age Discrimination in Employment Act
    c. Civil Rights Act of 1964
    d. Immigration Reform and Control Act

**91. An integrative HRIS can help to alleviate the time and labor associated with basic administrative HR tasks. Which of the following is NOT a typical function found in an HRIS?**

    a. Employee information management
    b. Vacation time requests and approvals
    c. Pay record and document management
    d. Learning storage and applications

**92. Which of the following visual displays would be most effective to demonstrate the links between different organizational data and their respective relationships to the organization's strategic goals?**

    a. Pie chart
    b. Histogram
    c. Organizational structure chart
    d. Measurement map

**93. When utilizing financial statements to inform HR strategy, practices, and organizational decisions, which of the following should be considered first?**

    a. Statement of change in equity
    b. Balance sheet
    c. Cash flow statement
    d. Income statement

Copyright © Mometrix Media. You have been licensed one copy of this document for personal use only. Any other reproduction or redistribution is strictly prohibited. All rights reserved.

**94. Which of the following standards or descriptions about the Sarbanes-Oxley (SOX) Act is true?**

a. The SOX Act only covers the activities of high-ranking company leadership
b. The SOX Act requires companies to establish a Code of Ethics to be communicated with the company's employees
c. The SOX Act applies to any public or private company with over $100,000 in annual profit
d. The SOX Act establishes protections for whistleblowers who assist in federal investigations into illegal company practices

**95. Which of the following steps in training implementation comes first?**

a. Training design
b. Participant selection
c. Needs assessment
d. Pre-training survey

**96. Under the Americans with Disabilities Act of 1990 (ADA), individuals with disabilities are protected from discrimination in the workplace; in order to qualify for this protection, an individual must have the required skills and experience for the job and be able to perform the essential job functions. Which of the following would NOT be considered an essential job function?**

a. A manuscript editor's ability to accurately proofread
b. A firefighter's ability to move heavy equipment
c. A secretary's ability to replace the toner cartridge
d. A soldier's ability to wield a weapon

**97. Which of the following annual reports that are required to be filed with the overseeing agency are also required to be provided for the individual employees?**

a. Form 5500 – Financial conditions, operations, and investment information required by the Employment Retirement Income Security Act (ERISA)
b. Form 1095-B – Employee proof of insurance required by the Affordable Care Act (ACA)
c. Form 1120 – Corporation filing of income taxes required by the Internal Revenue Service (IRS)
d. Form 300A – Annual summary of workplace-related injuries and illnesses required by the Occupational Safety and Health Act (OSHA)

**98. In which of the following scenarios is it MOST appropriate to conduct an exit interview?**

a. Prior to an employee's involuntary termination for poor performance
b. Following an employee's communication of their two-week notice
c. During a financially driven workforce layoff
d. After an employee no-call no-shows for three consecutive shifts

**99. Which of the following should be the fundamental starting block when formulating an organization's total rewards strategy?**

a. Internal pay rate alignment
b. Environmental scan
c. Market salary rates
d. Organizational strategy

Copyright © Mometrix Media. You have been licensed one copy of this document for personal use only. Any other reproduction or redistribution is strictly prohibited. All rights reserved.

**100. In the wake of an extreme expansion of remote work options and opportunities, which of the following employee data points or sources is the MOST critical to update regularly to ensure compliant payroll processes?**

    a. Banking information
    b. Photo identification
    c. Home address
    d. Emergency contacts

**101. Different recruitment methods can be more or less efficient at targeting different types of candidates. Which of the following candidate pools is the LEAST likely to be targeted when attending a job fair?**

    a. Military veterans
    b. Entry level workers
    c. College graduates
    d. Supervisory professionals

**102. Which communication medium would be the most effective means by which to introduce the company's new health insurance options that come at greater cost to the employees than in previous years?**

    a. Companywide email detailing the benefits of the new plans
    b. Colorful newsletter that breaks down the details for each option
    c. Posted video on the company's internal social media platform discussing the upcoming changes
    d. In-person meetings between benefits representatives and each company department or work team

**103. When performing a job analysis, a Human Resources professional may take a job-based approach or a person-based approach. In which scenario is it more appropriate to take a person-based approach?**

    a. A position with a stable set of responsibilities and duties
    b. A position that is dependent on learning and obtaining new skills
    c. A position that can be found across an industry
    d. A position with performance measures rooted in output volume

**104. When monitoring the work of remote employees, what strategy is MOST effective at implementing legally and socially acceptable monitoring techniques?**

    a. Written releases for camera tracking
    b. Primary focus on active and idle time monitoring
    c. Required time spent in the office
    d. Transparency in supervision policy implementation

**105. Which of the following statistical tools would be the MOST effective to sort and manage basic descriptive statistics?**

    a. Oracle
    b. Python
    c. R
    d. Microsoft Excel

Copyright © Mometrix Media. You have been licensed one copy of this document for personal use only. Any other reproduction or redistribution is strictly prohibited. All rights reserved.

**106. Which type of privacy risk occurs when computer or technology users are tricked into disclosing private, personal, or organizational information to a malicious source?**

    a.  Decryption
    b.  Hacking
    c.  Encryption
    d.  Social Engineering

**107. Which of the following is a DISADVANTAGE to workplace observation as a data gathering tool?**

    a.  The observation method is expensive
    b.  The data is affected by memory bias
    c.  The data quality is dependent on the skill of the observer
    d.  The observation method is inconvenient for subjects

**108. Which of the following visual displays would be most effective for demonstrating the relationship between performance ratings for individual employees between one rating period and the next?**

    a.  Regression model
    b.  Bar chart
    c.  Line chart
    d.  Venn diagram

**109. Which of the following survey types would be MOST effective at gauging employee satisfaction, commitment, and morale?**

    a.  Attitude survey
    b.  Opinion survey
    c.  Engagement survey
    d.  Culture survey

**110. Which of the following is TRUE about applicant flow tracking?**

    a.  Applicant flow tracking is required by the EEOC for all private employers with 50 or more employees
    b.  Applicant flow tracking is used to analyze selection rate for a position and ensure fair hiring outcomes
    c.  Applicant flow tracking is the process of collecting data on the race and gender of job applicants
    d.  Applicant flow tracking data is collected and stored with the corresponding candidate applications

**111. When recognizing employees in the workplace, which of the following practices is the MOST effective?**

    a.  Publicly announcing recognition throughout the organization
    b.  Tying recognition efforts to organizational values
    c.  Budgeting adequate funds for individual recognition
    d.  Ensuring all employees are recognized

Copyright © Mometrix Media. You have been licensed one copy of this document for personal use only. Any other reproduction or redistribution is strictly prohibited. All rights reserved.

**112. For job candidates and new employees, their initial exposure to an organization's culture occurs at what step of job search process?**

    a.  Job posting
    b.  Job application follow up
    c.  Initial interview
    d.  First day on the job

**113. Which of the following orientation activities confirms an employee's authorization to work in the United States?**

    a.  Code of conduct sign off
    b.  I-9 verification
    c.  Employee background check
    d.  Meeting with HR representative

**114. Which of the following goals would be most effective when measuring employee performance?**

    a.  To improve overall performance by 10% within 6 months
    b.  To increase total product output by 500 units
    c.  To increase the net promoter score by 6 points before May 1
    d.  To decrease total waste output by 100% within 2 months

**115. While working remotely, an employee is struggling to collaborate with a peer over email. The employee seeks the advice of his or her HR representative and describes the peer's email responses as short, abrupt, and lacking in detail. Which of the following would be the most effective advice that the representative can provide?**

    a.  The employee should report this behavior to his or her supervisor to let an authority figure fix the situation
    b.  The employee should attempt to call or videoconference with his or her peer to discuss project details but not address the challenges with email
    c.  The employee should attempt to call or videoconference with his or her peer to address frustrations regarding the emails and seek communication alternatives or solutions
    d.  The employee should move ahead with the project on his or her own in order to meet deadlines

**116. When conducting employee surveys or feedback activities, which of the following steps or characteristics is the MOST important to employee trust and engagement in the process?**

    a.  Easy to understand survey purpose
    b.  Convenient survey style or feedback schedule
    c.  Effectively designed questions
    d.  Transparent results and subsequent action plans

**117. The availability of employee records should be limited to those with a legitimate business need and which of the following?**

    a.  Company senior leadership such as executives and vice presidents
    b.  Mid-level leadership such as managers and supervisors
    c.  Employee emergency contacts as designated by the employee during the hiring process
    d.  Parties in specific situations designated by federal, state, and local laws

Copyright © Mometrix Media. You have been licensed one copy of this document for personal use only. Any other reproduction or redistribution is strictly prohibited. All rights reserved.

**118. Which progressive discipline prevention method most closely aligns with the roles and responsibilities of a Human Resource practitioner?**

a. Enforce consistency in workplace behaviors and decisions
b. Encourage and practice multi-directional communication
c. Use job descriptions, employee handbook, and other organizational policies to set clear behavior expectations
d. Regularly review, revise, and implement employee codes of conduct

**119. When faced with the decision to terminate an employee for poor performance, which of the following is the LEAST effective practice?**

a. Verify accurate contact information to be able to accurately complete payroll, tax documents, or other end of employment matters
b. Meet face-to-face with the employee and a witness when delivering news of termination
c. Inform the employee that he or she has the option to quit to avoid being fired
d. Inventory equipment or supplies to be returned before the employee's departure

**120. Which of the following alternative staffing practices can help to facilitate both increased institutional knowledge transfer and improved recruiting outcomes?**

a. Phased retirement
b. Temp-to-hire programs
c. Joint employment practices
d. Utilizing gig workers

**121. When analyzing employee engagement and retention, which of the following interview types would be MOST effective for a human resources professional to use during the data collection phase?**

a. Screening interview
b. Stay interview
c. Selection interview
d. Stress interview

**122. Which medium is the most EFFICIENT way to collect employee opinions regarding a recent change in workplace policy?**

a. Company town hall
b. Online multiple-choice survey
c. Emailed questionnaire
d. Focus groups held over video conference

**123. Which technology function or apparatus is most effective to align the company brand with the employer brand of a company?**

a. HRIS
b. Social media
c. Company intranet
d. Television advertisement

Copyright © Mometrix Media. You have been licensed one copy of this document for personal use only. Any other reproduction or redistribution is strictly prohibited. All rights reserved.

**124. When cleaning up data about benefits utilization across an organization, which of the following functions in Microsoft Excel would be MOST useful in reviewing the variety of unique responses within a column?**

  a.  Text to columns
  b.  Remove duplicates
  c.  Filter
  d.  Concatenate

**125. Which of the following functional descriptions would NOT qualify an employee to be classified as exempt under the Fair Labor Standards Act (FLSA)?**

  a.  Production
  b.  Executive
  c.  Administrative
  d.  Professional

Copyright © Mometrix Media. You have been licensed one copy of this document for personal use only. Any other reproduction or redistribution is strictly prohibited. All rights reserved.

# Answer Key and Explanations

**1. A:** The Drug-Free Workplace Act requires federal contractors with contracts valued at or in excess of $100,000 and any federal grant recipient to establish policies that prohibit unlawful use, possession, or distribution of controlled substances in the workplace. The Drug-Free Workplace Act also sets standards for drug-free awareness programs, notification standards for employees to inform employers of a breach in policy, and consequences for policy breach.

**2. A:** Referral programs can run in the background of day-to-day operations for low to no cost and yield high-quality candidates. Internships and alumni networks can be cost-efficient when recruiting new and experienced candidates but require time and resources to design and maintain. Online job boards can reach a broad audience but can be expensive to post and maintain and do not always yield high-quality or relevant candidates.

**3. B:** Multifactor authentication can utilize biometric scanning, passwords, or other means of access verification but rely on any combination of two or more means in total. A virtual private network (VPN) can be used in addition to heightened login protections to redirect Internet traffic through more secure channels. A random password generator may help to create stronger passwords for users but that still requires remembering or recording the passwords somewhere. Biometric technology such as face scans, fingerprint scans, or voice recognition eliminates the use of passwords for logging into systems or accessing organizational data or property.

**4. B:** SWOT analyses and growth-share matrix analyses can be utilized as part of systems thinking, but are specific tools used to scan the external environment for conditions that may affect internal processes and outcomes. Strategic thinking aligns decisions and actions with the organization's overall strategy and goals but does not always span a variety of departments or teams. Systems thinking involves focusing on how various business functions interact with and influence each other.

**5. B:** A mechanistic organizational culture is defined by its formal policies, rules, and procedures. This strict definition of communications and operations fosters consistency and stability, but can serve as an obstacle to innovation. While authoritarian organizational cultures may also lead to slower innovation rates, this potential trait is dependent on the organization's leaders and industry.

**6. A:** External HR service providers are useful for reducing the administrative workload of an HR team and increasing the time and attention available for the strategic responsibilities of HR. Workers compensation and payroll processing are each administrative in nature and furthest in function from strategic HR functions. Workforce recruiting can be either administrative or strategic in nature, depending on the roles being recruited and goals of the team recruiting. Workforce planning is a purely strategic HR task that focuses on the style, skills, structure, and business alignment of an organization's workforce.

**7. C:** Line managers are directly in charge of front-line staff teams and will have the most up-to-date information regarding the number of roles to fill for each team that they supervise; line managers may also report to senior managers in regards to their staffing needs and operations. Line managers may also work closely with the current reception desk attendants so they can collect data regarding current attendant opinions and attitudes. Executive leadership can advise to the general philosophy of staffing and workforce structure but are typically too far removed from front line workers to advise regarding the specific number of positions to fill. Finance and administration

Copyright © Mometrix Media. You have been licensed one copy of this document for personal use only. Any other reproduction or redistribution is strictly prohibited. All rights reserved.

staff can advise regarding recommended salary rates and staff team budgets but will not always be able to adjust that data to the real-time needs of the team in question.

**8. C:** While each option represents a benefits broker function or area of expertise, an organization that has or is currently expanding geographically will need to take extra care when ensuring insurance compliance. Laws and requirements for insurance can vary from federal to state to local levels and selecting a benefits broker with a proven track record of providing services across a wide range of regions will be important to support new and continued company growth.

**9. C:** Employee self-service technologies focus on the needs of the employee such as benefits management or time-off requests. Software as a service refers to the service being delivered remotely instead of as product installed onto a device or computer. Best of breed systems and enterprise resource planning systems refer to varying degrees of system integration across organizational functions. An enterprise resource planning system connects different functions across the organization but may sacrifice functionality for that integration. Best of breed systems offer a higher level of specification to the needs of each business function but may sacrifice each function's ability to communicate with the other.

**10. B:** Disparate treatment and disparate impact are both types of discrimination. Where disparate treatment is outright discrimination based on a protected class like sex, religion, or color, disparate impact is when a job condition or requirement is not discriminatory in text but can have discriminatory outcomes. An entry level position at a department store does not likely require college level education to be completed, but can be an obstacle to employment for members of a protected class who may not have the same access to education as other applicants.

**11. A:** Video surveillance can be an effective mitigation method but can also cause discomfort or legal challenges in the workplace. Team meetings that review theft policies can help to mitigate theft but does not necessarily provide employees with the means to hold one another accountable. Encouraging employees to confront theft in the workplace may be appropriate in some situations but can also potentially lead to unhealthy conflict or violence in the workplace. Strong whistleblower policies and practices can give employees the means to anonymously report unethical behavior in the workplace while maintaining their personal safety.

**12. D:** Signage and policy communication are essential parts of establishing and teaching the desired response to an emergency. However, employees learn best by doing and by practicing the various responses. Practical drills and exercises give employees the visual experience and muscle memory to respond more quickly in the event of an emergency. After-action debriefs are a critical piece to assessing an organization's response to an emergency but take place after the emergency has already occurred.

**13. C:** Pay for performance has been shown to improve performance by motivating current employees to improve their overall output or results (incentive effect). Additionally, this compensation plan can lead employees to self-select out of the organization who are not able to or do not desire to improve their performance (sorting effect). Competitive position refers to how an employer's compensation plan compares within the market and the spillover effect occurs when union benefits or working demands spill over into nonunion environments in an attempt to discourage unionization.

**14. C:** Post-offer medical exams can only be required as a result of the physical demands of a job's essential functions. The exam must be performed by a third-party medical provider, the exam

Copyright © Mometrix Media. You have been licensed one copy of this document for personal use only. Any other reproduction or redistribution is strictly prohibited. All rights reserved.

results may not be used to discriminate against a candidate due to a disability, and the exam data must be kept separate from the employee's personnel file.

**15. D:** The Internet can be a powerful tool for reaching a wide audience that is geographically and demographically diverse. Utilizing the company intranet would be more appropriate if the position to be filled was best done by an internal candidate. In-person job fairs and open houses can limit potential candidates based on availability and awareness of the event, but may produce candidates who are a good fit depending on the details and design of the hiring event.

**16. D:** A forced distribution system of performance appraisals utilizes a bell curve with forced performance labels to identify top performers, middle of the road performers, and performers who must improve. Relative percentile methods of performance appraisal also use the 50th percentile as the midpoint when comparing employee performance but can vary based on the competency measured and determine a specific percentile placement for each employee. Paired comparisons and alternation rank order are systems that compare individual employee performance to the performance of others: paired comparisons pit one employee's performance against each individual performance of other employees and alternation rank order determines the top performer, then the bottom performer, followed by the second top performer and the second bottom performer, and so on and so forth.

**17. C:** Both employers and union members must give effort during collective bargaining, a principle known as the duty to bargain. Secondary strikes occur when employees from a related industry who are not involved in the labor dispute participate in a strike. Healthcare institutions require specific notification and consideration timeframes before striking to determine the potential damage that may occur locally if healthcare is affected. A Taft-Hartley injunction occurs when the size and/or scope of a strike poses a threat to national health or safety.

**18. A:** When determining compensation practices, an employer is required to comply with all applicable laws. According to the pay rates described in the question, the employer must pay the highest required rate across the three, which is the municipal law of $15.00 per hour.

**19. D:** Written and mutually agreed upon employment contracts can set an agreed-upon time for the employment relationship to last or can set the standards that termination can only occur for cause or under predetermined circumstances. Public policy exceptions, implied contract exceptions, and good faith and fair dealing exceptions are considered or not considered according to various state laws and precedents.

**20. D:** The posters required for organization can vary by state, organization size, and other factors. Under federal regulation, a Fair Labor Standards Act poster is required to be posted in a conspicuous area for employees to review details. Other posters that may be required depending on the organization include the Occupational Safety and Health Act, Family and Medical Leave Act, Migrant and Seasonal Agricultural Worker Protection Act, and more.

**21. B:** While all organizations should ensure compliance regardless of the law source, guidelines are the specific interpretation of statutes and regulations as they pertain to an organization's day-to-day operations. Guidelines explain regulations and statutes and can provide additional material directly related to how the law will be enforced.

**22. C:** When selecting employees for training or development opportunities, it is essential to do so in a fair and consistent manner in order to avoid possible discrimination or unfair treatment. Time between training opportunities, performance appraisals, and seniority are all work-related qualifications for selecting an employee for training. Selecting or not selecting an employee for

Copyright © Mometrix Media. You have been licensed one copy of this document for personal use only. Any other reproduction or redistribution is strictly prohibited. All rights reserved.

training based on what is perceived to be happening outside of the work environment may involve judgment based on a protected class and can lead to a discrimination charge. For example: if a manager knows that one of his subordinates is a mother with small children at home he may favor her male counterpart for a development opportunity because he assumes the mother will not be able to travel due to her childcare responsibilities. While the manager may see this as being considerate for the mother's home life, it deprives her of the opportunity for development and advancement.

**23. C:** Job sharing and temporary employees are appropriate alternative staffing practices for predictable and stable work needs. Contract workers should only be utilized for specialized jobs and projects and are not appropriate to fill in for positions typically manned by part- or full-time employees. On-call workers are the most appropriate for difficult-to-predict spikes in staffing needs as they can be brought in at the last minute and are able to step in for regular employee positions.

**24. D:** Each of the options caters to different styles of learning; however, the most effective approach to teaching combines a variety of learning styles regardless of what the student perceives their individual learning style to be. By combining independent learning with team learning and reading materials with hands-on training, the trainer exposes the students to the new material in a variety of mediums and learning environments.

**25. B:** Per guidance set forth in the Civil Rights Act of 1964 (Title VII), the Americans with Disabilities Act (ADA), and the Age Discrimination in Employment Act (ADEA), employers must retain pre-employment documentation for one year in order to demonstrate fair and non-discriminatory hiring practices.

**26. C:** An employee's performance appraisal can reveal a wide variety of data points such as what work the employee performed, how this work contributed to the team or organization at large, and supervisor comments on the role played by the employee, as well as comments on the work challenges and successes by the employee themselves. This data can suggest which jobs and which job tasks most closely align with desired organizational outcomes. Environmental scans and customer feedback can provide valuable data but the data is limited to external conditions and views. Employee timesheets can be a valuable tool to assess working conditions but lack the qualitative data required for substantive job description information.

**27. D:** Direct accounts of the job functions from incumbents and supervisors of the position in question are the most accurate data sources for the current day-to-day tasks, environment, and expectations of the job. HR observations of the job in question can provide a more objective account of the job functions as well as context as to where the job does or should fit within the workforce as a whole. The senior management vision gives a strategic context to work being performed as it relates to the goals and direction of the organization as a whole.

**28. D:** The most effective way to elicit employee buy-in to new policies, procedures, practices, and other company messages is to utilize interactive (and genuine) workshops, focus groups, and other feedback mechanisms between organizational leadership and the organization's front line. High quality communication in the form of supervisor role models and town halls can be effective but may take longer for the intended employee buy-in effect. Executive expertise is an important part of crafting organizational values that align with the organization's strategy, but without employee feedback, it may be challenging for employees to develop a sense of ownership over the organizational values.

Copyright © Mometrix Media. You have been licensed one copy of this document for personal use only. Any other reproduction or redistribution is strictly prohibited. All rights reserved.

**29. B:** An employee's Weingarten rights refers to a union employee's right to request a union representative be present during an investigatory interview. While a union representative present for an investigatory interview is not permitted to cause severe disruption to the investigation process, he or she may protect employees by clarifying questions or objecting to intimidation attempts by the employer. An employer is not required to bargain with the union representative during the investigation process.

**30. B:** The first step to effective communication is listening to the other party in a genuine and non-judgmental manner. Asking open-ended questions can be a highly valuable tool to better understand the other party, but questions should be informed by the data collected while listening (as well as any data gathered or confirmed when using reflection techniques as well.) Pre-planning a response to the employee regarding the policy benefits does not acknowledge the message that the employee is trying to communicate and can create additional frustration if used too soon (or inappropriately) during the conversation. While taking a break can be a viable tool during heated conversations, giving the employee an ultimatum early in the conflict sends the message that what the employee has to say is not important; this can do more damage than good.

**31. A:** Matrix-style reporting structures set employees at a cross between a functional and a product-based supervisor. However, reporting to two different supervisors with varying perspectives can create reporting inconsistencies and unclear communications, and lead to increased time spent in meetings to create cohesive plans and expectations.

**32. D:** A negative correlation between data points means that as one data set increases, the corresponding data set decreases (it is also important to note that a correlation suggests a link between the two data sets and not necessarily a causal relationship). As the roll out and use of a wellness initiative increases, a decrease in the employee absence rate may suggest increased health outcomes for current employees, improved engagement outcomes from current employees, or a shift in the health demographics of newly hired employees. A decreased rate of grievances may be indicative of a positive shift in the working environment but it is not as strongly linked to a wellness initiative as the absence rate. Decreased employee satisfaction ratings and retention rate are each indicative of negative outcomes that may or may not be linked to the wellness initiative.

**33. C:** Each of the tools listed can be helpful in their own way to inform the design of a performance appraisal but a balanced scorecard is unique in its holistic approach to measuring organizational performance. The balanced scorecard, informed by an organization's strategy and vision, breaks performance down into four main categories: customers, learning and growth, financial, and internal business processes. These categories each list the metrics and indicators of success associated with the big picture of organizational operations. Employee performance evaluations that are derived from their organization's or team's balanced scorecard are subsequently aligned with the organization's financial and non-financial objectives.

**34. C:** Mitigating defamation risks can be a challenging task that is best met with adequate training, practice, honesty, and discretion. A no-referral policy may backfire and result in negligent referral lawsuits and discontent among the workforce. Closely monitoring written workplace interactions can help to discover libel-related risks but can also negatively impact workplace culture and camaraderie. While opinions on performance reviews and in referrals can present tricky legal waters, in general this is protected speech if the opinions are fact-based and business-focused.

**35. C:** Successful unlimited vacation policies are built on high quality communication regarding behavior expectations, individual work outcome expectations, and team outcome expectations. A high-quality Performance Management approach clearly defines what 'high performance' looks like

Copyright © Mometrix Media. You have been licensed one copy of this document for personal use only. Any other reproduction or redistribution is strictly prohibited. All rights reserved.

and gives individuals and teams the leverage needed to focus more on actual business outcomes instead of the number of hours spent in the office.

**36. B:** International assignments may be an important aspect of the strategic plan if global expansion is deemed of high strategic importance, but international assignments can also be factored within succession planning if that is the case. Employee mentoring and tuition reimbursement programs can help to improve the quality of individual employees (and consequently their organizational outcomes), but that is a small piece of the strategic plan. Succession planning identifies and develops employees whose work specialties and leadership potential align with the organization's strategic vision for the future.

**37. B:** In order to calculate the yield ratio of highly qualified candidates, one must add the total number of highly qualified candidates (12) and divide it by the total number of candidates (64) and multiply by 100. This indicates an 18.8% yield of highly qualified candidates.

**38. D:** By setting the base pay at the 50th percentile of the market, the organization is stating that, of the similar jobs within the labor market, approximately 50% of the jobs will have base pay rates below the determined rate and 50% of the jobs will have base rates above the determined rate. Despite being set at the 50th percentile of the market, the compensation philosophy suggests a lead pay-level strategy (as opposed to a lagging or matching strategy) strategy due to the total incentive pay being set at the 75th percentile of the market.

**39. B:** Independent contractors are free to set their own work hours, purchase their own work tools, and take on whichever projects they are offered—regardless of whether they will make money or not. One key difference between contractors and regular employees is the type of work being completed. Regular employees typically perform work that is a function of the organization's mission and is closely tied to the organization's day-to-day operations. Contractors, on the other hand, specialize in project-type work as opposed to core operations and maintain their own autonomy as workers.

**40. C:** A total rewards statement is a tool that organizations can use to communicate the rewards available to employees. Total rewards statements can communicate direct compensation practices like base pay as well as indirect compensation like dental plans and material perks. Social Security deductions, while related to compensation practices, are not perks offered by the employer but required federal taxes and would not be highlighted in a total rewards statement.

**41. D:** While each of the options may have various levels of effectiveness at balancing the cost-reward balance of benefits, personalizing the benefits options to the needs of employees is the most effective. The personalization process can be accomplished by catering offerings based on the workforce demographics, gathering data through employee surveys, or offering cafeteria-style benefits plans. Reducing the availability of the benefits by passing on costs, tying availability to tenure, or restricting which employees are eligible can positively affect the cost-reward balance, but can also lead to tension from employees who may feel they are missing out or that there is inequity in benefits administration.

**42. C:** Unemployment insurance is intended to assist employees who are involuntarily unemployed as they transition to a new job and to encourage employers to create a more stable work environment. Unemployment insurance is paid out at a fraction of what the worker's salary was with their previous employer and is only intended to assist the transition, not to support the unemployed worker for an extended period of time.

Copyright © Mometrix Media. You have been licensed one copy of this document for personal use only. Any other reproduction or redistribution is strictly prohibited. All rights reserved.

**43. D:** While Marketing and Sales may contribute to building and advertising the employer brand in some scenarios, the other options have direct contact with a remote working policy. Line managers and employees will be utilizing and supervising the policy and can lend knowledge to the practical needs and considerations of teleworking. The IT department will be a critical collaborator in the necessary hardware and possible software needed for teleworking. The Legal department will be an essential partner to advise regarding any best practices to avoid disparate treatment in selecting which employees may telework; additionally, the Legal team will be essential to partner with when tackling unforeseen outcomes of a telework policy such as employees moving out of the local area.

**44. B:** Dual career ladders provide alternate journeys of advancement for high-performing employees who do not have an interest in or would not perform well at supervising others. Dual career ladders are designed to give senior staff somewhere to advance internally so they are not forced to leave the company in search of better opportunities.

**45. C:** While all of the options are capable of collecting qualitative data, a focus group data collection method elicits not just the viewpoint from one observer or interviewee but back-and-forth dialogue between interviewer and interviewees regarding the topic at hand. Interviewees can react to and build on the opinions and observations of each other to paint a more dynamic and integrative picture of the data being collected.

**46. C:** Behavioral interview questions focus in on past behavior and experiences that the applicant has had that may demonstrate a good fit for the open position. The other questions may be more appropriately used for attempting to gauge the applicant's work values, approach to work relationships, and self-confidence.

**47. D:** Field reviews and behavior observation scales can provide valuable qualitative data regarding the work an employee is doing, but do not cover the quantitative data from production over time. A behaviorally anchored rating scale asks the supervisor or manager to rate the frequency or volume of different employee behaviors on the job. This rating scale can be useful for providing quantitative data, but the data is subjective to the opinions and experiences of the rater. Each of these appraisal methods is an absolute system, with the exception of straight ranking. By using a comparative system, the competitive culture is enforced and production volume can be used as a simple metric to anchor the ranking scale.

**48. C:** Job enlargement entrusts employees with a larger quantity of work but does not necessarily require leadership or additional critical thinking skills. Job rotations and job transfers can be useful to give employees a wider perspective of the organization from a different role or location but do not necessarily develop leadership skills. Job enrichment gives employees additional decision-making responsibilities and leadership experiences that can be valuable for employees hoping to climb the organizational ladder.

**49. B:** With few exceptions, the FLSA covers workers in both the public and private sector in organizations that report at least $500,000 in sales annually or who do business across more than one state. Employers are not responsible under the FLSA for independent contractors who are utilized for project-based work, provide their own tools, training, and expertise, and who set their own work hours and standards.

**50. A:** A pension program is a type of defined benefit plan in which the employer is responsible for a predetermined payout amount or rate once the employee retires. Stock ownership plans, 401(k)s, and profit-sharing plans are all types of defined contribution plans in which the employer is responsible for a predetermined contribution rate during the time that the employee is working. In

172

Copyright © Mometrix Media. You have been licensed one copy of this document for personal use only. Any other reproduction or redistribution is strictly prohibited. All rights reserved.

a defined contribution plan, the employer and employee contribute at different rates and in different ways, depending on the program, but it is the employee's burden to make the financial decisions that will lead to their desired retirement date and lifestyle.

**51. D:** Virtual and modular style reporting structures lack a formal chain of command and do not resemble typical reporting hierarchies; also referred to as a boundary-less structure, these styles are utilized to increase speed, collaboration, and flexibility among work teams. Matrix style reporting structures create a cross-function reporting structure where an employee works for both a functional and a divisional supervisor. Traditional vertical reporting structures most closely align with an authoritarian organizational culture as both value power and decision-making coming from the few leaders at the top of the structure.

**52. B:** Cost per hire and time to hire measure the efficiency and effectiveness of hiring processes but not necessarily the efficiency or effectiveness of the jobs themselves. Measuring retention rate can be suggestive of effective management policies and workplace environments; however, a team's retention rate does not necessarily indicate whether there is the correct number of jobs and/or types of jobs on a given team. Revenue per employee can be a leading indicator as to what number of employees per team is the optimal level to maximize financial returns.

**53. C:** Each of the options are metrics that can suggest a certain level or scope of success in training outcomes. However, return on investment best demonstrates a training optimization as it translates participation, learning, and behaviors into tangible business outcomes. Measuring return on investment empowers an organization to efficiently plan and fund the most effective training methods and programs for positive organizational outcomes.

**54. D:** Group interviews with multiple interviewers can help to combine the time and resources of hiring managers and organizational leaders, especially when assessing multiple candidates for a position that interacts with a variety of organizational functions. Group interviews can also involve multiple candidates to demonstrate in real time how candidates work with one another. Situations with multiple interviewers or candidates interacting with one another can be a stressful and intimidating experience if a welcoming tone is not set.

**55. B:** Weighing possible costs of mitigation against costs of the risk itself is an element of cost-benefit analysis. Enterprise risk management may eliminate or reduce the likelihood of certain risks and may also be executed in a way that accounts for a variety of organizational functions and locations; however, these outcomes are a product of the strategic approach to assessing a variety of risk characteristics such as the probability of risk, speed of risk onset, and the potential severity of risk if it were to occur.

**56. C:** The EEO-1 Component 1 report collects data for the EEOC and the Office of Federal Contract Compliance Programs (OFCCP) to utilize when determining hiring and employment patterns for women and minorities.

**57. B:** While mission statements can be updated over time to reflect the direction and strategy of an organization, this is not an annual process and the mission statement content does not cover policies and procedures. Job descriptions detail the duties, skills, and knowledge required of different positions but are not an inclusive picture of organizational policies and procedures. Organizational charts demonstrate the chain of command and team structure within the organization but not necessarily how the teams or reporting relationships operate with one another.

Copyright © Mometrix Media. You have been licensed one copy of this document for personal use only. Any other reproduction or redistribution is strictly prohibited. All rights reserved.

**58. B:** Concerted activities are considered actions taken or communications participated in by employees in regards to working conditions or seeking to improve working conditions. Protected concerted activities are applicable to both union and nonunion employees. Limitations to a protected concerted activity can arise when it interferes with an employer's right to conduct business on his or her personal property; therefore, employers and employees alike must stay aware of what is and what is not considered a protected activity. Employers are not permitted to issue blanket bans on or policies intended to prevent employees from discussing pending sexual harassment investigations.

**59. C:** Role-playing is the most effective example, as it gives students the chance to practice their skills with other live humans. In role-playing scenarios, the instructor can posit a variety of situations so that the students can go back and forth to practice their skills under different conditions and stressors. A video example or case study may be more useful when taught prior to the role-play as it can introduce the new skills or extreme scenarios not appropriate to act out in the classroom (such as if a customer were to become violent). Concept mapping is more useful in complex learning environments that require understanding of multiple factors and overlapping scenarios.

**60. B:** Negligent hiring refers to an employer failing to do his or her due diligence to protect employees, customers, and the community from new hires who may cause harm or damage to those around them. Background checks can reveal potential threats to the workforce and should be conducted within federal, local, and state regulations.

**61. B:** Progressive discipline should be conducted privately and with the intent to give the employee an opportunity to improve and succeed. Progressive discipline conducted with the intent to remove or punish an employee hurts both the employee and the organization as a whole.

**62. B:** Workers' compensation claims can be paid out in medical benefits, wage replacement payments, death benefits, and/or rehabilitation benefits for an injury or illness sustained at work. Benefits for dependents are part of Social Security payouts and can cover benefits for the dependents of disabled or retired workers.

**63. D:** Furloughs and pay reductions would be more appropriate in situations where there is financial strain that requires a downsize in staffing levels and not necessarily a restructure. A hiring freeze may be appropriate in some situations where the restructure calls for reduced numbers of positions at certain jobs but can also lead to frustration or confusion by the current workforce if that freeze negatively impacts the workflow or work outputs. Early retirement options can give experienced, long-standing staff the option to choose whether or not they want to stay on through major change. Early retirement options can create a situation where there is natural downsizing prior to the restructure and may result in a smoother transition if the staff left behind are more open to change.

**64. D:** The importance of the learning tools and materials and content visualization is going to vary based on the training content; additionally, adapting the tools and visuals can be considered part of the structure of the training and less so the strategic impact of the training. It is essential that facilitators are able to reach and interact with students over learning platforms, but depending on the content and facilitator, this difference may not always require consideration for consistency. When moving from an in-person training to a virtual training, student attention span (and the lack thereof in a virtual environment) is the greatest strategic threat to a poor training design. Students in a virtual learning environment can struggle with the unchanging environment, lack of peer interaction, and accessibility of other work materials that can divide their attention. Virtual

Copyright © Mometrix Media. You have been licensed one copy of this document for personal use only. Any other reproduction or redistribution is strictly prohibited. All rights reserved.

learning opportunities can overcome this by breaking up the learning material into digestible bites, introducing asynchronous learning opportunities they can engage in on their own time, and utilizing other presentation methods that break up the monotony of web conferencing as a training method.

**65. C:** The Job Evaluation step of compensation design assesses a position's relative value within an organization and/or within the job market. An internal or external compensation and benefits survey can provide a Human Resources professional with the data required to compare the relative value of multiple positions.

**66. D:** Orientation is typically one piece of the onboarding process. New employee orientation takes place over a few hours or a few days and covers the most immediate details of what the new employee can and should expect: position duties, direct contacts, tools and systems to be used, etc. Onboarding is a more strategic process that takes place over a longer period of time and depending on the organization can be either a formal or an informal process. Informal onboarding processes consist of the employee figuring out the company culture and his or her place by him/herself, whereas formal onboarding processes can include structured training and events that cover the organizational culture, policies, relationships, and expectations.

**67. B:** Change, especially organization-wide change, can be frightening for employees who are unsure for their futures. In order to successfully navigate that change, HR and organizational leaders must build trust and understanding with the workforce through honest and timely communication practices—even when the message may be bad news. Strong communication practices build strong relationships with employees who remain with the organization, demonstrate strong organizational culture for any incoming employees, and can ease the process of leaving for outgoing employees.

**68. A:** The OSHA Form 300 details specific information from all work-related injuries and illnesses throughout a year. Hearing loss during employment is a required condition for documentation on the form. Additionally, any illness or injury deemed work-related in a work-related establishment requires documentation. For an employee working from home, the worker's establishment is considered the office to which they report and therefore injuries sustained in the home do not need to be documented on the OSHA Form 300.

**69. B:** With the evolution of technology and the subsequent transformation of cybercrimes, employers are not able to 100% guarantee the absolute safety of employee records. In order to demonstrate the employer's dedication to data protection, their confidentiality policy should outline what data gets shared when and with whom, what type of data is collected and how it is stored, as well as to whom employees should reach out if they have questions or suspect a breach of data.

**70. C:** Employer rules when providing a pension were set by the Employee Retirement Income Security Act (ERISA). Standards for leave for companies with 50 or more employees were set by the Family Medical Leave Act. Prohibition of discrimination in benefits administration is addressed in a variety of legislation pieces such as the Civil Rights Act, the Pregnancy Disability Act, or the Age Discrimination in Employment Act.

**71. A:** Addiction such as alcoholism can be considered a disability and, therefore, may require the employer to provide reasonable accommodations for the employee. However, the ADA does not protect employees under federal law who are using illegal drugs. Employers may establish random testing procedures for current employees so long as the procedures comply with federal and state

Copyright © Mometrix Media. You have been licensed one copy of this document for personal use only. Any other reproduction or redistribution is strictly prohibited. All rights reserved.

laws. When requiring drug tests as part of a pre-employment screening, it is best practice to require all candidates of a certain job to get tested and not just some.

**72. A:** Market- and outcome-based salary structures can be appropriate for some industries and organizations but do not necessarily aid the transition to a flatter organizational design. A broadband salary structure takes the traditional pay grade structure typically found in a vertical organizational hierarchy and combines various grades to create differ pay bands. This combination of pay rates and options gives employees more opportunity for growth where there is no longer a figurative ladder to climb within the organization. Broadband structures can also encourage employees to move laterally and potentially increase the skills, retention rate, and flexibility of a workforce.

**73. A:** It is important to cater the onboarding experience to the individual joining the company in order to improve engagement and retention. An assigned mentor from a leadership role can be highly impactful for a new professional with aspirations of growing within the industry and company. Role-specific training and teambuilding events can be effective tools for teaching the day-to-day operations and introducing the new employee to team members, but they do not hone in on the employee's background. Job rotation can be a unique onboarding tool for new managers overseeing a new team but is less effective with entry-level individuals or positions.

**74. A:** While each answer can indicate possible comparability between internal and external positions, comparing positions with similar leadership responsibilities, daily duties, and long-term goals will yield the most specific comparison. Data compared by geographical origin, effective data age, and labor market coverage can be leveled to create a more accurate comparison.

**75. B:** The Sarbanes-Oxley Act of 2002 limits the potential stock profits of executives based on ethical conduct and reporting standards. The Lilly Ledbetter Fair Pay Act of 2009 was passed in response to Ledbetter v. Goodyear Tire Supreme Court ruling that employees who wish to sue for pay discrimination must do so within 180 days of the initial pay decision (the 180-day limit to file suit restarts with each discriminatory act, consequence, or paycheck). The Patient Protection and Affordable Care Act sets standards for employers and individual to maintain essential health insurance coverage and other health care, coverage, and availability-related standards.

**76. D:** An employee resource group (ERG) is a type of networking group in which employees can choose to participate that links employees who share a particular dimension of diversity. Employee resource groups can contribute to a variety of organizational functions such as employee development, recruiting, diversity training, and product or services advisement. A diversity council is a formal group that is led by a high-ranking executive and is responsible for aligning goals, operations, and processes with diversity and inclusion goals and needs. Employee assistance programs and company wellness programs can contribute to employee engagement and support, but do not include a social element for diversity-linked connections.

**77. B:** An organization's mission statement describes the organizational strategy in terms of its primary actions, processes, and stakeholders. Business Goals and Objectives are typically limited to measurable, financial outcomes. An organization's Vision Statement describes the desired future state of the organization as a realization of the organization's strategy. The vision statement may include the organization's future impact on its community, future desired financial or operational states, or future achievements for internal and external stakeholders as a whole.

**78. B:** For a low-level conflict between a newly introduced supervisor and employee, the legal process of arbitration and the formal process of a grievance hearing would be inappropriate. While

Copyright © Mometrix Media. You have been licensed one copy of this document for personal use only. Any other reproduction or redistribution is strictly prohibited. All rights reserved.

involving peers in a type of peer review may be appropriate in the future if it is discovered that the conflict is systemic across the team, it would not be appropriate in in the initial stages of conflict resolution. Acting as the mediator, the Human Resources representative can help to guide conversation between the manager and employee. Mediation empowers the conflicting parties to communicate more effectively, discover the root of disagreements, and create the solutions that best fit each party without having solutions imposed on them by a third party.

**79. A:** Consistency is a key element in effective progressive discipline (especially across a team). Because the employee had not been previously counseled for a relatively mild transgression, it is essential to acknowledge the undesired behavior prior to formal counseling or warnings. Ideally, the verbal counseling step can serve as an opportunity to problem solve and improve overall communication.

**80. B:** Retaliation does not need to be filed with a corresponding discrimination charge and can be filed individually. Because retaliation does not need to affect the terms and conditions of the job and does not need to be discriminatory in nature, it can be easier to prove. Any negative change in the treatment of an employee from how they were treated prior to filing a discrimination charge can be considered retaliation and can lead to a retaliation charge.

**81. D:** In a perfect world, diversity and inclusion trainings would eliminate discrimination and create understanding empathetic workplaces; unfortunately, deeply held beliefs and ingrained behaviors are unlikely to be changed due to diversity and inclusion training. However, training can help to raise employee awareness of the challenges faced by people different to themselves and how those differences and challenges can affect productivity and performance in the workplace. This increased awareness can lead to improved workplace relations and communication skills. While demonstrating commitment to shareholders is not a bad goal for diversity and inclusion training, it should not be the primary goal.

**82. A:** According to the Americans with Disabilities Act (ADA), one of the keys to a successful reasonable accommodation is that the individual is able to experience the same opportunities as his or her peers who do not require accommodations. While a virtual training or separate training still provides the employee with additional knowledge and reward for their part on the sales team, they are ostracized from the rest of their team and miss out on the social learning and interactions that would come of the team-based learning. For a one-time event, building a ramp for the employee may not be financially possible and may also pose a challenge if the training facility is not owned by the employer. By seeking an alternate location for the training, the organization can ensure that the employee is able to learn from the training and also network and build stronger relationships with the team members.

**83. A:** Job bidding is the process by which employees can communicate their interest in a job that is not currently posted but may be posted in the future. Part of succession planning does include determining the interest for future leadership positions, but the primary goal is to identify the talent needed for these roles. Once the potential talent is identified, candidates are then groomed, trained, and prepared for future roles in leadership.

**84. C:** The WARN Act sets the standards for employee notification regarding mass layoffs. For organizations with 100 or more full-time staff (or part-time staff who work at least 4,000 cumulative hours in a week), a 60-day notice is required when the downsizing changes affect at least one-third of the facility or team in question and when unpredictable financial strain is not a factor.

Copyright © Mometrix Media. You have been licensed one copy of this document for personal use only. Any other reproduction or redistribution is strictly prohibited. All rights reserved.

**85. B:** The two benefits proven most effective at improving the employee turnover rate are pensions and medical coverage. The high, long-term impact of each of these two benefits can create scenarios where it would cost an employee more to leave an organization than he or she would stand to make elsewhere.

**86. B:** Low-Cost Leadership and Focused Cost Leadership strategic positions seek to establish a competitive advantage by offering the lowest possible price for customers by creating efficient processes and reducing waste. Differentiation and Focused Differentiation strategic positions seek to create a competitive advantage by setting their product or services apart from competitors through quality, performance, advanced/new age design, or some other unique or defining characteristic. A Focused Differentiation strategic position seeks to create this competitive advantage within a niche or specialized market or industry.

**87. B:** Outsourcing certain staffing needs can enable an organization to cut staffing costs, focus on the core business functions, and tap into knowledge or expertise that would otherwise be difficult to hire and maintain. However, outsourcing can also result in damage to employee morale, compromised data security, and relinquishing of control over procedures and processes.

**88. B:** Companies that effectively shift from annual performance reviews to quarterly, monthly, or weekly performance feedback formats by definition increase the engagement with employees and establish an expectation of a feedback culture. The more frequently managers and employees meet regarding performance, the more quickly they are able to respond to changes in the business and correct performance challenges the employee may be facing. While shifting from an annual review to a regular review method can produce desirable organizational outcomes, the change can bring with it time and financial costs when learning a new system, investing in any required technologies, and finding the time to regularly meet with employees more than once a year.

**89. D:** Flexible work hours, or flextime, refers specifically to the employee's authority to set his or her start and end times to fit their home needs while ensuring his or her work day includes the core business hours. Telecommuting and a variable workweek can include flextime scheduling but do not guarantee flextime. Job sharing is when two or more employees split the hours and share the responsibilities of one position.

**90. B:** Using terminology such as 'fresh face' and 'new energy' can be suggestive of discrimination against older candidates. The Age Discrimination in Employment Act protects employees and job candidates who are forty years of age or older from employment decisions based on age.

**91. D:** Employee information management, vacation time management, and pay document management are all functions that can be found in a modern HRIS. Learning functions such as knowledge storage and training management are more likely to be found in a learning management system (LMS) or knowledge management system (KMS).

**92. D:** A pie chart or histogram can be a useful visual depiction of a single type of descriptive data. An organizational structure chart may be aligned with an organization's strategy but it is only one visual tool that demonstrates information like chain of command and functional makeup. A measurement map displays the measurable links between an organization's big picture strategy and its operational practices.

**93. D:** The income statement is the basic breakdown of an organization's revenue and expenditures. The income statement gives the most accurate idea of an organization's overall financial health. The statement of changes in equity can provide information regarding shareholders' equity over a certain period of time. The balance sheet can provide information

Copyright © Mometrix Media. You have been licensed one copy of this document for personal use only. Any other reproduction or redistribution is strictly prohibited. All rights reserved.

regarding the organization's assets, liabilities, and equity. The cash flow statement can provide information regarding how much cash is available to an organization at any given point in time based on the incoming and outgoing cash.

**94. D:** The SOX Act established regulations overseeing corporate governance and other financial oversight as a reaction to widespread unethical practices by publicly traded companies. The SOX Act applies to publicly traded companies and all of their employees. The SOX Act requires companies to report their code of ethics (or why they don't have a code of ethics) to the US Securities and Exchange Commission. The SOX Act prohibits retaliation for whistleblower employees or supervisors who participate or aid in federal investigations.

**95. C:** Prior to a training program, an organization first needs to complete a needs assessment, then determine the training design, then select participants, and then complete the pre-training survey. A needs assessment is an essential first step to designing employee training. Needs assessments enable organizations to accurately identify problems; determine what causes the problems; identify skills, knowledge, and abilities needed to solve the problem; and define the metrics that will indicate training effectiveness.

**96. C:** An essential job function is one that is the reason the job exists, one that cannot be done by other people, and one that may be highly specialized. A secretary's essential job functions may include answering phones and greeting customers; however, changing a toner cartridge is a task that may be performed by other employees and is not the reason that the job exists.

**97. B:** The Affordable Care Act requires the annual filing of the IRS Form 1094-C, which details employer information and the details of coverage for employees, as well as the IRS Form 1095-B, which provides details on individual employees and their health insurance coverage for the year. Form 1095-B is required to be provided annually to the individual employee to whom it pertains.

**98. B:** Exit interviews are a valuable tool for gauging an exiting employee's perspective on the culture in an organization and determine what factors led to their departure. This information can help supervisors and HR professionals to improve workplace conditions or processes to improve future retention rates. Exit interviews may be inappropriate or impractical in cases of involuntary termination or in instances where the employer is unable to reach the employee in question.

**99. D:** Internal and external data are critical to setting compensation practices that are fair and attract top talent in the industry. However, it is essential to start at the organizational strategy before analyzing additional data in order to understand where the organization is going. Aligning the total rewards strategy with the organizational strategy helps to determine which positions are critical to future organizational outcomes.

**100. C:** Payroll taxes and requirements can be affected by where an employee is living. For an organization that transforms positions from office-reporting positions to purely remote work, it is important to keep up-to-date records of where employees choose to live and where new employees are recruited from.

**101. D:** Job fairs are useful at finding a diverse group of candidates who are early in their careers or may be going through a specific type of transition such as leaving the military or graduating college. Job fairs are attractive for candidates within these pools due to the volume of employment options available and the direct interaction with potential employers. For a supervisory professional, other recruiting methods should be considered due to the experience and knowledge specifications of those types of positions.

Copyright © Mometrix Media. You have been licensed one copy of this document for personal use only. Any other reproduction or redistribution is strictly prohibited. All rights reserved.

**102. D:** When the message in question is of higher complexity, has higher stakes, or may elicit an emotional response, it is more effective to utilize information-rich means of communications such as in-person meetings, videoconferences, or presentations. The information-lean mediums of communication such as social media posts, newsletters, or emails can be helpful as supplemental sources of information in this instance, but the primary form of communication should be in person in order to provide opportunities for real time questions and feedback.

**103. B:** Job-based job analysis focuses on defining the content and needs of the job at hand and guides staffing practices to place the best person fit for the job into that position. Job-based analysis is traditionally used in positions that are relatively predictable and require a stable set of skills and competencies to complete. Person-based job analysis is more appropriate for positions that require flexibility in the skills and competencies needed and rewards individual learning and upskilling. Person-based job analysis guides staffing practices to assign specific job duties to the person most skilled to accomplish the task.

**104. D:** Different monitoring methods will be more or less effective, depending on the company and position in question. Requiring time in the office may help with building relationships but can also backfire if employees are not physically able or willing to comply. Having written record of policies and policy acknowledgement is a recommended practice but not necessarily one that will impact employee views on the policy in question. By being honest and transparent with the policy development and implementation, an employer can build both trust and understanding with the employees.

**105. D:** Descriptive statistics paint a basic picture of data sets and can be useful for setting the foundation for higher level analysis. Oracle, Python, and R as statistical tools are useful for handling large volumes of complicated data. Microsoft Excel can be used as an entry-level analytic tool for sorting and organizing basic data and statistics.

**106. D:** Decryption is the process by which digital information is returned to its original state from the privacy and security safeguard known as encryption. Hacking and computer viruses are processes and tools by which unauthorized individuals access secured information. Social Engineering is the phenomenon in which users are fooled into sharing sensitive, personal, or professional information with an unauthorized individual; it can take the form of phishing, spear phishing, pretexting, piggybacking, and more.

**107. C:** The observation method does not typically carry high costs. The observation method is advantageous because the data is firsthand and immediate and therefore is not affected by memory bias. Because this method depends on subjects being in their typical location performing their typical tasks at the typical time, it can be more convenient for subjects than other major data collection methods. It is critical that the observer is an objective party who is skilled and experienced in this method of data collection in order to increase the quality of data collected.

**108. A:** Bar charts and Venn diagrams are useful for displaying different types of categorical data. Line charts can be used to demonstrate a data point or set over a period of time. Regression models are useful to demonstrate the relationship between two sets of data; a positive or negative correlation can be observed based on the positioning of the data points.

**109. C:** An employee engagement survey seeks to measure satisfaction, commitment, and morale. An attitude survey or culture survey seeks to measure employee opinions regarding the state of the company, issues affecting the company, and the overall culture of the company. An opinion survey

Copyright © Mometrix Media. You have been licensed one copy of this document for personal use only. Any other reproduction or redistribution is strictly prohibited. All rights reserved.

is narrower in scope and seeks to measure how employees feel about specific policies or practices within the organization.

**110. C:** Applicant flow tracking is required of any employer with a federal contract in order to analyze the race and gender data of applicants. It is critical that applicant flow tracking data is kept separate from the corresponding application and that the data is not used in hiring decisions. Applicant flow tracking is important for analyzing what candidates are applying for jobs to ensure that there is a fair sourcing process for openings.

**111. B:** Publicly recognizing staff or recognizing all staff can backfire if the employee being recognized does not enjoy public attention or if employees feel the recognition is less genuine when everyone is recognized regardless of performance. Planning a budget for an individualized recognition program can be a helpful tool but is not always practical or possible, depending on the team or organization. By tying recognition efforts to the organization's values and mission, employees see not just how they or others are doing well but how their choices and behaviors positively affect organizational outcomes. This approach to recognition also reinforces the desire for employee behavior to align with company values and may encourage other employees to make similar choices or efforts.

**112. A:** An organization's employer brand and culture can be experienced before a job candidate ever speaks with or connects to the organization. Companies can communicate their culture and values through what is included in the job posting. Each of the following steps can confirm and add depth to the candidate's understanding of the organization's culture.

**113. B:** The I-9 Form is a document required by the Immigration Reform and Control Act that verifies an employee's identity and authorization to work in the United States. While this form can be completed with an HR representative, the supervisor or a representative on the employer's behalf can complete the form as well. A background check verifies an employee's criminal history and not his or her employability status as it relates to the employee's authorization to work in the United States.

**114. C:** Performance goals that are SMART are specific, measurable, achievable, relevant, and timebound. Measuring 'overall performance' is not specific to what needs to be improved or how that improvement could be measured. Increasing the total product output by 500 units may be a useful measure but without a deadline, it does not hold weight. Decreasing total waste output by 100% within 2 months is highly unlikely to be achievable. Increasing the net promoter score by 6 points by a stated date is specific to customer service, measurable with the number of data points, achievable as a goal, relevant to organizational performance, and states a clear deadline.

**115. C:** While it can be challenging during conflicts, honesty is one of the cornerstones to effective communication. Email can be a tricky form of communication due to the lack of context clues and other elements of nonverbal communication; if employees are not on the same page regarding communication expectations and email etiquette then the overall outcomes of collaboration attempts can be negatively affected. When working as a team, it is important that teammates are honest with one another in order to build collaborative trust prior to seeking more extreme responses or alternate intervention avenues.

**116. D:** Employee surveys and feedback activities are only as effective as what happens after the feedback has been collected. If employees feel their opinions matter and see the tangible results from participating in surveys, they are more likely to engage truthfully and energetically in future feedback collecting activities. Action plans based on employee feedback communicates to

Copyright © Mometrix Media. You have been licensed one copy of this document for personal use only. Any other reproduction or redistribution is strictly prohibited. All rights reserved.

employees that their opinions matter and that they have a stake in company policies and operations.

**117. D:** Federal, state, and local laws can dictate who is eligible or should receive what information in different situations (e.g., HIPAA, GINA, ADA, etc.). Senior leadership, managers and supervisors, and employee emergency contacts may only access employee records and information within the context of a legitimate business need or as stated by a federal, state, or local law.

**118. D:** Each of the answers do describe prevention methods; however, answers A, B, and C indicate methods in which Human Resources would likely act as an advisor, mediator, or partner. Human Resources professionals should take leadership roles in the review, revision, and implementation of employee codes of conduct.

**119. C:** Transparency and respect are important characteristics of a successful involuntary termination. Attempts to get the employee to quit before being terminated can be attempts to avoid unemployment disputes, to avoid the documentation responsibilities of firing an employee, or to avoid further confrontation. However, this approach is also referred to as constructive discharge and is legally viewed as firing an employee, even if the employee does quit. A constructive discharge can lead to the same legal or moral challenges of involuntary terminations; therefore, it is in the organization's best interest to be honest with the employee through the termination process and to be consistent with documentation of behaviors and treatment of staff.

**120. A:** Both phased retirement and temp-to-hire programs can facilitate improved recruiting outcomes, with the former allowing an organization time to recruit for a departing senior staff member and the latter allowing for a trial period of sorts before committing to a new employee. Phased retirement facilitates the transfer of institutional knowledge as the departing senior staff member can take a measured approach of sharing information with colleagues and training their replacement before leaving the company. Joint employment refers to the shared control and responsibility between two or more employers and one employee. Gig workers are a type of independent contractor performing one or more short-term jobs.

**121. B:** Stay interviews are utilized with active employees to determine what they value in their employment experience and what can be improved. Stay interviews can provide valuable insight into company culture, opportunities, and challenges. Screening, selection, and stress interviews are all recruiting style interviews for assessing candidate experience and potential.

**122. B:** While company town halls and focus groups can be rich in information exchange, they take time and focus on qualitative feedback that must be recorded and interpreted. An emailed questionnaire can also provide valuable information but requires data compiling, cleaning, and interpretation; additionally, a questionnaire will elicit different quality responses from different employees and require additional time to complete. An online survey can be a quick feedback tool that employees can easily and swiftly complete; additionally, the multiple-choice format allows for quantitative analysis and can be more quickly used to identify challenges or trends.

**123. B:** Social media can be a dynamic tool to visually and interactively demonstrate how the employment practices align with the company mission and brand. Key elements to an effective brand are its visibility, recognizability, and alignment between a visual representation and reality; social media can communicate each of these elements through images, videos, chat options, and more. The other options can (and should) be used in ways that align with company and employer branding but are not as effective at drawing clear, visible connections between the two.

Copyright © Mometrix Media. You have been licensed one copy of this document for personal use only. Any other reproduction or redistribution is strictly prohibited. All rights reserved.

**124. C:** The "text to columns" and "concatenate" commands are most useful for manipulating what data appears in what columns. While removing duplicates would reduce the data to unique values only, it would do so at the expense of data volume. Using the filter tool can help the user see at a glance the different unique values in a column without sacrificing data volume integrity.

**125. A:** Under the FLSA, white-collar exempt positions are considered those that function as executive, administrative, or professional positions. These jobs must have the majority of their work classified as such in order to qualify (in addition to other pay requirements). There are other exemption classifications within the sales and computer industries. However, positions that are considered 'production' and non-management are considered blue-collar jobs and are not eligible for overtime exemptions.

Copyright © Mometrix Media. You have been licensed one copy of this document for personal use only. Any other reproduction or redistribution is strictly prohibited. All rights reserved.

# How to Overcome Test Anxiety

Just the thought of taking a test is enough to make most people a little nervous. A test is an important event that can have a long-term impact on your future, so it's important to take it seriously and it's natural to feel anxious about performing well. But just because anxiety is normal, that doesn't mean that it's helpful in test taking, or that you should simply accept it as part of your life. Anxiety can have a variety of effects. These effects can be mild, like making you feel slightly nervous, or severe, like blocking your ability to focus or remember even a simple detail.

If you experience test anxiety—whether severe or mild—it's important to know how to beat it. To discover this, first you need to understand what causes test anxiety.

## Causes of Test Anxiety

While we often think of anxiety as an uncontrollable emotional state, it can actually be caused by simple, practical things. One of the most common causes of test anxiety is that a person does not feel adequately prepared for their test. This feeling can be the result of many different issues such as poor study habits or lack of organization, but the most common culprit is time management. Starting to study too late, failing to organize your study time to cover all of the material, or being distracted while you study will mean that you're not well prepared for the test. This may lead to cramming the night before, which will cause you to be physically and mentally exhausted for the test. Poor time management also contributes to feelings of stress, fear, and hopelessness as you realize you are not well prepared but don't know what to do about it.

Other times, test anxiety is not related to your preparation for the test but comes from unresolved fear. This may be a past failure on a test, or poor performance on tests in general. It may come from comparing yourself to others who seem to be performing better or from the stress of living up to expectations. Anxiety may be driven by fears of the future—how failure on this test would affect your educational and career goals. These fears are often completely irrational, but they can still negatively impact your test performance.

> **Review Video: 3 Reasons You Have Test Anxiety**
> Visit mometrix.com/academy and enter code: 428468

Copyright © Mometrix Media. You have been licensed one copy of this document for personal use only. Any other reproduction or redistribution is strictly prohibited. All rights reserved.

# Elements of Test Anxiety

As mentioned earlier, test anxiety is considered to be an emotional state, but it has physical and mental components as well. Sometimes you may not even realize that you are suffering from test anxiety until you notice the physical symptoms. These can include trembling hands, rapid heartbeat, sweating, nausea, and tense muscles. Extreme anxiety may lead to fainting or vomiting. Obviously, any of these symptoms can have a negative impact on testing. It is important to recognize them as soon as they begin to occur so that you can address the problem before it damages your performance.

> **Review Video: 3 Ways to Tell You Have Test Anxiety**
> Visit mometrix.com/academy and enter code: 927847

The mental components of test anxiety include trouble focusing and inability to remember learned information. During a test, your mind is on high alert, which can help you recall information and stay focused for an extended period of time. However, anxiety interferes with your mind's natural processes, causing you to blank out, even on the questions you know well. The strain of testing during anxiety makes it difficult to stay focused, especially on a test that may take several hours. Extreme anxiety can take a huge mental toll, making it difficult not only to recall test information but even to understand the test questions or pull your thoughts together.

> **Review Video: How Test Anxiety Affects Memory**
> Visit mometrix.com/academy and enter code: 609003

# Effects of Test Anxiety

Test anxiety is like a disease—if left untreated, it will get progressively worse. Anxiety leads to poor performance, and this reinforces the feelings of fear and failure, which in turn lead to poor performances on subsequent tests. It can grow from a mild nervousness to a crippling condition. If allowed to progress, test anxiety can have a big impact on your schooling, and consequently on your future.

Test anxiety can spread to other parts of your life. Anxiety on tests can become anxiety in any stressful situation, and blanking on a test can turn into panicking in a job situation. But fortunately, you don't have to let anxiety rule your testing and determine your grades. There are a number of relatively simple steps you can take to move past anxiety and function normally on a test and in the rest of life.

> **Review Video: How Test Anxiety Impacts Your Grades**
> Visit mometrix.com/academy and enter code: 939819

Copyright © Mometrix Media. You have been licensed one copy of this document for personal use only. Any other reproduction or redistribution is strictly prohibited. All rights reserved.

# Physical Steps for Beating Test Anxiety

While test anxiety is a serious problem, the good news is that it can be overcome. It doesn't have to control your ability to think and remember information. While it may take time, you can begin taking steps today to beat anxiety.

Just as your first hint that you may be struggling with anxiety comes from the physical symptoms, the first step to treating it is also physical. Rest is crucial for having a clear, strong mind. If you are tired, it is much easier to give in to anxiety. But if you establish good sleep habits, your body and mind will be ready to perform optimally, without the strain of exhaustion. Additionally, sleeping well helps you to retain information better, so you're more likely to recall the answers when you see the test questions.

Getting good sleep means more than going to bed on time. It's important to allow your brain time to relax. Take study breaks from time to time so it doesn't get overworked, and don't study right before bed. Take time to rest your mind before trying to rest your body, or you may find it difficult to fall asleep.

> **Review Video: <u>The Importance of Sleep for Your Brain</u>**
> Visit mometrix.com/academy and enter code: 319338

Along with sleep, other aspects of physical health are important in preparing for a test. Good nutrition is vital for good brain function. Sugary foods and drinks may give a burst of energy but this burst is followed by a crash, both physically and emotionally. Instead, fuel your body with protein and vitamin-rich foods.

Also, drink plenty of water. Dehydration can lead to headaches and exhaustion, especially if your brain is already under stress from the rigors of the test. Particularly if your test is a long one, drink water during the breaks. And if possible, take an energy-boosting snack to eat between sections.

> **Review Video: <u>How Diet Can Affect your Mood</u>**
> Visit mometrix.com/academy and enter code: 624317

Along with sleep and diet, a third important part of physical health is exercise. Maintaining a steady workout schedule is helpful, but even taking 5-minute study breaks to walk can help get your blood pumping faster and clear your head. Exercise also releases endorphins, which contribute to a positive feeling and can help combat test anxiety.

When you nurture your physical health, you are also contributing to your mental health. If your body is healthy, your mind is much more likely to be healthy as well. So take time to rest, nourish your body with healthy food and water, and get moving as much as possible. Taking these physical steps will make you stronger and more able to take the mental steps necessary to overcome test anxiety.

Copyright © Mometrix Media. You have been licensed one copy of this document for personal use only. Any other reproduction or redistribution is strictly prohibited. All rights reserved.

# Mental Steps for Beating Test Anxiety

Working on the mental side of test anxiety can be more challenging, but as with the physical side, there are clear steps you can take to overcome it. As mentioned earlier, test anxiety often stems from lack of preparation, so the obvious solution is to prepare for the test. Effective studying may be the most important weapon you have for beating test anxiety, but you can and should employ several other mental tools to combat fear.

First, boost your confidence by reminding yourself of past success—tests or projects that you aced. If you're putting as much effort into preparing for this test as you did for those, there's no reason you should expect to fail here. Work hard to prepare; then trust your preparation.

Second, surround yourself with encouraging people. It can be helpful to find a study group, but be sure that the people you're around will encourage a positive attitude. If you spend time with others who are anxious or cynical, this will only contribute to your own anxiety. Look for others who are motivated to study hard from a desire to succeed, not from a fear of failure.

Third, reward yourself. A test is physically and mentally tiring, even without anxiety, and it can be helpful to have something to look forward to. Plan an activity following the test, regardless of the outcome, such as going to a movie or getting ice cream.

When you are taking the test, if you find yourself beginning to feel anxious, remind yourself that you know the material. Visualize successfully completing the test. Then take a few deep, relaxing breaths and return to it. Work through the questions carefully but with confidence, knowing that you are capable of succeeding.

Developing a healthy mental approach to test taking will also aid in other areas of life. Test anxiety affects more than just the actual test—it can be damaging to your mental health and even contribute to depression. It's important to beat test anxiety before it becomes a problem for more than testing.

> **Review Video: <u>Test Anxiety and Depression</u>**
> Visit mometrix.com/academy and enter code: 904704

Copyright © Mometrix Media. You have been licensed one copy of this document for personal use only. Any other reproduction or redistribution is strictly prohibited. All rights reserved.

# Study Strategy

Being prepared for the test is necessary to combat anxiety, but what does being prepared look like? You may study for hours on end and still not feel prepared. What you need is a strategy for test prep. The next few pages outline our recommended steps to help you plan out and conquer the challenge of preparation.

## STEP 1: SCOPE OUT THE TEST

Learn everything you can about the format (multiple choice, essay, etc.) and what will be on the test. Gather any study materials, course outlines, or sample exams that may be available. Not only will this help you to prepare, but knowing what to expect can help to alleviate test anxiety.

## STEP 2: MAP OUT THE MATERIAL

Look through the textbook or study guide and make note of how many chapters or sections it has. Then divide these over the time you have. For example, if a book has 15 chapters and you have five days to study, you need to cover three chapters each day. Even better, if you have the time, leave an extra day at the end for overall review after you have gone through the material in depth.

If time is limited, you may need to prioritize the material. Look through it and make note of which sections you think you already have a good grasp on, and which need review. While you are studying, skim quickly through the familiar sections and take more time on the challenging parts. Write out your plan so you don't get lost as you go. Having a written plan also helps you feel more in control of the study, so anxiety is less likely to arise from feeling overwhelmed at the amount to cover.

## STEP 3: GATHER YOUR TOOLS

Decide what study method works best for you. Do you prefer to highlight in the book as you study and then go back over the highlighted portions? Or do you type out notes of the important information? Or is it helpful to make flashcards that you can carry with you? Assemble the pens, index cards, highlighters, post-it notes, and any other materials you may need so you won't be distracted by getting up to find things while you study.

If you're having a hard time retaining the information or organizing your notes, experiment with different methods. For example, try color-coding by subject with colored pens, highlighters, or post-it notes. If you learn better by hearing, try recording yourself reading your notes so you can listen while in the car, working out, or simply sitting at your desk. Ask a friend to quiz you from your flashcards, or try teaching someone the material to solidify it in your mind.

## STEP 4: CREATE YOUR ENVIRONMENT

It's important to avoid distractions while you study. This includes both the obvious distractions like visitors and the subtle distractions like an uncomfortable chair (or a too-comfortable couch that makes you want to fall asleep). Set up the best study environment possible: good lighting and a comfortable work area. If background music helps you focus, you may want to turn it on, but otherwise keep the room quiet. If you are using a computer to take notes, be sure you don't have any other windows open, especially applications like social media, games, or anything else that could distract you. Silence your phone and turn off notifications. Be sure to keep water close by so you stay hydrated while you study (but avoid unhealthy drinks and snacks).

Also, take into account the best time of day to study. Are you freshest first thing in the morning? Try to set aside some time then to work through the material. Is your mind clearer in the afternoon or evening? Schedule your study session then. Another method is to study at the same time of day that

Copyright © Mometrix Media. You have been licensed one copy of this document for personal use only. Any other reproduction or redistribution is strictly prohibited. All rights reserved.

you will take the test, so that your brain gets used to working on the material at that time and will be ready to focus at test time.

## STEP 5: STUDY!

Once you have done all the study preparation, it's time to settle into the actual studying. Sit down, take a few moments to settle your mind so you can focus, and begin to follow your study plan. Don't give in to distractions or let yourself procrastinate. This is your time to prepare so you'll be ready to fearlessly approach the test. Make the most of the time and stay focused.

Of course, you don't want to burn out. If you study too long you may find that you're not retaining the information very well. Take regular study breaks. For example, taking five minutes out of every hour to walk briskly, breathing deeply and swinging your arms, can help your mind stay fresh.

As you get to the end of each chapter or section, it's a good idea to do a quick review. Remind yourself of what you learned and work on any difficult parts. When you feel that you've mastered the material, move on to the next part. At the end of your study session, briefly skim through your notes again.

But while review is helpful, cramming last minute is NOT. If at all possible, work ahead so that you won't need to fit all your study into the last day. Cramming overloads your brain with more information than it can process and retain, and your tired mind may struggle to recall even previously learned information when it is overwhelmed with last-minute study. Also, the urgent nature of cramming and the stress placed on your brain contribute to anxiety. You'll be more likely to go to the test feeling unprepared and having trouble thinking clearly.

So don't cram, and don't stay up late before the test, even just to review your notes at a leisurely pace. Your brain needs rest more than it needs to go over the information again. In fact, plan to finish your studies by noon or early afternoon the day before the test. Give your brain the rest of the day to relax or focus on other things, and get a good night's sleep. Then you will be fresh for the test and better able to recall what you've studied.

## STEP 6: TAKE A PRACTICE TEST

Many courses offer sample tests, either online or in the study materials. This is an excellent resource to check whether you have mastered the material, as well as to prepare for the test format and environment.

Check the test format ahead of time: the number of questions, the type (multiple choice, free response, etc.), and the time limit. Then create a plan for working through them. For example, if you have 30 minutes to take a 60-question test, your limit is 30 seconds per question. Spend less time on the questions you know well so that you can take more time on the difficult ones.

If you have time to take several practice tests, take the first one open book, with no time limit. Work through the questions at your own pace and make sure you fully understand them. Gradually work up to taking a test under test conditions: sit at a desk with all study materials put away and set a timer. Pace yourself to make sure you finish the test with time to spare and go back to check your answers if you have time.

After each test, check your answers. On the questions you missed, be sure you understand why you missed them. Did you misread the question (tests can use tricky wording)? Did you forget the information? Or was it something you hadn't learned? Go back and study any shaky areas that the practice tests reveal.

Copyright © Mometrix Media. You have been licensed one copy of this document for personal use only. Any other reproduction or redistribution is strictly prohibited. All rights reserved.

Taking these tests not only helps with your grade, but also aids in combating test anxiety. If you're already used to the test conditions, you're less likely to worry about it, and working through tests until you're scoring well gives you a confidence boost. Go through the practice tests until you feel comfortable, and then you can go into the test knowing that you're ready for it.

## Test Tips

On test day, you should be confident, knowing that you've prepared well and are ready to answer the questions. But aside from preparation, there are several test day strategies you can employ to maximize your performance.

First, as stated before, get a good night's sleep the night before the test (and for several nights before that, if possible). Go into the test with a fresh, alert mind rather than staying up late to study.

Try not to change too much about your normal routine on the day of the test. It's important to eat a nutritious breakfast, but if you normally don't eat breakfast at all, consider eating just a protein bar. If you're a coffee drinker, go ahead and have your normal coffee. Just make sure you time it so that the caffeine doesn't wear off right in the middle of your test. Avoid sugary beverages, and drink enough water to stay hydrated but not so much that you need a restroom break 10 minutes into the test. If your test isn't first thing in the morning, consider going for a walk or doing a light workout before the test to get your blood flowing.

Allow yourself enough time to get ready, and leave for the test with plenty of time to spare so you won't have the anxiety of scrambling to arrive in time. Another reason to be early is to select a good seat. It's helpful to sit away from doors and windows, which can be distracting. Find a good seat, get out your supplies, and settle your mind before the test begins.

When the test begins, start by going over the instructions carefully, even if you already know what to expect. Make sure you avoid any careless mistakes by following the directions.

Then begin working through the questions, pacing yourself as you've practiced. If you're not sure on an answer, don't spend too much time on it, and don't let it shake your confidence. Either skip it and come back later, or eliminate as many wrong answers as possible and guess among the remaining ones. Don't dwell on these questions as you continue—put them out of your mind and focus on what lies ahead.

Be sure to read all of the answer choices, even if you're sure the first one is the right answer. Sometimes you'll find a better one if you keep reading. But don't second-guess yourself if you do immediately know the answer. Your gut instinct is usually right. Don't let test anxiety rob you of the information you know.

If you have time at the end of the test (and if the test format allows), go back and review your answers. Be cautious about changing any, since your first instinct tends to be correct, but make sure you didn't misread any of the questions or accidentally mark the wrong answer choice. Look over any you skipped and make an educated guess.

Copyright © Mometrix Media. You have been licensed one copy of this document for personal use only. Any other reproduction or redistribution is strictly prohibited. All rights reserved.

At the end, leave the test feeling confident. You've done your best, so don't waste time worrying about your performance or wishing you could change anything. Instead, celebrate the successful completion of this test. And finally, use this test to learn how to deal with anxiety even better next time.

**Review Video: 5 Tips to Beat Test Anxiety**
Visit mometrix.com/academy and enter code: 570656

## Important Qualification

Not all anxiety is created equal. If your test anxiety is causing major issues in your life beyond the classroom or testing center, or if you are experiencing troubling physical symptoms related to your anxiety, it may be a sign of a serious physiological or psychological condition. If this sounds like your situation, we strongly encourage you to seek professional help.

Copyright © Mometrix Media. You have been licensed one copy of this document for personal use only. Any other reproduction or redistribution is strictly prohibited. All rights reserved.

# Tell Us Your Story

We at Mometrix would like to extend our heartfelt thanks to you for letting us be a part of your journey. It is an honor to serve people from all walks of life, people like you, who are committed to building the best future they can for themselves.

We know that each person's situation is unique. But we also know that, whether you are a young student or a mother of four, you care about working to make your own life and the lives of those around you better.

**That's why we want to hear your story.**

We want to know why you're taking this test. We want to know about the trials you've gone through to get here. And we want to know about the successes you've experienced after taking and passing your test.

In addition to your story, which can be an inspiration both to us and to others, we value your feedback. We want to know both what you loved about our book and what you think we can improve on.

**The team at Mometrix would be absolutely thrilled to hear from you!** So please, send us an email at tellusyourstory@mometrix.com or visit us at mometrix.com/tellusyourstory.php and let's stay in touch.

192

Copyright © Mometrix Media. You have been licensed one copy of this document for personal use only. Any other reproduction or redistribution is strictly prohibited. All rights reserved.

# Additional Bonus Material

Due to our efforts to try to keep this book to a manageable length, we've created a link that will give you access to all of your additional bonus material.

Please visit https://www.mometrix.com/bonus948/aphr to access the information.

Copyright © Mometrix Media. You have been licensed one copy of this document for personal use only. Any other reproduction or redistribution is strictly prohibited. All rights reserved.